An Introduction to
Algorithm Design
and
Structured Programming

An Introduction to Algorithm Design and Structured Programming

THOMAS A. REED

University of Maryland, European Division

WITHDRAWN

PRENTICE HALL

New York • London • Toronto • Sydney • Tokyo

First published 1988 by
Prentice Hall International (UK) Ltd,
66 Wood Lane End, Hemel Hempstead,
Hertfordshire, HP2 4RG
A division of
Simon & Schuster International Group

© 1988 Prentice Hall International (UK) Ltd

Printed and bound in Great Britain by
A. Wheaton & Co. Ltd, Exeter

Library of Congress Cataloging-in-Publication Data

Reed, Thomas A., 1928 –
    An introduction to algorithm design and structured
programming.

    Includes index.
    1. Electronic digital computers – Programming.
2. Algorithms.   3. Structured programming.   I. Title.
QA76.6.R42   1988   005.1   87-7173
ISBN 0-13-477779-4

British Library Cataloguing in Publication Data

Reed, Thomas A.
    An introduction to algorithm design and
structured programming.
    1. Algorithms   2. Electronic digital
computers – Programming   I. Title
005.1'2'028   QA76.6

ISBN 0-13-477779-4
ISBN 0-13-477720-4 (pbk)

---

1 2 3 4 5   92 91 90 89 88

ISBN 0-13-477779-4
ISBN 0-13-477720-4 PBK

To

H.K.

who risked his life to save mine

Contents

Preface   ix

Glossary   xiv

1   Pseudocode and Computers   1

2   Constants and Variables   21

3   The Assignment Operator   31

4   Flowcharting and Elementary Algorithm Development   44

5   Flowcharting and Standard Flowchart Forms   62

6   The Details of Pseudocode and Program Solution Layout   81

7   Development of Algorithms   103

8   Nested Control Structures   116

9   Boolean Algebra and Nested Control Structures   133

10   Arrays and Array Processing   155

11   The DOFOR Control Structure and Two-Dimensional Arrays   173

12   The Subroutine   194

Answers to Selected Problems   216

Appendix   Translating Pseudocode into Computer
                Languages   257
                1: Pseudocode into BASIC   258
                2: Pseudocode into FORTRAN   264
                3: Pseudocode into COBOL   269
                4: Pseudocode into PASCAL   272

Index   274

Preface

Today, the computer industry has no problem with hardware; the average user can buy for a relatively small price virtually as much memory and speed as he or she is likely to need for normal programming. But there is a problem in obtaining good software. Of course, there are a number of excellent languages. However, much of the existing software and, unfortunately, a significant portion of the software being written is not properly organized, and it is difficult to understand and to maintain or update.

Furthermore, programs are not expensive to prepare because of the amount of space they occupy in computers; they are expensive to prepare because of the number of worker-hours spent in developing them.

Finally, many programmers spend the majority of their time updating or correcting programs written by someone else. This is called maintenance programming. It is unimportant whether the programmer is a professional working in a large team or a non-professional working for his or her own enjoyment. Maintenance takes up a lot of time that could better be used creatively. In some organizations this can be as much as 80 percent of the available programming time. This happens because many programs are written in such a manner that they are hard to understand and, once understanding has been painfully achieved, hard to repair.

All of the above problems are solved or minimized by using modern logical techniques to organize the programs. The problem is broken down into small, easily understood tasks. The division into tasks is known as modular programming or modular structure, and the organization of tasks into a logical order is known as top-down programming. These techniques hold the key to most of the software problems that plague industrial and private programmers today. They work for all languages, and they are taught and practiced in this text.

ix

The second step for all working and would-be programmers is to translate the tasks into a logical series of steps that lead to the problem's solution. This is called algorithm design. Part of the difficulty here is that the logical structure of a computing language is ideal for program execution in computers, but it is ill-suited for problem analysis and algorithm design by human beings.

Fortunately, people-friendly technology exists for problem solving and algorithm design. One of the most comfortable ways to handle the tools of this method is in the form of structured English or pseudocode. The pseudocode approach is not only helpful for the design of algorithms, it is also an efficient way to design programs with proper structure. Since this method solves so many problems, we use it in this text.

There is another reason for learning programming via pseudocode. Most languages contain common techniques. Thus a skill developed in pseudocode can be easily transferred to many languages. That's nice, but the real advantage is that you don't need to learn on a machine. Learning a language on the machine is enjoyable, but you have to learn the machine operating system and some kind of typing to get the program in through the keyboard. Further, you must write the language exactly, so that the machine will not continually interrupt your learning with minor grammar corrections. All these problems are present in addition to learning structuring, problem analysis and the logic that is common to most computer languages.

In the early stages of language learning a computer hinders more than it helps. For this reason this text teaches algorithm analysis and construction, common computer language devices and program structure in pseudocode, all without a computer.

It might be asked why we spend so much time on flowcharts. Since the pseudocode statements are written in English, they don't give a clear picture of how the ideas are controlled and moved around in a program. So we provide a picture of this idea manipulation. That's what a flowchart is. Once our concept of idea movement is well developed, we will move on to pseudocode since it is more efficient for design work.

This text is organized in twelve chapters, which move from a general overview of computing and the primitive ideas of programming to the development of simple arithmetic procedures.

Chapter One begins with a general evolution of software and computers. We will see that the working definitions of 'computer' and 'program' may differ somewhat from what they are popularly conceived to be. Types of input and output have also varied widely, depending on available technology and the type of problem to be solved.

Problem analysis will concern itself first with everyday tasks, and our exercises will concentrate on breaking these down into lists of step-by-step instructions. These in turn will be shown to exhibit the structures of programs and their characteristic logic, as we make use of subroutines and loops. From these simple examples it will be possible to derive generalized solutions of greater complexity.

Chapter Two examines the relationship between the three steps of input, process and output. We will also distinguish the elements of numerical problems (numerical variables and constants) and start to outline the hierarchy of numerical operations and other rules programs must follow to be coherent to the computer.

We will construct our first programs in the third chapter. Here, we will define the assignment operator and the rules governing its use with variables and constants. A few short programs will provide examples of print, END and GOTO statements.

The geometry of the flowcharts becomes more complicated in Chapter Four. Decisions and tests are used to exit from loops, and prompts inform the user about the state of the program as it runs. We will translate these more complex algorithms into programs, and vice versa.

Three standard computing structures were created by Bohm and Jacopini: sequence, selection (IF–THEN–ELSE) and iteration (DOWHILE). Chapter Five introduces these and two additional forms (DOUNTIL and CASE). The use of these forms with top-down programming and modular structures simplifies the task of program design.

After Chapter Five we refine what we have learned so far. Chapter Six focuses on problem solution layout and the details of pseudocode.

Chapters Six, Seven and Eight introduce nested control structures. We will have a closer look at the difference between algorithms and programs in Chapter Seven, as well as the development of algorithms. Here variables are used to state the basic ideas of a program.

In Chapter Eight we use multiple decisions or conditions to move from one loop to another. A thorough review of indentation and numbering procedures will help to clarify multi-loop structure and operation.

Programming structures make use of the formal rules of logic.

Boolean algebra (a system of logical operators) provides an alternative to some of the nested control structures introduced in previous chapters. We will describe these new operators with 'truth tables' and Venn diagrams in Chapter Nine.

We will start to use one-dimensional arrays in Chapter Ten. Counting loops and DOFOR structures are applied to two-dimensional arrays in Chapter Eleven. These will give us the power to manipulate variables with the ease with which we deal with constants.

Chapter Twelve gives us one final tool in the form of the subroutine. This is a procedure that can be called up by name to perform a task, after which control can be passed back to the main program.

We end with the answers to selected problems, and an Appendix of translations from pseudocode into FORTRAN, COBOL, BASIC and Pascal.

The text is intended for a one-semester course at the university or junior college level. It should also be suitable for high school seniors. Knowledge of a computer language is not required, but it is not a hindrance. The mathematical background required is elementary high school algebra. Persons who already program, but wish to improve their appreciation of algorithm design and program structure, should find it comfortable reading. The text is intended to be used from cover to cover, with the chapters taken in the order in which they occur. Each problem set is discussed in an individual introduction. Many of the problems are answered at the end of the book.

My special thanks to the following people: Dr B. Oellers, chief of accident surgery at the Theresien Hospital in Mannheim, for permitting me to have a computer in my room during my protracted stay. Thanks to the staff of ward 3E and particularly Sister Corsina, for putting up with the screen, keyboard, cables and printer. For critical word-by-word editorial reading and a massive series of suggestions for improvement I am grateful to Joe Shapiro, Jim Harrison and Ron Salley of the University of Maryland. The students in my various classes were extremely patient and helpful in finding bad grammar, unclear passages, and nonstandard spelling. I should like to particularly thank Sandy Miquelon, Ruth Frye and Nancy S. Harmon. For faith and encouragement, much thanks to Maggie McDougall of Prentice Hall International. Copy editor David Stebbing did a sympathetic job of smoothing many rough edges. Finally, I feel special gratitude to my wife Dr Jennifer Reed and my elder son Christopher for patiently putting up with missed appointments, delayed vacations and a tremendous physical mess.

T.A.R.

Glossary

THIS glossary contains computer terms and slang used in this text. It is particularly intended to provide a way of looking up the meaning of terms that are used in the text prior to being defined. For completeness, a few words not included in the text are examined. This glossary is not intended to be exhaustive.

*   *   *

Algorithm   This is a set of steps, a rule or a recipe that provides the solution to a problem. It is not necessary for the person using it to know *why* it works but a correct solution must result whenever it is applied to the particular type of problem for which it is designed. In computer work, algorithm is *not* a synonym for program. A program normally consists of an algorithm to solve the problem being considered *plus* sections to provide for the acquisition of necessary data and the output of results.

Array   An array is a programming structure that allows a set of data to be referred to by a single variable name. Each item of the data list is located by numbers within parentheses that are usually added on at the end of the array name. Such numbers are called *Pointers* or *Subscripts*.

Assignment Operator   The symbol (:=) represents the assignment operator in the version of pseudocode used in this text and in many standard computer languages. Some languages use the equals sign (=) or another symbol such as an arrow. Whatever symbol is used, it does not indicate a state of equality, but causes certain events to occur. First, the expressions on the right-hand side of this operator are evaluated to produce a single constant value. When this has been completed, that value is caused to be contained in the single variable on the left-hand side of the assignment operator. *See* Assignment Statement.

Assignment Statement   This statement causes a value to be assigned to a particular variable. It consists of three parts. A single variable is located on the left-hand side of the assignment operator. The right-hand side of the statement consists of a set of variables, constants and operators that interact in a manner valid in the language being used. The two sides of the statement are separated by an assignment operator. The statement indicates the activity of assigning a value to a variable, it does not indicate equality between the two sides. *See* Assignment Operator, Variable (numerical and nonnumerical).

BASIC   The name is an acronym for Beginners' All-Purpose Symbolic Instruction Code. It is a high-level language using instructions written in a restricted form of English. Developed at Dartmouth College, it was first used in 1965. It is relatively easy and flexible to work with, and it allows excellent interaction between the user and the computer.

Boolean Algebra   This is a type of logical algebra developed by the British mathematician George Boole. It consists of a set of variables which take the value either 'true' or 'false'. The variables having these values are combined by a special set of operators which permit new variables to be assigned the value ('true' or 'false') resulting from such combinations. Boolean algebra underlies much of circuit, computer and computer language design as well as the logical and decision aspects of problem solving with computer programs. *See* Logical Operator, Truth Table and Venn Diagram.

Central Processing Unit   This device is hardware that is essentially the heart of the computer. It consists of two parts: the Arithmetic-Logic Unit (ALU) and a unit called Control. The ALU conducts arithmetic activities, compares values and makes simple logical decisions. Control takes care of communication with data storage devices and input/output devices. Central Processing Unit is often abbreviated as CPU.

COBOL   COBOL is an acronym for Common Business-Oriented Language. This language is unusual in that the sentence structure of the programming statements and the syntax to organize them are extremely flexible. When properly written, the section that actually does the computing resembles a relatively unstructured English which seems to clearly describe the activities to be conducted. Thus, the language is said to be 'self-documenting'. This high-level language was first introduced in 1959.

Code   A general term widely used to refer to statements or expressions written in any computer language. A person who has just converted a program design into a program written in COBOL, BASIC or some other high-level language might say, 'I've just written 30 lines of code.' The language that the computing machines actually 'understand' is referred to as *machine language* or *machine code*.

Compiler   This is a special program which takes a computer program written in a high-level language and converts it into a program written in machine language so that it may actually be run on the machine. The translated program is run as a complete unit on the computing machine. When execution is complete the machine code program is saved. When it is necessary to run the program again, the machine code program is run directly. This is much faster than recompiling the high-level language. Compilers are often contrasted with interpreters as a way of translating high-level languages.

Constant (nonnumerical)   A nonnumerical constant is a combination of letters, spaces or other symbols whose meaning or value is fixed. Alphabetical examples would be the letter 'a', the nonsense word 'FREEP', the word 'bench' and the phrase 'sandy beach'. Numerical structures may be used, but it should be understood that these are considered labels in the sense of an automobile licence plate and may not be combined arithmetically. Mixtures of symbols may be used such as '35+6', but the structure has no significance as an implied calculation or as numbers to be used in calculation. Those collections or strings of symbols are called *strings*. Another type of nonnumerical constant is the value 'true' and the value 'false' which may be assigned to variables used in Boolean statements. In this case, though the values are nonnumerical, they may interact according to the rules of Boolean algebra.

Constant (numerical)   Numbers are constant. Their values are accepted and not considered to change. Three is always three. It does not matter whether the numbers are whole numbers, decimal fractions, positive or negative. They follow the rules of arithmetic. The term 'numerical constant' is used to avoid confusion with constants which are not numbers.

Data   Data consists of numbers, letters or words and/or strings of symbols which are entered into a computer to be processed in some way. Of course, in disciplines other than computing, the word *data* has slightly different meanings, but we are interested in computers and computing, so we will stick to this context.

DOUNTIL   In a *loop*, an activity controlled by the structure is caused to repeat until a test condition, which is included in the structure, becomes true.

DOWHILE   An activity in a *loop* is caused to repeat only as long as a given condition is 'true'. When the condition becomes 'false', the activity is no longer repeated. *See* DOUNTIL and Loop.

END Statement   In many computer languages it is necessary to have an END statement to mark the end of a program. If the program contains *subroutines* which are written after the main part of the program, the END statement is usually placed at the end of the main program, but before the subroutines. Even in languages which do not require this statement for operation of the program, proper use of this statement contributes to the structural integrity of the program.

ENIAC   This is an acronym for Electronic Numerical Integrator and

Computer. Brought into operation in 1946, it was the first general-purpose electronic digital computer. It used 18,000 electron tubes.

Error Prompt   An error prompt is a notice the computer presents to the programmer or operator to tell him/her that something is not understood by the computer. Usually it means that an instruction has improper syntax or that a piece of data supplied to the computer is not organized properly.

Flowchart   A flowchart is a geometrical representation of the organization of steps in a computer program or in an algorithm. By the use of appropriate symbols and connecting lines it is possible to indicate the means by which intermediate results are tested, the repetition of steps and operations which cause input and output.

FORTRAN   Is an acronym for Formula Translator. FORTRAN, the first high-level language, was developed by International Business Machines Corporation, and first put into service in 1954. Intended more for scientific than for business problems, it is still widely used today.

GOTO Statement   This is sometimes referred to as an 'unconditional jump'. It always includes the address of another statement. When this statement is met it causes the step indicated by the attached address to be the next statement executed, irregardless of the location of the step in the program. Use of this statement can make it very difficult to follow the effective order of steps in a program. Use of the GOTO statement is to be avoided whenever possible.

Hard Copy   Refers to any programs, data or information presented in a form that may be interpreted or read directly by a human user and which may be transported away from the location of the computer. Thus a picture on a computer screen is not hard copy, but the same picture printed out on paper is hard copy. Hard copy is usually thought of as referring to something printed on paper, but there is no reason it could not be chiseled on a stone tablet if your computer had an appropriate printing device.

Hardware   Refers to those parts of your computer that are mechanical, electrical or electronic devices. The Central Processing Unit is hardware, as is the screen, main storage and any other devices that you can pick up or physically manipulate. Hardware is normally contrasted with software, which is a set of instructions. It has been said that if you can drop it and it goes 'klunk,' it is hardware. This is probably as good a definition as any, though in practice it can be a bit destructive.

High-Level Languages   These are languages normally written in a restricted form of a human language like English. Examples are FORTRAN, BASIC, COBOL and Pascal. One command or statement in such a language may cause many individual steps in machine language to be executed. High-level languages are sometimes spoken of as *higher languages*.

Hollerith Card   This is the traditional stiff paper card with holes punched in it. It has 80 columns in which holes may be punched. The position of the holes tells a card-reading machine what data are contained on the card. The card-reading machine may then transfer the information to a computer. For many years this was the principle way in which data and programs were entered into a computer. It is named for Herman Hollerith, who invented it in combination with machines that could punch, read and manipulate data obtained from such cards. *See* Punch Card.

IF–THEN–ELSE   This structure begins with the test of a given variable against some condition defined by the programmer. The condition is chosen so that there are only two possible results. Two alternative actions are provided within the body of the IF–THEN–ELSE block. Which of the choices is executed depends on the results of the test. On completion of execution of one of the choices, program control is returned to the main program. *See* Selection.

Input   Input refers to any type of information that is introduced into a computer. Obviously, data and programs are input. Instructions typed in from a keyboard qualify as input. Strictly speaking, even turning on the power switch is a form of input. Input can also be data that is typed into a hand calculator. In fact, it is information entered into a device for processing or to aid in processing. Come to think of it, there is no reason the device couldn't be a horse, or even a human being. As you read these words, they serve as input for you! Input is usually contrasted with output.

Interpreter   An interpreter is a program that translates instructions written in a high-level language into machine code so that it can be executed by the machine. The translation occurs in a special manner. A single line or statement in the higher language is translated. The instructions from this line are executed. After execution, the line of machine code is discarded. Then the next line of higher language code is translated and executed. This process continues until the program is finished. When the program must be run again, the line-by-line translation process must be carried out again. An interpreter is usually contrasted with a compiler. Programs executed with an interpreter run more slowly than programs executed with a compiler.

Iteration   This is another way of saying repetition. It normally refers to repetition of steps within a program or algorithm.

Logical Operator   Just as arithmetic operators are symbols which indicate interaction between numerical variables or constants, logical operators are symbols which indicate interaction between logical variables or constants. The logical constants have the value 'true' or 'false' while the logical variables are variables restricted to containing the values 'true' or 'false'. Typical operators are AND, OR and NOT though a number of other logical operators exist. *See* Boolean Algebra.

Loop   A loop is a structure built into a program that permits the same process to be repeated again and again. An example would be printing your name 20 times. Loops may also be designed to permit modification of the process as it is repeated. *See* DOWHILE, DOUNTIL and GOTO.

Machine Language   Machine language is the language that the machine actually reads and works in. It is written out only rarely. When this is done, it must be written in binary numbers. Translators such as compilers and interpreters are used to convert programs into machine language.

Magnetic Disk Storage   Magnetic storage disks may be flexible disks made of thin plastic (floppy disks) or rigid disks made out of metal (fixed disks). In either case, the surface of the disk is coated with a film of material containing extremely fine metal oxide. The metal involved in the oxide is usually iron or chromium. This is the same type of material that is on the surface of the tape used to record music. The disk drive of the computer contains a magnetic device that causes alterations in the metal oxide film. These are organized in tiny spots or swirls, each corresponding to either 0 or 1. In this way information may be stored on the surface of the disk. The information is organized in circular tracks, which the head 'writes' onto the disk as the disk revolves. The magnetic head may also be used to detect the magnetic spots placed on the disk. In this way, information stored on the disk may be 'read' back into the computer. A great deal of information may be stored on a magnetic disk because the magnetic spots are small and placed close together.

Magnetic Tape Storage   Magnetic tape for use by computers is essentially the same as the magnetic tape used for the storage of music or speech. Like the magnetic disk, the tape is coated with metal oxide film. The principle of information storage and recovery is also the same as in the case of magnetic disks; the difference lies in the geometry of the organization. Magnetic tapes store the data one item after another, on the tape. The magnetic disks store the data in concentric tracks or circles. The tape must be drawn through an assembly containing the magnetic read/write head. The operation is just as in the case of an ordinary tape recorder. In fact, some computers permit a conventional tape recorder working with an ordinary music tape cassette to be used as a storage device for programs and data.

Menu   A computer menu operates rather like the menu in a restaurant. Just as the waiter in the restaurant presents a menu with a list of choices, the screen of the computer may present a display listing a series of choices. When the user selects an activity from the menu, the computer may begin the selected activity immediately, or it may present a new menu in order to obtain more details of the exact action or conditions required. In any event, after presenting a set of choices or a series of such sets, the computer has obtained sufficient information and executes the action desired by the operator. This is quite similar to the restaurant situation, though the waiter often requests further information verbally rather than by presenting additional menus.

Module   A module is a block of computer code that performs a specific activity or a small number of closely related activities. Information and data passing through this block of statements enters at a single location and leaves at a single location. In this way the program module is like a module in a piece of mechanical or electrical equipment. It does one job or a small number of related jobs. Such structures facilitate the design of equipment and programs. If a particular aspect of a program must be updated or altered, a single module may be removed and replaced.

Object file   *Object file* refers to a set of computer information that is intended to be run on the machine and which is written in machine code. *Object code* implies the same meaning. A program written in a high-level language is translated by a compiler to produce an object file that will be run on the machine. We might also say that it is translated to produce object code to be run on the machine.

Operating System   The operating system is software. It has three purposes. It controls the operation of input and output devices; it provides an environment in which programs may be executed or run; and it controls the allocation of main storage within the computer. The operating system may be thought of as being located between the hardware of the computer and the various programs run by the operator. It may also be likened to the top of one of the newer electric stoves. No matter how the energy is controlled within the modern stove, the stove top has a rather standard set of burners or hotplates and switches which permit the cook to prepare dishes in a prescribed manner, independent of the make of stove. The operating system of a computer creates an analogous standardization for the user and his/her programs.

Output   Obviously, this is what the computer puts out. It may be information on the screen, printed tables of answers to computations, a weather prediction, a light signal, a funny sound or a simulation of the human voice.

Pascal   Pascal is a high-level programming language named for the French mathematician Pascal. It is notable for its extremely good logical structures and for being a language in which it is easy to write well-structured programs. It was designed by Niklaus Wirth in 1971.

Pointer A pointer is a number that a gives the address in memory where a specific piece of data may be found. It may be a number in machine code that indicates the actual physical location of data within main storage, or it may be a number which in conjunction with certain aspects of the higher language being used will refer to such a location. The subscript or index of an element in an array, in conjunction with the language being used, points to a specific location in the memory system of the machine on which it is being used. In this text, we have used the word *pointer* for this purpose so that the student becomes accustomed to this idea.

Print Statement Information such as requests for data, the results of computation or a comment are sent from the program to an output device such as the screen or a printer by a print statement.

Program A program is a list of instructions in a language that can be made understandable to the computer. It tells the computer what to do to solve some specified problem and how to test and respond to intermediate results. More generally, it is a recipe or instruction set to solve a problem in the real world.

Prompt A prompt is information provided by the computer to indicate what state it is in at a given moment. Often when you turn on a computer it emits a beep. This may signal that the computer is active and ready to receive input. Such a prompt may be accompanied by a notice on the screen giving more information. The screen notice is also a prompt. If hardware failure should occur, many modern machines will notify the user with a screen message. This is a prompt. When the program in the computer is waiting for data, it may send a request in one form or another. This is a prompt.

Punch Card This term usually implies an 80-column punch card or Hollerith card. At one time this was the most common way to get information into the machine. Instead of talking about a source file or source program, one still often talks about a source deck to refer to a program in high-level language ready for translation by a compiler. This refers to the deck of punch cards once used to hold such a program. There are still a number of computer installations in the world which depend, at least in part, on punch card input. The organization of computer data derived from punch cards or decks of punch cards is with us as a fossil structure built into most data manipulation programs used today, even though these data manipulation systems actually use other sorts of data input such as keyboards, magnetic disks and magnetic tape. *See* Hollerith Card.

Punched Paper Tape Such tape is now much more familiar to users of teleprinter communications systems than users of computers. It consists of paper tape with a single line of holes across the tape for each character. Various coding patterns have been used. The earliest involved patterns based on five positions which might or might not have holes. Later designs used eight- and nine-hole patterns. Punched paper tape has been used in computing operations, but it is now rarely seen in this application. It was relatively slow to read and quite fragile.

Screen   This is just the television-like device on which many computers present information. I used it in the text because it was obvious. I included it in the glossary so that I could refer to the more 'computerish' names. It is often called a *monitor*. This is especially true when the screen itself is not a part of the computer chassis. I prefer the old-fashioned terms, cathode-ray tube (CRT), which is still widely used. It refers to the time in the not too distant past when a box of electronic tricks was used to feed output information through a screen rather like a laboratory oscilloscope. Thus *screen* is an excellent word for the glowing output device associated with your computer, but CRT is still widely used.

Selection   This is a more formal name for the IF–THEN–ELSE control structure. *See* IF–THEN–ELSE.

Sequence   A series of program steps one after the other or a series of process symbols in a flowchart may be referred to as a *sequence*. The use of the terminology in this way is to bind the steps or processes together to form a single structure which may be considered as a unit for purposes of program or algorithm structure.

Software   Computer programs are software. They don't go 'klunk' when you drop them unless they have been written on stone tablets or something of the sort. Even then it is not the software itself going 'klunk', it is just what the software is written on. The software is the program. The paper or screen or magnetic disk or tablecloth it is written on is really not a part of it. Then why bother to call it software; why not just say 'program'? It works like this. Many of the programs we use in computing are anything but obvious. They may be part of the operating system. They may be even deeper beneath the surface of the machine than that. There may be programs that simulate pieces of hardware to make design of the computer easier or more efficient. Of course, some kind of hardware must underlie it all to provide something on which to run the programs, which may be pretending to be hardware. Just the same, there are many programs that we would not think of in the same terms as programs that edit copy or do computations or play games. To encompass this whole range of programs, we use the term *software*. Besides, it leaves the term *program* relatively unencumbered, so that we can use it to refer to our latest effort without being confusing.

Source Code   *Source code* refers to programs or parts of programs written in a high-level language by a human being. It must be translated by a compiler or interpreter before it can be read and executed by the machine. Source code is not necessarily a complete program; it may only be a few lines of it. The source code may be organized in a file and will then be referred to as a *source file*. Often, in order to be romantic or just because it has a certain ring to it, we refer to a 'source deck', even though we are years away from writing out source code on Hollerith cards.

Subroutine   The best metaphor here is a tool in a toolkit. A subroutine is a small program separated from the main program. It usually does a rather specific job that must be repeated often in various parts of the main program. Rather than rewrite the particular block of code again and again, high-level languages provide facilities permitting us to write this block as a special kind of program separated from the main program. When the activities of the subroutine are needed, it is called by mentioning its name or location. At this time, control of program execution is shifted from control of the main program to control of the subroutine. When the subroutine's operations are complete, control of execution is returned to the main program in a position immediately following the statement that called the subroutine. Thus it is like a screwdriver that you take from the toolkit when you need to tighten a screw and that you return when the job is done. Subroutines may also be used to improve the program structure. A subroutine might be designed to read data, another to process the data, and yet another to print out the results. The main program would just call each subroutine in turn. Such a use permits us to write out the program in a logical fashion, improves structure and reduces the number of mistakes introduced by the programmer.

Subscript   This term refers to the reference numbers in parentheses that indicate the particular element of an array that is being considered. The terminology comes from mathematics. We have used the term *pointer* in this text to mean the same thing.

Terminal   A terminal is a single keyboard-and-screen combination. Properly, it refers to such a device which connects to a large computer which runs many terminals. It is sometimes used casually to refer to a keyboard and screen that are only part of a microcomputer.

Terminal Time   This is time an operator spends working on a terminal. For larger machines, it is part of a computation that may be used to determine the charge for computer use.

Terminator   This refers to an oval-shaped flowchart symbol which is used to mark the beginning and end of a program. At the beginning of the program the symbol contains the word 'BEGIN' and at the end of the program, the same shaped symbol contains the word 'END'.

Truth Table   A truth table is a table which lists logical variables, combinations of logical variables, and the values the individual and combined variables have as the result of assignment and combination. It is used to define logical operators and to determine the value of combinations of logical variables and operators in Boolean algebra. In constructing a truth table only the values 'true' and 'false' are used. *See* Boolean Algebra and Logical Operator.

Variable (numerical and nonnumerical)   A variable is a symbol which takes the place of a value in an expression. It does not have a value until one is assigned to it. When a value has been assigned, it replaces the variable in the expression. A numerical variable only accepts assignments which are numbers. These numbers may be integers (whole numbers without a decimal part or decimal point); they may be decimal fractions or may be presented in a format using exponents. However they are presented, they must obey the accepted laws of arithmetic and combine by use of arithmetic operators such as plus, minus, etc. Nonnumerical variables may be assigned only non-numerical constants as values. These include string constants and logical constants (true, false). *See* Assignment Statement, Constant (nonnumerical), Constant (numerical).

Venn Diagram   This picture represents a class of all objects having a particular character by an area in two dimensions. The area is sometimes presented as a circle, but it may be a square, or it may be any shape. Areas defined by the overlap between two areas, or by the sum of two areas or as the space not included in an initially defined area may be used to represent the effect of the logical operators AND, OR and NOT respectively. The Venn diagram method may be applied to any number of variables and to combinations of any number of variables and logical operators, provided they represent an expression which is valid in Boolean algebra. *See* Boolean Algebra, Logical Operator, Truth Table.

CHAPTER ONE

Pseudocode and Computers

IT SEEMS to me that one of the great pleasures of this world is just playing with computers. Sitting in front of a screen and working through the mysteries of an operating system is exciting. Writing one's own program directly on the screen and then running it right away gives a great feeling of accomplishment. The joys of exploring the computer frontier in this way must be like the experiences of the early airplane pilots. However, an interesting transition occurred. As flying became more complex, the pure seat-of-the-pants pilot became not just obsolete, but an actual menace. Pilots today still have that almost intuitive 'feel' that characterized the early air pioneers, but they have additional layers of instrument, navigation, planning and communication skills that permit them to handle complex modern aircraft with the same consummate technique that their predecessors displayed on the 'old crates'. The native abilities are still with us; there is just a lot more besides.

A similar change has occurred in computer programming. Computers are being used to solve more complicated problems; the computers themselves have become more complex. It was soon apparent that languages evolving in close association with computer hardware development did not provide efficient ways of handling logical situations in mathematics or in the real world. A need for more formalized structures, designs more suited to problem analysis and standardized logical devices became obvious.

Today the competent computer programmer has a well-developed collection of logical devices, techniques, problem analysis procedures and structuring methods that are analogous to the flight management tools of the competent pilot. Just as in the case of the pilot, all the intuitive skills are still present. In beginning our introduction to algorithm design and structured programming, we will follow the evolution of modern structure and analysis from earlier methods.

It is all well and good to talk about the romance of computers, but there are still a great many people today who do not have a realistic idea of what a computer is. Of course, one sees computers in movies and on television. These machines may be anything from a modernistic room full of electronics gone mad in a science fiction story, to a desk-top machine run by some confident and casual pre-teenage youngster in an advertisement.

People may work with a computer and still not have an idea of what it really is. In this case, it is a screen on which one types information from a keyboard. The fact that the information put into the machine may be manipulated by following the commands on a menu or some other prompting device does not mean that the operator has any real idea about the nature of the computer.

We can have a fantasy computer. In this machine, the user enters instructions and/or data through a keyboard and a TV screen. This user believes the computer is a mass of electronics (albeit with a rather slow response time). In fact, the orders and information entered are read off another screen by ordinary people. If they don't like the way information is entered, they send error notices. If they need to look up information, they use an encyclopedia or a set of numeric tables. If they have to do a calculation, they count on their fingers. When the job is complete and the patient user asks for a printout of the results, they put it out on an electric typewriter, or maybe they scrawl it in pencil on an old paper bag and speed it off to the user via a pneumatic tube. It drops into a basket under the user's TV screen with a klunk.

This, of course, cannot be a computer. Are you sure? We could make things even simpler and avoid the TV screen. The questions are supplied on old paper bags and the answers return on old paper bags. Speed and accuracy excluded, how different is this from typing a question into an electronic computer and getting an answer?

Let's look at a normal four-function pocket calculator that simply adds, subtracts, divides and multiplies. It is becoming difficult to find a simple device like this outside of an antique shop, but again we can have it as a primitive fantasy. Is this pocket calculator a computer? It can certainly calculate rapidly enough. It has a keyboard for input. It has a simple screen or printer for output, but even if it is electronic, we must probably exclude it from consideration as a computer. What does it lack?

Actually, it's not too hard to define a computer. It must have some means of taking in and putting out data. It must have the capacity to change the sequence of operations on the basis of input and/or intermediate results, and it must be capable of being adjusted to solve a particular problem. That is, it must be programmable. But then, assuming there is a means of programming things, our paper-bag processor is a computer! Certainly – why not? You might even wish to get together with some friends and build one. After all, for such a machine, you don't have to know much about electronics.

This brings us to the problem of a program. What is a program? It is just a set of instructions or directions explaining how to achieve a particular result. Is a recipe a program? Absolutely, and the computer in this case is the kitchen and the cooking staff.

The input may be raw materials like eggs or salt and the output could be a cake or a stew. We would change the recipe depending on what was desired. There would even be a set of rules to make the recipes function properly. A recipe written in Hindustani would cause a normal English-speaking staff and kitchen to send the prescription for culinary delight back to the person submitting it.

Although, as we have seen, it is possible to describe a computer that runs without electronics and uses a MOCG (manually operated character generator – or pencil) as an output, we will restrict ourselves to something that operates with electronics in the form of tubes or relays or transistors. We will think in terms of input and output on devices similar to typewriters, TV screens, cards coded by means of holes punched in them, or on magnetic materials such as tape or disks. However, while we are restricting our immediate thoughts to this electronic world, it is essential to remember that our simple calculator would be quite like a computer if we were to include an intelligent operator. In this case, the electronic calculator might be replaced by an abacus.

Machines that pass information to the world by blinking colored lights, opening doors or blowing whistles can also be computers. The only tricky place in the definition is evaluating flexibility of response and programmability. It is, of course, quite possible for the program to be physically built in by the manufacturer. Thus, we have an input, an output, a means of calculation, the chance for the machine to make decisions and/or alter its own behavior on the basis of internal results and, finally, a means of being programmed to adjust to some particular environment.

We are particularly interested in the program, so we will examine various types of programming. One of the first computers was ENIAC. It had everything, including thousands of electron tubes just as found in the old-fashioned pre-transistor radio. Programming was very interesting. Every time one changed the problem type, one reprogrammed the machine by rewiring it with a great many cables and plugs.

As more advanced machines were built, they were programmed by inserting a code written in binary numbers. Binary numbers are written in base 2. An individual digit is allowed to be only 0 or 1. Long strings of these digits can represent any number we are used to seeing as our everyday numbers in base 10. The binary digits have another property. Since they have only two states (1 and 0) they are ideal for setting switches, which are usually limited to being either 'on' or 'off'.

Computers are almost entirely made up of large collections of interconnected on–off switches. Therefore, binary numbers are ideal for setting the switches inside a computer. This is what is involved in programming a computer. The early use of cables and plugs was only a crude way of arranging interconnections that could be more easily made by changing the internal switching, once it was discovered how to do it. Teaching the properties of binary arithmetic is not our interest in presenting this book. Thus, having noted that binary numbers exist, roughly what they are, and the way they are useful to computers, we will leave them here. You will not really need them in pseudocode work and algorithm design at this level. When you need them, you will find they are easily learned.

The next step, then, in the improvement of computer programming after rewiring was to program the machine by inserting long lists of instructions written in binary code. The program, of course, is just a list of instructions to do a job. It even includes instructions to say what tests and alternatives should be presented during the course of machine operation. Code insertion might be done by means of a keyboard, punched paper tape, punched cards or magnetic tape. A typical series of commands might look like:

010011101011
101110110101
011010110101

Checking and correcting such commands is clearly a nightmare. Means were developed for translating these commands into simple abbreviations called mnemonic code. Essentially, one abbreviation would represent one binary command number or command word. The organization of the binary number words and the program was based almost entirely on the physical arrangement of electronic switches in the computer, and designed for convenience of operation from the point of view of the computer. The simple numerical command words themselves caused movement of a number, simple operations like addition or subtraction, comparisons between two numbers, storage of an intermediate result, introduction of another number for processing, and similar simple activities. The abbreviations for these command words were a bit easier to work with because they had a crude relation to what was going on, but there was still one mnemonic command for each of the old numerical commands. The mnemonic 'LD' might be used in place of a binary number command that caused a number to be loaded into a particular location. 'AD' might stand for addition. The numbers or location addresses to be manipulated would stand in specific relation to the abbreviations according to a set of conventions designed for the particular machine using the language.

A program loaded into the machine would translate all these mnemonic commands into binary commands, because binary number code is really the only thing the machine can understand. If the mnemonic code abbreviations were not perfectly written with the necessary addresses and numbers in exactly the right place, the translation would produce a mess that would cause chaos when the machine attempted to run it. Since the abbreviation code corresponded more or less exactly to the machine code, command and program organization was convenient for the machine, but not necessarily convenient for the people who had to develop and insert the program.

Between 1950 and 1960 more advanced languages were developed. The first computer languages of this type were FORTRAN and COBOL. These were much more like English; whole words were used. Single command words or statements might cause several related machine code words to be executed. The construction and logic were much more acceptable to human operators.

While these so-called high-level languages were easier to understand for the programmers, they required a great deal of precision to write properly. Each error, no matter how trivial, was noted by the translation device. The programmer then had the task of correcting the error. This remains true today, no matter what language is being used.

Just as a paragraph in English may be organized in different ways and yet say the same thing, programs in the higher languages had many possibilities for organization while still giving the same instructions to the machine in good grammatical form. Some organizations were difficult to understand and might be very long. Other organizations of the same program might be quite clear. The programming languages still dimly reflected the calculation methods involved in generalized computer hardware. It was the special organization of the programs that permitted them to reflect logical procedures for problem solving. It is this organization which is the domain of the human programmer.

A number of methods were developed to facilitate program design and understanding. These included several different graphical systems and various simplified versions of English. The search for what constituted good program structure and methods by which it might be achieved was a continuing theme of computer literature. Such efforts resulted in organizing the statements of the program to reflect the logic of the problem and its solution rather than structures derived from internal machine logic and architecture. Charting procedures were effective, but suffered the drawback of requiring extensive redrawing as the programmer optimized his or her program structure. They were not a major factor in design, but were and are important in documentation, analysis and teaching.

In this text, charting procedures will be restricted to these purposes. On the other hand, specialized versions of English in the form of so-called pseudocode have become important in design as well as teaching, although the documentation role is left to charting and to notes within the program itself.

Learning a computer language in the conventional way involves learning proper logical organization to produce well-structured, modular code. It involves acquiring entirely new concepts of data manipulation such as loops and arrays. Formal problem analysis and solution will probably be a new experience for the student.

Acquiring a computer language means learning a special set of commands and, at the same time, learning to introduce particular variables and parameters that properly mesh with the command structure and make everything work. This is immersed in a mechanical environment that involves learning how to operate a computer, getting it all straight with the keyboard even if one is not an experienced typist, and learning some editorial procedure to correct mistakes in the program. This complex learning experience is conducted in the presence of the translation system within the computer, which converts the language being used by the student into something that the internal parts of the computer can handle. Every missed comma, extra space, and syntax or grammatical error is ruthlessly brought to the attention of the student, but often in terms that take a bit of understanding.

It's hard to get the music correct when, each time you start to play, the teacher points at your toe and grunts. Maybe you're tapping your foot to the wrong beat, which is a matter of importance to the music, or maybe your shoelace is untied, which doesn't really matter until you get on the concert stage. But all these interruptions inhibit an easy understanding of the music. In the case of computer languages, the critic is a remorseless machine, the inhibition is real and some of the language developed may be right outside the machine's vocabulary. You can't even get the machine angry. It just sits there and burps out error prompts, often accompanied by a ridiculous beeping sound. When you get things right, it goes on to the next mistake without even a friendly nod or a pat on the shoulder. This lack of personality may be comfortable for the professional, but it is unnerving for the person learning his or her first computer language.

Pseudocode has a number of advantages. Chief among these is that although the programmer writes a proper program, this pseudocode program is never intended to be translated by electronic means for use in the computer. Thus, all the problems of perfect syntax and grammar can be set aside while the overall line of the program as well as many of the details are developed. As pseudocode matured, advanced logical structures were introduced. These could be used to design programs, even if the result, to be run on a machine, might be written in a language without the logical refinements of pseudocode.

As pseudocode became more and more standardized, conversion of specific logical structures to equivalent statement blocks in real computer languages became quite straightforward. We will not worry about conversion to real computer languages until the end of the book.

A couple of remarks about the computer world and language learning are important. First, the bottleneck in computer application today is software, not hardware. This is true whether the application is a simple program run by an individual on a personal computer, or a huge program system run by a large institution on a main-frame computer. At both levels, the solution is careful problem analysis to produce well-designed algorithms realized as properly structured, understandable programs. Pseudocode is a tool that connects all of these endeavors and allows easy transition from preliminary analysis to the final program.

Second, there are many situations where the amount of computer time available is limited. Of course, when people know enough about computers and, particularly, can demonstrate some understanding of programming, they will find that one way or another actual hands-on computer time will come their way. But this is a catch-22. How can you learn about computer programming on limited computer time? That's precisely why we are here. In fact, it is actually easier to learn the fundamentals of computer programming without the distraction of an electronic box of tricks telling you to start from scratch because you used 'ain't' instead of 'isn't' in what was otherwise the beginning of a decent piece of literature.

Let's review things. Then we will consider a few actual programs before going on to more detail in the next chapter. First of all, a computer consists of some kind of hardware and some kind of software. The hardware is the box of switches and electronics and mechanical devices. The software is a set of instructions telling the hardware how to function, how to translate the instructions it is given and, of course, it is these instructions themselves.

This list of instructions is the program. Developing a program is generating a list of instructions that permits the rest of the software and the hardware to work on problems that interest us. The program must fit between our idea of the real world and the rest of the computer. It must be organized in a fashion that follows the logic of problem-solving processes that we can understand. In this text, we are interested in developing problem-solving routines in a way that displays the logic behind the routines in a clearcut, economical fashion.

We care so much about the clarity and logic of the situation that we are not going to bother with a computer at all. This is because getting the grammar of the program perfect enough to avoid noisy electronic criticism by the rest of the computer is distracting.

The way that the program is translated for the computer is of no interest at all. This is software that is not part of the program. What the hardware of the computer can do has some interest for us, since we have to tell the computer how to gather information and present results.

For our purposes, at this time, a computer has some way to take in information. This is a typewriter keyboard, a card-reading device or some device based on magnetic tape or magnetic disks. There may be other special ways of taking in information, particularly in situations involving physical situations such as the control of traffic lights. There is some way of reading out results. This could be a console screen, a printer, a graphical plotter or more specialized devices like some of the traffic lights mentioned above. Of course, the devices that take in data may also be used to enter the program, but since the program will not control its own entry in the situations we consider here, this is outside our interest. The physical means by which the data is manipulated inside the hardware is also of no interest to us. This happens in the central processing unit. There is a large memory system called main storage. This is also of no interest to us at the moment. That narrows it down just to devices that take in data and those that put out results. Still, so that you have an overall picture of a computer, we present a simple diagram in Figure 1.1.

We will now examine several lists of instructions or programs related to the physical world. These are selected with some care. If you examine such apparently simple operations as putting on a shirt or tying your shoes, you will find that they are very complex, with a lot of built-in tests and steps that you never fully define on a conscious level. Analyzing these is quite tricky. It

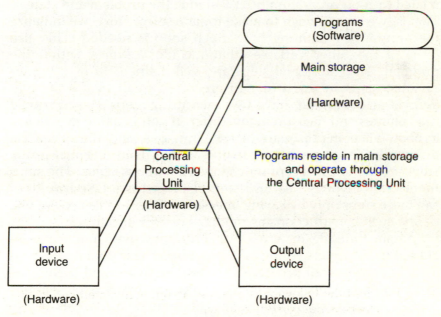

Fig. 1.1   A simple computing machine

is because the analysis of such operations is complex that we have no robots that help with the housework or serve as valets or ladies' maids.

A kitchen recipe is a good example of a simple program, provided we do not try to include all the details of using spoons, moving dishes from one counter to the other and breaking eggs. So here is a recipe for cream of tomato soup:

1. Decide how much soup you will need.
2. At room temperature measure out a volume of Sauce Supreme equal to three-quarters of the desired volume of soup.
3. At room temperature measure out a quantity of good quality commercial tomato paste (not catsup) equivalent to one-quarter of the volume of the desired volume of soup.
4. Mix the ingredients from steps 2 and 3.
5. Bring the mixture to a temperature slightly above serving temperature on a steam table, or in a double-boiler.
6. Dilute with milk until the consistency of thick cream. Maintain temperature.
7. Adjust seasoning.
8. Serve.

There are a number of important aspects of this recipe that are related to good programming. We define the problem and state it. That is, we say we wish to make tomato soup. Next, we initialize the program by defining how much soup is needed. This also fixes all the other variables that include volumes within the program. The individual steps are well defined. In fact, the individual steps in this program are often small blocks of well-defined activities. We have two measuring steps in which only the volumes and measurements differ. If you imagine the chef as a robot, it is going through the same motions; only the size of the measuring spoon and the contents differ. Thus the measuring steps are identical, except for changes in two variables. The steps themselves involve a set of identical procedures. We invoke or call these steps only by saying 'measure.' Later in this text we will define such constructions as modules or as subroutines.

Again, thinking in terms of subroutines, we could have included the complete recipe for Sauce Supreme or tomato paste as a part of the overall program. As it is, we just called them. The preparation of Sauce Supreme, which we store in the refrigerator, represents a subroutine that we might use in many recipes or programs. The same applies to the tomato paste we get in a can from the grocery store. We use it a lot – in spaghetti, in lasagna and in this soup. Why make it fresh every time? Buy a couple of cans and keep it on the shelf to call for when we need it. Tomato paste is a subroutine.

We have another computer structure here. It is found in different forms in both steps 5 and 6. This is a loop. In step 5 we will start warming the mixture. We will test the temperature. If the temperature is too low, we will execute a well-known operation. We will wait a bit. Then, we will test again. Then we will wait. We keep looping through a waiting period and then retesting until the test is successful. Then we exit the 'wait loop' and proceed to the next step.

Step 6 is another loop and test system. We add a bit of milk, stir it in, test the thickness, and if the soup is too thick, we add some more milk and test again. This dilute-and-test loop will be kept up until the test is successful, when we will exit and proceed to the next step.

Step 7 is another of those subroutines. It may also be a loop in the event that we add a little salt, test the taste and add a little more. The variables that establish the test standard will be changeable, but the testing routine will involve many activities similar to testing routines used in other dishes. Again, it will constitute a procedure that will be called up instead of described each time.

The serving routine in Step 8 is another modular structure. You probably lay out the bowls and spoons and fill the bowls in the same way you would for any hot soup without lumps. Again, it is a routine that you invoke.

Notice the many looping structures in which you conduct an activity, check to see if it is successful, repeat the activity and check again. This testing and looping is common in all program design.

You may feel a bit robbed at this point. You wanted a program-like activity and I gave you a list of activities each of which called a simple routine procedure that you could do elsewhere or get off the shelf. This is very important in programming. It represents what is called modular thinking. We will refer to it again and again until people develop a feel for it. Then it will be presented in a formalized manner as part of a more formal pseudocode.

Let's try one more problem from the real world. In the above program, we went through a procedure to establish a known result, we had to make adjustments along the way, but it was like writing up a table of values automatically. There was not the sense of problem solving. However, whether one likes it or not, this is one of the main aspects of computer programming.

For the second program, we will solve a problem from the physical world. Like so many such problems, it turns out to be very complex, and specific strategies must be adopted to deal with it. The problem is this: We are outside a house. The house may be of any size. It is all on one floor. We must enter the house, turn out the lights in every room of the house and leave the house.

Certain details will be ignored. When we have turned out the lights in a room, how will we navigate? We can assume that daylight comes in from other rooms or windows, or we can assume that we have a large flashlight with us. An examination reveals that we are dealing with a problem in which we have to visit every room of the house and that doing this is the real problem. Since this is a generalized problem, we are beset with difficulties of recognition. All the rooms might look the same. There do not have to be too many rooms before it becomes clear that recognition and memory will be difficult.

As soon as we begin to think about the problem, it also becomes clear that it is not a simple one if we are to arrive at a procedure that will get us into every room of this house. This is one of the major difficulties with the physical world. It is very complex. For this reason we will stick to problems that are essentially numerical. In general such problems are easier to handle than nonnumerical ones.

But back to the house. We must now consider techniques that will lead us to the solution of this house problem. One technique is to invert the thinking and use some trick. For example. Why go in at all? We could just use the main switch, provided we have a routine that guarantees we find it. Of course, if the lighting is candles we are stuck, but if some trick solves the general problem, so much the better.

An important part of problem solving is to stand back and ask what the question really is and see if we cannot solve it by turning the problem upside down or looking at it in another way. I have built this problem so that this approach won't work, but this is still worth mentioning.

Another way to handle problems is to break them down into parts. In a sense we did this by recognizing that in this case we really wanted to get into each room of the house. Without saying it explicitly, we meant that if we could get into each room, then in each room we would invoke a light-turning-off routine and when the lights were out, we would return to the room-accessing routine.

Here is another general technique. We can define a carefully simplified version of the problem. We will solve this and then expand it stepwise, in stages, until we can handle the main problem. In this presentation we will consider a simplification, but the main problem is a bit more sophisticated and we will not solve it at this time. This is a bit disappointing, perhaps, but many physical problems are so difficult that the general solutions, even when known, are rarely used.

The simplified house is defined in the following way. It is still a one-level house. It may have as many rooms as we wish. There is at least one entrance between the inside of the house and the outside world. All rooms have either one or two doors.

Within the house, there is some route that connects any room to any other room. This is a pretty simple house. You may be surprised at how simple it really is when you think about it a bit. However, we can work up a routine to solve the problem by starting the process and analyzing the activity as we progress. This is the hallmark of a good simplification. It gives us a place to start and subsequent actions are easy to analyze.

1. Enter the house by any external door.
2. If the lights in this room are on, turn them off.
3. Look around and see how many other doors there are. There will either be one other door, or none.
4. If there are no other doors, leave the room by the way you came in. If there is another door, leave the room by this one.
5. You are now either in a room, or you are outside the house. If you are in a room, go to Step 2 of this routine and carry on. If you are outside the house, you have turned off all the lights and your task is completed.

Try this out on a few sample houses and you will find it works. I have included one such house in Figure 1.2. You will also realize that the type of house we can handle by this routine is very limited. Still, it is surprising how many houses fit this category.

The next step is to increase the level of complexity. A good way to do this is to say that every room may have up to three doors, but that at least one of the doors must always lead to a one-door room like a closet.

With three doors in each room, when you have chosen a door

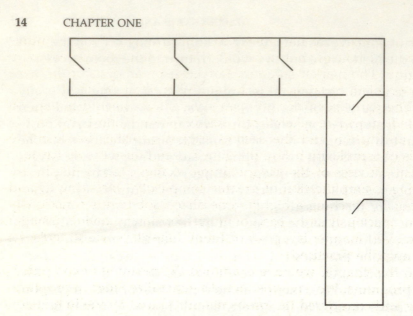

Fig. 1.2   A very simple house

leading to a dead-end room as your first choice, you must choose between the two doors that may remain in the room. One is the one you entered by and the other is not the one you entered by. This could get confusing. One tactic that may come to you is to mark the door you entered by with a marker of some sort placed on the floor. A refinement would be to mark the doorway twice (two markers on the floor). Mark it once when you go in and once when you pass through again. Thus, going into a one-door room would immediately put two markers in the doorway and you would not want to go in that way again. Leaving a room by a door that you had not used before would result in one marker. When you finally want to backtrack the way you came, you need only go through the doorways with one marker and you will be exiting along ways you have used, but only once. This is a good plan. There is one hitch: if you go out a door that leads outside without trying the other door in the room (this door is automatically a closet), you might leave one light in the house that has not been turned off. You must have a special rule determining a test and activity regarding doors leading outside. This is a test not required in the first, simpler example.

Now we have a second, more advanced simplification. I did not write the program, but you will find it at the end of the book with the answers to the questions concerning this chapter. The class of houses we have described includes quite a large number of real houses, but not all of the one-story houses we may imagine. The marker solution derived from analysis of the two-door problem certainly gives a clue to handling greater complexity. The early-exit difficulty also suggests routines that may be needed in a more generalized house. The relation between the first abstraction and the second suggests further intermediate levels of complexity before the generalized house can be treated.

This process of choosing a simple example, analyzing it, designing a simplification of greater complexity, analyzing it, and eventually reaching a highly generalized solution is consciously or unconsciously at the basis of much of problem solving. Using it in an overt manner is a powerful tool. Like all powerful tools, its use must be practiced.

In this chapter we have examined the meaning of computers and programs. We have abstracted a generalized idea of programming and considered the problems introduced by the interaction between the programmer, the programming language and the machine on which the language runs. This has led us to consider a language that resembles a generalized computer language, but does not run on a computer, as a learning and design tool.

Programs themselves have been considered as lists of instructions that have specific feedback properties. These properties permit the program to adjust its behavior to initial requirements or intermediate results. While examples have been taken from the physical world, it has been noted that such an environment often requires a particularly complex type of program; and that for simplicity, our teaching examples will generally be numerical in nature. Finally, we briefly examined various types of strategies that might be used in approaching solutions to problems.

In the next chapter we will begin to examine the elements that make up numerical problems and the development of programs to solve them.

PROBLEMS

At this time you probably do not have the formal tools required for problem solving, but you can write programs by listing the necessary steps in the form of a recipe as was done in Chapter 1. You should take a crack at these problems, but remember that the idea is to get you thinking about the difficulties of problem analysis and the need for comfortable techniques to describe what the analyst wishes done. Many of these problems will be presented in slightly different forms throughout the rest of the text when their solution can help you understand particular techniques or problems. So enjoy attacking them in a rather serious manner, but don't worry too much about any difficulties you may have. These are good problems for group effort and class discussions. Since these problems are intended to stimulate thinking, solutions to them will not be found in the answer section at the end of the book.

*   *   *

1.1   You have a job polishing the floor of a large rectangular gymnasium. The floor polisher is an electric device with a built-in battery that you will not have to recharge. It is just a simple unit with a soft rotating buffing wheel, a small motor housing and a long handle that you use to guide the polisher along the floor. Using a simple program written in ordinary English, describe the movements of the polisher that will accomplish this task.

There are no tricks in this problem. You may walk across the floor when you are done, if you wish. Just polish the whole floor without missing any of it. If there is a small bit an inch or two wide along the wall that does not get polished, don't worry about it. You just have to think in terms of moving the polishing wheel across the floor. Never mind about what you need to do with the handle or the person pushing the unit when turns are made. The operator can always walk over the area to be polished or the area that has been polished.

1.2   A fairly common practice is to maintain a 'running average' for some kind of measurement. That is, as each new measurement comes in, the average of all numbers that have come in so far is determined. Computationally, the way to do this is to maintain a running total of the number of values that have come in.

Each time a new value comes in, you increase the 'number of values' by one. Then, at the same time, you total up all the numbers that have already come in. Each time a new value is brought in, you also add it to the sum of those numbers that have already come in. When you have done this, you divide the updated sum by the updated number of values and print the updated average.

Write a stepwise recipe or program to calculate the running average. Begin with a statement that says something like '1. Accept the next value.' Include the necessary loop or loops to keep this routine going forever.

1.3   You have broken your left arm. It is useless and in a sling, so you may use only one hand. You are alone in the kitchen and have two live and very unfriendly lobsters in two separate pots. Unfortunately, you realize that the large lobster is in the small pot and will never cook properly and the small lobster is in the large pot. Although you can successfully grasp one lobster, there is no way you can hold two lobsters at one time.

If the lobsters are accidentally placed in the same pot they will grab each other and never be separated. If you set a lobster on the table, it will scuttle to the floor and hide under the icebox, becoming lost forever unless you wish to take a chance on losing a finger getting it out.

Write a program in simple English indicating the steps in getting the big lobster in the big pot and the small lobster in the small pot.

Hint: Nobody has said you cannot use another pot and there are plenty of pots in the kitchen.

Restriction: Tossing a lobster into the air is not allowed.

1.4   You are given a particular street address and told to go there if it exists. If you find the address you must take the doorknob along with you (the doorknob is unique and will be readily available). If the address does not exist, you must write in your notebook that it does not exist. When you have got the knob or written the message you are done.

The house is on a long street. The house numbers are organized from smallest to largest though some numbers may be missing. You do not know in which direction the numbers run. You do not know how large the largest is or how small the smallest is. You do not know how long the street is, though it will not take more than a few hours to walk its entire length so the task is not impossible. The houses are far enough apart, or their numbers are so arranged, that you can see only one number at a time. To make life simple, all houses are on the same side of the street and face in the same direction. There is no street map.

Assume that the Simplistic Bus Company drops you off at the only stop on this street. The stop is approximately midway between the ends of the street. Write a set of instructions indicating your actions, the questions you ask yourself and your responses based on what you find. Needless to say, you wish to do the job with the least possible effort. You cannot see any house numbers from the bus. The number you seek is given to you on a piece of paper by the bus driver as you get off the bus. Good luck!

1.5   In determining the alphabetical order of two words, we select the first letter of each word. If they are unequal, the word with the letter lying nearer A in the alphabet is taken as the first word. If the letters are the same, the second letter of each word is tested.

We must consider what must be done if one word is shorter than another. Can we define the lack of a letter as a letter in some way? Write a program in numbered steps in simple English which sets two words of any length in alphabetical order. It should include the selection of letters, appropriate questions and responses depending on answers.

Remember, there are two outcomes. In one, the words are different and they are set in alphabetical order. In the other, the words are the same and some notification of this must be made. In any event, the process must repeat as many times as there are letters in the shorter word. This will involve loops with some way of escaping from the loops at the end of the shorter word. If the letters are the same do one thing. If they are different, do something else.

Hint: Think in terms of 'less than', where letter A is 'less than' B. What happens to a 'blank'?

Comment: In this· problem and the next, the structures of the questions which cause repeat loops or program end get a bit complicated. If they bother you, don't worry. Getting the feel of a stepwise program is the main point of the exercise. The text will straighten out choice situations for you later on. So don't worry, but have a good try and if things don't work, try again.

1.6   Repeat Problem 1.5, but this time the task is to determine whether the words are alike or different. In general, must we go through all the letters of each word to end the program? There will be subtle differences. Here, the information put out by the program is 'SAME' or 'DIFFERENT'.

1.7   You have been given a large bin containing ropes. They fall into two categories. One type of rope is circular; that is, its ends are invisibly spliced together in some manner. The second type is a normal rope with two ends. The ropes are of many different lengths. These are all dumped together in a jumbled manner, but they are special in that if you take hold of a piece of rope, you can follow along it without causing a tangle.

You have a rope-sorting machine that works in the following manner. The machine takes hold of a loop of rope. When it first fastens onto this rope it makes a mark on the rope. After it has made this mark it moves the mark through the switched off detection assembly, then turns the detection assembly on and continues to move the rope in the same direction. It can move the rope in only one direction. The detection assembly is capable of responding to and telling the difference between a rope end and the mark if the mark should pass through again.

The controls may be set to determine how much rope is drawn

through the feeler assembly, what the device will do on detecting a rope end and what it will do when it meets the mark again. If the machine does not have a piece of rope in its feeler assembly it can search the bin for more rope. If it cannot find any more rope, then there is no more in the bin.

The information that may be derived from the detector assembly is as follows. If a rope end is detected, the rope is a normal rope. If the mark is detected, the rope is circular. If the rope is still passing through the detector, without a mark or an end being detected, when the amount of rope set for passage has been surpassed then the rope is too long. Based on the findings of the detector, the rope being tested will be set aside in containers designated 'normal', 'circular' or 'too long'. If the device runs out of rope to test it will sound a horn.

Your task is to write a program in simple English showing the action of the sorter as it finds a rope, tests the rope by passing it through the detector, disposes of the rope on the basis of the test results, searches for more rope and responds on the basis of its search. You should think in terms of modules or groups of operations and indicate loops by referring the action back to appropriate earlier steps.

1.8   Consider a simple four-way intersection. Each direction is controlled by a traffic signal. Each street also has a crosswalk associated with the signal lamp controlling it. You wish to organize the traffic at this intersection with a computer. You are not interested in any other intersection. You might be interested in traffic density, cars waiting, pedestrians waiting, etc.

a. Indicate the output information that might be needed to control traffic and pedestrian movements.

b. Indicate a set of output devices and the various states and combinations of states which these might have, in order to provide the information shown in **a**.

c. Indicate the kind of input information that might be useful as a basis for making decisions on traffic and pedestrian control.

d. Indicate the devices that might be used to acquire the information discussed in **c**.

e. Make a drawing of the intersection with the inputs and outputs in place.

f. Write a simple program in words to show the interaction of the input information to provide the output information you need.

g. Run a few simple traffic situations to see how the system should work.

Comment: It is a good idea to design this first as a pure traffic problem without pedestrians. In working with this problem, don't try to build a 'super' system. Initially produce a relatively simple set of inputs, outputs, desired transitions and controls. If you don't keep it fairly simple, you will not have time to get through all the activities suggested. If you get hooked on the problem, then take time to build a fancy system.

1.9   A problem in turning out the lights of a house was discussed in the text. A very simple version of the problem was designed in the text, and the program for solution was developed. To continue toward the production of a general solution, a somewhat more advanced simplification was developed. The house design in this case was as follows.

Every room may have up to three doors. At least one door in each room leads to a room with a total of only one door – a closet. The house has at least one door connecting the inside and the outside. There is some route connecting all rooms by the conventional doors.

Your problem is to devise a program that will cause the user to enter every room of the house, including closets. Needless to say, all lights must be turned off. The person involved must end up outside the house.

Hints: You will probably want to use some kind of marking technique as discussed in the text. Thinking about which door is the best one to use when you finally exit the house will provide insight. Behavior in the rooms may be reduced to a small number of repeated modules or subroutines.

1.10 Consider the house problem again. The generalized problem was presented in the text along with a very simple version and a second more complex simplification. This more complex simplification was presented in Problem 9 as a programming problem.

Your task is to define a 'next' higher level of simplification. Consider carefully how the rules for house design should be changed to result in a higher, but still not impossible, level of complexity. You should defend your choice in a brief discussion by comparing your choice with other choices you might have made. Remember, it is possible to introduce new limitations, if you wish, as well as to just reduce some of the limitations or enlarge the number of doors. In this case, you only define the problem. You need not devise the solution program. Of course, if you think it might be fun to devise such a program...

CHAPTER TWO

Constants and Variables

Everything, or perhaps almost everything, evolves in a series of relatively small alterations from a predecessor. As change continues, the current, apparently perfected stage serves as the predecessor for the next development. Regardless of the size of the steps between the stages, the newly emerging stage will have many of the characteristics of its predecessors. Some of these built-in fossil/structures will be essential; others, while not essential, will be convenient, and still others will have merely remained because it was too much bother to eliminate them. Fortunately, in a highly competitive environment the really obsolete aspects of a design are rapidly eliminated because they represent an inefficient use of a scarce commodity such as energy, material or space.

A major driving force in the emergence of computers as we know them today has been the need to produce large numerical tables for such applications as marine navigation, astronomy and ballistic calculation. Production of such tables has been a prominent activity of the more mathematically involved members of humanity at least as far back as Babylon, and it has been one of immense importance to commerce, health and our understanding of the universe.

In the pre-computer era, the person generating the numerical table first selected the numbers to serve as the start of the calculation. These were the numbers that would be entered into the calculation process. This represents the 'input' stage of the overall calculation process.

The next stage was to perform the calculation, which might be straightforward or might consist of a rather complex set of inter-related parts. The calculation process might generate a need to change certain aspects of the computation, as a result of decisions arising from intermediate results. This second major step, in which the actual calculations are made or the results of the input activity are processed, is normally called the 'process' step.

Finally, when the calculation or process step was complete the result was recorded. In the case of making tables, whether they were for a reference handbook for the British Admiralty or a clay tablet for the temple archives, we needed to show the results. We were required, therefore, to place this result away from the details of the calculation so that it could be easily read. This third stage of the overall process of calculation is called the 'output' stage. (Once again, of course, our calculation technician may have to make some decision such as: 'If there are still numbers to be input, I must do so and do another calculation.')

If a time before computers is too remote, just imagine someone doing his or her income tax. Having assembled all the information, the taxpayer begins to fill in the various blocks on the form with information from external sources. These involve gross income, number of family members, special deductions, and the like. This is the input stage.

With all the external information supplied, calculations are begun which involve such activities as subtracting Box 22 from Box 17 if Box 16 is larger than $1,500. This is the process stage of operations. Finally, once again, the answers are inserted in boxes that will be examined by the tax office. This is the result of the calculations; it is intended for human use in the world outside the computer and is, therefore, the output stage.

Two major concepts result from these somewhat informal analyses: (1) The complete calculation involves three steps: input, process and output. (These three steps and related concepts will be discussed in this chapter.) (2) The person making the calculation must make decisions and act on them. A description of the calculation process that may be used to drive a computer must have decision and testing options. (This concept will be discussed in detail in later chapters.)

Of course, we know that these concepts are not new. Anyone with a reasonable knowledge of computers is more or less aware of them. Let us concentrate on input, process, and output. They represent an element carried over from manual calculation or calculation with simple calculators to modern computing. They are one of our essential fossil structures.

The application of the three steps is obvious from our table and tax models. But there were many other reasons besides table generation for inventing computers, all of which involve activities utilizing the input, process, output organization. This structure may not always be so straightforward. As more general computer problems are examined, we will expand the meaning of this three-step concept.

Leaving aside the process step for the moment, let's look rather specifically at what the input and output will consist of. For starters, consider the case where they are just ordinary numbers like 5 or −75.36 or 0.0086. In computing and mathematics, numbers such as these are referred to as 'numerical constants' ('numerical' because they are numbers; 'constant' refers to the fact that they have a fixed meaning). No one goes around and says, 'Hey, let's take that funny symbol 5 and let it stand (holds up three fingers) for this many fingers.' It could be done, but part of the meaning of numbers involves this property of sameness and lack of change – five fingers, five elephants, five beans. We can line them up in columns of fingers and elephants and beans. We may match just one bean to one finger to one elephant and keep this up. We will run out of beans and elephants and fingers all at the same time and we will have five of each. The numbers are constants because they have fixed values.

So why bother to talk about numerical constants when we could just use the shorter term 'numbers'? The term 'numerical constant' is utilized to distinguish these constants from other types of constants that are not numerical. We will initially concentrate on numerical constants and then, when we are used to working with them, work with other types of constants will evolve more smoothly.

Numerical constants are essentially numbers and we can do with them anything we can do with numbers. Sometimes the operation signs are slightly different from the ones we are used to, but this is only because it makes the symbols easier to produce on the average computer keyboard. Here are the 'big four':

$$\text{addition: } 2.85 + 378.3$$
$$\text{subtraction: } 92.58 - 65$$
$$\text{multiplication: } 38.5 * 54$$
$$\text{division: } 77/59.8$$

The signs for addition '+' and subtraction '−' are the same as those normally used in writing mathematical expressions. The sign for division is '/', which is often used under ordinary conditions. It is used in this case because it exists on the standard keyboard and may be used in conjunction with parentheses to write fractional expressions all on a single line without resorting to upward or downward shifting. The multiplication sign, '*', which is a bit unusual, is used because it is on the keyboard and is not likely to cause confusion with the letter X.

Finally, there is the problem of indicating that some number is raised to a power, like the square of 5, which is 5 * 5, or the seventh power of 3, which is 3 * 3 * 3 * 3 * 3 * 3 * 3. The notation for a short symbolic version of this varies somewhat between computer languages, but the notation is not generally necessary for our development of algorithms or pseudocode programs as written in this text, so we will ignore it until a specific need arises.

Parentheses '( )' also will be used in the usual mathematical way. Thus 3 * (5 + 1) will simplify to 3 * 6 or 18.

The last detail in our treatment of numerical constants will be the order of operations. This is correctly spoken of as the 'hierarchy of operations'. You might as well know it by this term since this is the precise one. Hierarchy of operations simply means the order in which operations are carried out. In evaluating an expression, you first solve everything inside parentheses. In working with the operations of division, multiplication, addition and subtraction, you do the multiplication and division first and then do the addition and subtraction. In the event you have two or more operations with the same priority, just work from left to right as you would read the line. The same order applies if you are working inside parentheses.

Consider the following simplification:

$$3 * 25 + (4 * 3 + 2)$$

Inside parentheses, multiply:

$$3 * 25 + (12 + 2)$$

Inside parentheses, add:

$$3 * 25 + (14)$$

Remove parentheses:

$$3 * 25 + 14$$

Multiply:

$$75 + 14$$

Add:

89

Following the steps in the prescribed order has produced simplification by a simple procedure. Many of you will have this technique down cold from other courses, but just in case you feel a bit shaky or it is new, you will find a set of examples, some of which are partially solved, at the end of this chapter.

By this time numerical constants and their manipulation should look like they are beginning to make sense. As I said, we will take on nonnumerical constants a bit later after we have become thoroughly comfortable with the numerical kind. Let's go to numerical variables next.

We know that to get the price of a bag of apples at a particular grocery store, we take the cost of a single apple of one of the many types sold in this store and multiply it by the number of apples in the bag. (Yes, I know this is rather a strange grocery store, but you were warned about such things at the start of this book.) One way to calculate the cost of the bag of apples is to have a complicated table. One axis of the table is the cost of a single apple of each type that the store sells. The other axis lists the numbers of apples that may be placed in a bag. Our store has large bags, so this scale runs from 1 to 25. Since the store handles 35 different kinds of apples, there are 825 (25 * 35) entries in this table. To get the price of a bag of apples, one selects the apple type and reads across to the column under the appropriate number of apples to find the cost.

A table with over 800 entries in which you have to look up apple type and number is a tough way to price bags of apples. Assuming you had some way to get apple type and number quickly, it would be a lot easier to stick a note up where the clerk could see it. All it need say is:

APPLE~COST * APPLE~NUMBER

Now all the clerk has to do is enter the unit price of the apple type in question in place of APPLE~COST, and enter the number of apples in the bag instead of APPLE~NUMBER. Now the multiplication is carried out as indicated by the '*' sign, and he or she has the price of the bag of apples.

Suppose the next customer has a bag with a different number of a different kind of apples. So who cares – there is nothing permanent about the numbers you put in for the first calculation. You just inserted them to do the first calculation. Enter the new unit price in place of APPLE~COST and the new number of apples in place of APPLE~NUMBER. Now with the new numbers in place, do what the * sign tells you to and you have the cost of the second bag of apples.

How can we get away with giving APPLE~NUMBER and APPLE~COST any numerical value we wish? Simple – APPLE~NUMBER and APPLE~COST are variables. Specifically, they are numerical variables because they take on numerical values. They are variables because, unlike constants, they may be given any numerical value we wish. Of course, there are other types of variables just as there are other types of constants. We will concern ourselves with variables other than numerical variables when we have become familiar with the numerical kind.

We know what numerical variables are, but how may they be represented? The various conventional computer languages have a wide variety of models that provide us with flexibility if we choose to use it. This is because, as noted in the preface, pseudocode is designed to present the common features of computer language, but it does not have the special narrow type of structural specificity required of languages that must actually undergo the electronic process of translation to machine language.

Despite this freedom to design as we wish, our variable nomenclature will be simple and reflect properties common to many computer languages. Written numerical variables will appear according to the following rules:

1. All variables will be written in upper case.
2. Allowable characters will be the 26 letters of the alphabet, numbers 1 through 9 and 0 and the squiggle (~).
3. The first symbol of any variable must be a letter.
4. Separate words may be connected by a squiggle (~), but no blank spaces may be included within variables because it would be hard to tell where the variable ends. The squiggle (~) is used instead of the hyphen to separate words in multiword variables since the hyphen can be confused with a minus sign.
5. Single-letter variables may be used, or words or word–letter combinations. I am not setting an overall length limit, but a bunch of 20 symbol variables can make life pretty messy.
6. Words like 'input' and others that we will encounter later have special meanings and will be designated as 'reserved

words'. It's not permitted to use them as variable names. Using them in this way causes confusion, just as naming your dog 'BITE' would. However, these words can be used as a part of a compound variable name. An example would be calling your dog 'MOSQUITO~BITE'.

Two questions present themselves. The first is, 'What operations may we carry out on numerical variables?' The second is, 'How do we assign a value to a numerical variable?'

The first question is delightfully simple, so we'll handle it first. The answer is straightforward. Any operation that can be carried out on a numerical constant can be done on a numerical variable.

Why not? A numerical variable is just a stand-in for a numerical constant. It occurs in some mathematical expression, showing by its presence and location what role is to be played, but the real action does not take place until the numerical variable is replaced with a numerical constant. This is because we may symbolically add MUFF and MEATBALL, but then we are stuck because there is usually not a relation that will allow us to simplify the statement further. We must have numerical values for MUFF (let us say 6) and MEATBALL (let us say −3) that allow us to replace MUFF + MEATBALL with 3. Of course, since numerical variables stand in the place of numerical constants, we may multiply or divide them by numerical constants, or add or subtract numerical constants to or from them, or use them in forming powers (though this will be relatively rare). Looking at some 'legal' expressions we find:

$$3 * A + MOXEY \qquad ROSE * ROSE * ROSE$$
$$ANT\sim HILL \qquad (MURF + SURF)/25$$

You will notice that we have used a number of short or modified words for variables. This is quite common and helps us maintain a better grip on what we are doing. There is a tendency among programmers that sometimes becomes almost a mental disease. This is to use humorous or nonsensical variable designators unrelated to the problem at hand. A humorous variable adds spice to a program, but the point where hysteria takes over is to be avoided.

We have reached a good place to pause in this saga leading us into the land of pseudocode and the algorithm. You will now be faced with a number of problems dealing with the manipulation of numerical constants and numerical variables and the translation of algebraic formulas into forms acceptable for computer or pseudocode format. In the sections that show preferred patterns or formats for laying out the solutions for these problems, you will note I have avoided using equals signs. I have not lost my senses or reverted to a more childish view of life. My reason for this stems from a common misconception that causes the developing computer student a lot of conscious and subconscious difficulty until he or she roots it out. Our sneaky approach to this difficulty is never to let the idea take root. Hence our non-use of anything resembling the equals sign. In the next chapter, the assignment operator will be discussed, thus clarifying the equals sign's ambiguity.

PROBLEMS

The problems in this group are designed to provide limited practice with variable naming, simple arithmetic manipulation of numbers, evaluation of formulas and the use of parentheses. We wish to provide a sufficient level of familiarization with these topics to enable the student to work with the ideas in the text. An in-depth knowledge of the borderline between arithmetic and algebra is not necessary at this time. The tools that are required are in Chapter 2 or will be developed along the way. Because it is important for the student that he or she be sure of being on the right track, all of the problems in Chapter 2 are answered at the end of the book.

*   *   *

2.1   Which of the following is a proper variable name according to the rules presented in Chapter 2?

    a. B   **b.** SNAP-LOCK   **c.** DOP3
    d. eagle   **e.** NERF3BAL   **f.** 5BOX
    g. A+DUCK   **h.** VisP4   **i.** B78434

2.2   Evaluate the following simple numerical expressions:

        a. $1 * 3 + 5$ **b.** $5 + 1 * 3$
        c. $1 + 4 * 3 + 6$ **d.** $8/2 * 3/6$
        e. $6/3 * 8/2$ **f.** $3 + 6/2 + 3$

2.3   Evaluate the following simple numerical expressions:

  a. $(3 + 2) * (8 + 1)$ **b.** $3 + (2 * 8) + 1$
  c. $3 + 2 * 8 + 1$ **d.** $3 + 2 * (8 + 1)$

2.4 Substitute as indicated and evaluate each of the following expressions. If the arithmetic gets complicated use a hand calculator, but show all steps and simplifications.

  a. $(M + K)/ZIP + 2$ M is 6, K is 8, ZIP is 7
  b. $BOB * BOB - 4 * ACK * CAT$ BOB is 7, ACK is 3, CAT
  c. $(A + 7 * C)/(B + 2 - A) +$ is 2
  $2 * B$ A is 3, B is 6, C is 4
  d. $(A + 5) * 3/2 * B - 6$ A is 3, B is 6

2.5 Translate each of the following English clauses into a mathematical expression using parentheses to control grouping where necessary. You need not evaluate the expressions.

  a. Six times the difference between eight and three
  b. The sum of seventeen and six divided by six, all divided by eight
  c. The difference between the product of 8 and 14, and the quotient of 16 and 4
  d. Eight minus five divided by the product of 2 and 3.

2.6 Write each of the following expressions in four different ways by introducing as many pairs of parentheses as you wish. However, do not have any nested parentheses, that is, parentheses inside of parentheses. Evaluate each version.

  a. $3 + 12 * 8 + 3 - 5/8 + 6$
  b. $6 * 3/4 - 3 + 5 * 3 - 1 + 4/3$

2.7 A car is driving from one city to another. The cities are 375 miles apart. When the car has driven 150 miles it has engine failure, and is loaded onto a truck and driven the rest of the way to its destination. The car gets 22 miles per gallon of gasoline. The truck gets 7 miles per gallon of gasoline. Gasoline costs $1.10 per gallon. What is the cost of gasoline for the entire trip?

  a. Solve the problem numerically.
  b. Using meaningful variable names for such quantities as the distance between the cities, the distance driven by the car, the distance driven by the truck, the rate of gasoline usage by the car and the rate of gasoline usage by the truck, write an expression to represent the total amount of gasoline required for the trip. You

may wish to use a different set of variables. The goal of this problem is production of an accurate expression.

2.8 Solve each of the following problems. Work stepwise, show all steps as in the examples in the text. You may use a hand calculator. In the case of decimal fractions, show the values accurate to two places to the right of the decimal point.

    a. $(3 + (8 - 2) + 4)/6$
    b. $5 * (75/15 + 4 * (4 - 1)) + 2 * (7 + 4)$
    c. $(15/(8 - 3) + 4 * (6 + 2)) * 2$
    d. $(8 + 3) * (40 - (7 * 4))$

2.9 Refer to the examples in Problem 2.6. Write each example four different ways, never using less than two levels of nested parentheses. Evaluate each variation, using a calculator if necessary. In the case of decimal fractions, show only two digits to the right of the decimal point.

2.10 In a particular food preparation plant, eggs are moved from one location to another in trains of 4 carts each. Each cart holds 62 cartons of eggs, each carton holds 12 eggs. There are 3 trains in motion at this moment in the plant.

    a. Using meaningful variables, write an expression that shows how many eggs are in transit at the present time. Use variables to represent number of trains, carts, cartons and eggs per carton.
    b. Calculate how many eggs are being moved in the example above.

CHAPTER THREE

The Assignment Operator

Until now, in order to prevent confusion, the use of anything remotely resembling an equals sign has been avoided. The second question raised at the end of Chapter 2 was 'How does a variable acquire a value?' The answer is, by having a value assigned to it. This requires a special sign just like a + (plus) sign or a / (division) sign, which indicates some kind of operation. These signs might also respectively be called the 'addition operator' and the 'division operator' with equal accuracy, since they are symbols that cause the operation of addition or division to occur. It's just that for these signs, the use of the term 'operator' never caught on.

The symbol that causes the operation of assigning a value to a variable to be performed is called the 'assignment operator'. Like most of the structures that form the basis for pseudocode, the assignment operator exists in all conventional computer languages. In the BASIC and FORTRAN languages the same sign is used as is used for the conventional equals sign (=). This creates some confusion, because there is a great deal of difference between the assignment operator and the equals sign.

In most other common languages, the symbol for the assignment operator is :=. This is the sign we will use. The complete assignment statement will look like this:

BUCKET := 79.5

It is read as: 'BUCKET is assigned the value of 79.5.' As long as a new assignment statement is not applied to BUCKET, whenever the variable BUCKET is used we will automatically replace it with the constant value 79.5.

In the event that a second assignment statement assigning a new value to BUCKET is entered, then the previous value that BUCKET held is 'written over', and BUCKET takes on its new assigned value just as if it had never held any other. There is no remorse in a computer. It simply takes the presently assigned values and 'runs with the ball'. Thus, if a new assignment statement shows up:

$$BUCKET := 14.2$$

then any time thereafter that BUCKET shows up in an expression, it has the value 14.2, and the previous value of 79.5 leaves no trace in the contents of BUCKET.

We should notice another property of the assignment statement. On the left-hand side of the assignment statement there is one variable and nothing else. There is no second variable related by some operations sign such as + or /. There is no constant that in any way modifies the variable. We don't have anything on the left-hand side of the statement except the variable, which will accept the assignment.

On the other hand, there are no restrictions on the right-hand side. It may be any mathematically valid combination of variables and constants that is consistent with the language we are writing. The first thing that will happen on the right-hand side is that the values of the variables will be determined and entered. The right-hand side will now consist of an expression of numerical constants, which will be evaluated in the usual way. After the evaluation is complete, the result of this will be assigned to the numerical variable that makes up the left-hand side of the assignment statement. This timing is of great importance, as we shall see.

It may seem that we have gone to a lot of trouble to examine the exact way in which the assignment operator and its corresponding assignment statement work. However, we don't have to worry about learning a new routine later, because assignment statements in all common computer languages work the same way.

The two expressions

$$2 * BUCKET := 14.2$$

and

$$BUCKET + 3 := 14.2$$

are illegal because there is more than just a single variable on the left-hand side of the assignment operator.

Now we have the requirements for the left-hand side and can concentrate on the right. First of all, we could have a constant as we have above. This is the simplest of the assignment statements. Another equally simple case would be to have another variable on the right-hand side instead of a constant:

BUCKET := SMERD

Now BUCKET has taken on whatever value SMERD has, but SMERD still retains whatever value it had. Remember, this assignment operation does not involve an interchange of contents, but a copy of contents.

A final special property of the assignment statement accounts directly and indirectly for some of its most important properties. If the assignment statement were to assign three times the value of SMERD to BUCKET, it would look like this:

BUCKET := 3 * SMERD

Clearly, numerical evaluation of the right-side of the assignment statement must be complete before the assignment process itself takes place. Were this not the case, there would be no single value (numerical in the case of numerical constants and variables) to assign to the variable on the left-hand side of the assignment. But really, directly and indirectly, we have said all this before. *But how about assigning BUCKET the value of three times the value of BUCKET!*

Well, it certainly wouldn't be very hard to write it. First of all, we just make sure BUCKET does, indeed, have a proper assignment by using the assignment operator to give it the value 25.

BUCKET := 25

With BUCKET properly assigned we can write the assignment statement that appears to be so special:

BUCKET := 3 * BUCKET

There really isn't anything so special if you just remember you are working with an assignment operator (:=) and not an equals sign. The statement is an assignment statement and is evaluated in the regular way:

1. Remember to do only activities on the right-hand side of the assignment operator (:=) until that side has been reduced to a single numerical constant, even if that constant is 0. *Then and only then* does the left side become involved.

2. The first real action is to replace the variables on the right-hand side with their assigned values. This seems to present a problem because the same variable BUCKET appears on *both* sides of the assignment statement. *Don't panic!* You're only working on the right-hand side, so don't try to get ahead of yourself. The last assignment statement in which BUCKET was involved was:

$$BUCKET := 25$$

So BUCKET has a value of 25. Thus when evaluating the right side of the assignment statement we have been given, we have no trouble:

$$BUCKET := 3 * BUCKET$$

Work the *right* side only. Replace variable BUCKET with the appropriate value:

$$BUCKET := 3 * 25$$

You are working on the right-hand side only; that's why the BUCKET on the left side remained unaltered.

So now just do what the right-hand arithmetic sign tells you and you're home free. You will have completely evaluated the right side of the assignment statement before doing anything else, and that's exactly the way the job should be done.

$$BUCKET := 75$$

Is the machine going to throw a fit and complain that BUCKET was used with another value to re-evaluate itself and that this is illegal? No, it did everything it was supposed to according to the operational rules of the assignment statement, and the correct value dropped out.

We are going to get a bit ahead of ourselves by writing a simple series of steps that some people might call an informal program. We want to do this to give an idea of the power of the special properties built into the assignment operator and its associated assignment statement. A second reason, alluded to in the preface, is that I like to expose students to new ideas in an informal manner so they can begin to accommodate to the ideas. In this way, when the ideas are formally presented, the shock is greatly reduced.

Before writing our informal program we are going to need some tools. In actual programming it is an excellent idea to know one's tools intimately. We are going to use a simple language, and so the problems of intimacy are not so great. Of course we have the assignment statement, but we know this pretty well. Now we need a statement to put out a result. This will be a 'print statement'. The statement is given with a word of command; you might call it a 'print operator'. It also needs something to print out. We will have to include a variable. It can be any variable. The purpose will simply be to hold a numerical constant that will be printed out in some undefined fashion.

A sample print statement might look like this:

Print BUCKET

Or it might be:

Print SMIRD

or:

Print B

Any of these would work. When a print statement is executed it will cause the present value of the variable to be printed. If we have forgotten to define the variable, '0' (zero) will be printed out. This is a common way of handling undefined variables. Just to keep life simple we have stayed with numerical variables as we have stayed with numerical constants.

The last statement we will build into our language is controversial. If this were an advanced language we would build the language without it, but it is a pretty primitive language we are building, so we will need this statement. It is called GOTO and enables us to change the order in which we execute a series of statements or a program.

If we want to GOTO a location, we have to have some way to identify the location. In this case, the location will be a statement line. The most logical method will be to assign each statement line a number so we can go where we wish just by addressing the number. For example:

GOTO 21

will transfer control to the statement labeled '21' no matter where '21' is, and afterward the progression of steps or statements will run along in a normal fashion from line 21 until we run out of work, or meet another GOTO.

We now have to add a few items that define the priority of operations. First, we will always use the standard hierarchy of operations for arithmetic. Second, we will list the statements in the order, from top to bottom, in which we want to run them unless a GOTO causes us to skip or repeat a statement. Third, we will be sure that the last statement of our series of statements or 'program' is the statement END. This is really just for neatness. Finally, for the moment, we will restrict ourselves to numerical constants and variables.

What we have done in the last few paragraphs is to create a very simple and somewhat sloppy computer language. There might be some room for criticism. First of all, we don't have a computer. Where is the screen of this particular machine, where is the memory, and so on? The answer is, of course, that they are imaginary. We know how they behave or how they behave ideally, so in simple cases we run the machine in our head and write the answers on a sheet of paper or the blackboard.

Next, even assuming we can imagine a computer, who says we have the right to design a computer language? More to the point, who says we can't? So we have designed one. It is not intended to be a universal language, but only to demonstrate certain ideas.

Let us quickly review the elements of our language.

1. The constants are numerical constants and the variables that may be designated by names such as SURF1 are also standard numerical variables.
2. Variables and constants may be combined according to the standard laws of arithmetic using the usual hierarchy.
3. The standard assignment operator ':=' is used to produce assignment statements in standard form.
4. The statements are executed in serial order, from top to bottom.

5. Each statement is sequentially numbered. The order of operation may be altered by a GOTO statement, which includes an appropriate statement number as an address.
6. Additionally, we have a print statement which in conjunction with a variable permits output of a result.
7. Finally, each program or series of statements that we wish to run as a whole finishes with an END statement.

This is a simple language and, therefore, it is easy to imagine a simple machine to run it. But this is a true pseudocode, so it has one nice advantage: it was never intended to run in a real machine with all the restrictions of translation and interpretation imposed by the rigid electronic interactions. If you spell GOTO as GoTo or Goesto, no lights flash or whistles blow. As long as you and your public are in reasonable agreement, everyone is happy. After all, you don't have to go around trying to please electronic logic circuits, which are notoriously limited, inflexible and intolerant.

Then why, as we proceed in this book, will you find me subtly (and otherwise) conning you into writing a fairly standard pseudocode? The reason is that a standard nomenclature is a lot easier for writing and thinking.

A few programs in our pseudocode are just what we need. We'll even tell you what kind of output we think you should get. For those of you who are purists, I am not going to rig up a fancy input from an imaginary card reader or some such gadget. We will just use the old reliable assignment statement.

1. A := 5
2. B := 6
3. C := A + B
4. Print C
5. END

When this grinds through our computer that really isn't there, the answer '11' is printed. Now a simple and mindless program using GOTO:

1. ARGO5 := 25
2. GOTO 5
3. MUD := 65
4. KRUD := 100
5. BOX := ARGO5 + MUD + KRUD

6. Print BOX
7. END

This time we don't get quite what we expect. The reason is that the forward GOTO statement causes the program to skip statements 3 and 4 and thus two assignment statements are not run.

KRUD is never assigned the value of 100. MUD is never assigned the value of 65. Thus the only variable assigned is ARGO5, which is assigned a value of 25. Now the control transfer statement 'GOTO 5' shifts control to statement 5, which is:

$$BOX := ARGO5 + MUD + KRUD$$

Since MUD and KRUD have not been assigned, even though they appear in other statements they are evaluated for purposes of calculation as 0. The value of the right-hand side of the assignment statement for BOX is 25. This, then, is the value assigned to BOX and printed out by the print statement.

In writing these short, informal programs that demonstrate specific properties of the common types of statement, we should present one particular combination of properties of the assignment statement and the GOTO statement. Consider the short program:

1. KOUNT := 1
2. Print KOUNT
3. KOUNT := KOUNT + 1
4. GOTO 2
5. END

This makes good sense if we stick to the simple rules for evaluating assignment statements. Since the program describes an unending loop we might want to write out the beginning steps on a piece of paper. We'll even save you the trouble, but it is suggested you make your own copy to get in the habit.

1. KOUNT := 1

Simply assign a value of 1 to KOUNT.

2. Print KOUNT

KOUNT has value of 1, so print 1.

3.   KOUNT := KOUNT + 1

Evaluate the right side; KOUNT has value of 1; add 1 and we have
2. Assign a value of 2 to KOUNT.

4.   GOTO 2

Do statement 2 just like it was the next one.

2.   Print KOUNT

KOUNT has a value of 2, so print 2.

3.   KOUNT := KOUNT + 1

Evaluate the right side; KOUNT has value of 2; add 1 and we have
3. Assign a value of 3 to KOUNT.

4.   GOTO 2

and here we go again.

   If you have any notion that this will stop on its own, you're
deluding yourself. We are running on an imaginary computer so
if you remembered to imagine a plug, you could try pulling it.
Seriously, this is an endless process provided you have defined
enough integers. It will just go on printing a virtually endless list
of sequential integers.
   Writing a series of reasonably exact programs in a simple
pseudocode has a number of advantages. It gets us used to the
idea of writing logical coded structures without the worry of detailed syntax problems which arise in a simple language designed
to run on a physical machine. It gives a feel for the type of statements we will have to build in to gain real control over a computer
language. For example, we need some form of control structures
to make useful devices from the combination of GOTO and the
special properties of the assignment statement. Finally, using a
simple pseudocode prepares us for writing the detailed pseudocode structures that we will need in the design of efficient, well-
structured programs in languages that will be run on real machines
with real problems.
   We now have an idea of the general outline of a pseudocode
based on a simple example. In fact the logical structure of

pseudocode is built from a relatively small number of elements. In the next chapter we will explore the nature of these structures and their interrelations. However, we will do so by means of 'flow diagrams'. Having developed a good feeling for the principal structures, we will once again resort to pseudocode for the actual creation of programs. Flowcharting will be reserved for program documentation and representation of detailed computational and logical procedures.

One additional powerful reason for using flowcharting to describe the various structures that we will eventually build in pseudocode is to avoid the overt use of the GOTO statement.

Having viewed the GOTO concept in appropriate historical context we will now strive to eliminate the need for this concept in program design procedures. The fact that I am aware of the history and importance of outdoor plumbing merely reinforces my reluctance to resort to the old 'two-holer' (and its associated wasp's nests) in all save the most dire circumstances. My sentiments about GOTO are similar.

PROBLEMS

The purpose of these problems is to familiarize you with the use of the assignment operator (:=) as a way of assigning values to variables. The problems also supply practice in using the idea of assignment in developing simple equations or statements and fitting them together into programs. Once again, extensive, correct practice is extremely important in building proper basic working techniques and self-confidence. For this reason, all the problems of Chapter 3 are answered at the back of the book.

You will notice that problems 3.9 and 3.10 are marked with an asterisk (*). The problems marked in this fashion are a bit more difficult than the average. In this sense they need not be emphasized as heavily as the others in a hurried treatment of the subject. On the other hand, they represent a rudimentary type of 'challenge problem', and attention to them will significantly increase your depth of understanding even if the solution attempts are not totally successful.

*   *   *

3.1   Which of the following is a proper assignment statement? If the statement is not correct, state why.

a. A + B := B + b
b. ROSCOE = ZAP + 1
c. NED := 9
d. K := K − 3.5
e. B := 17 − B
f. 5 := FERD
g. NECCO := ASP + MUCH
h. N + 1 := 8

3.2   Write assignment statements to complete each of the following tasks.

a. Assign the value 5 to the variable DROPSY.
b. Assign the value of the variable K to the variable PIP.
c. Increase the value that the variable NAN now has by 1.
d. Assign the sum of the variables X54 and BETA5 to the variable ZIP.
e. Decrease the value of the variable STING by the value of the variable FROST.

3.3   Using simple English, write a stepwise program that will print out the value of an unending series of odd numbers starting with the number 7.

3.4   Using simple English, write a stepwise program that prints out the phrase 'No Joy', then prints out the number 23, prints out 'No Joy', then prints out the number 28 and continues in this way alternately printing the same phrase and a number that increases by 5 each time.

3.5   What is the value printed out by the following program?

1. FOX := 25
2. ZAP := 15
3. K23 := 17
4. TED := K23 + FOX
5. Print TED
6. END

3.6   Write a program that presents the following word problem in symbolic form and causes the answer to be written out. The price of a pound of flour is 35 cents. The price of a box of eggs is 89 cents. The price of a quart of milk is 45 cents. A grocery order consists of the given amounts of each of the above foods. That is, of one pound of flour, a box of eggs and a quart of milk. What is the cost of the grocery order? The answer should be printed out in cents, but the units need not be included; only the number is required. Choose your own variable names.

3.7   Write a program in simple English to express the following word problem. Choose useful variable names. You will have to use GOTO. Bacteria are growing in a special colony. The colony starts with three bacteria. Every 20 minutes, each bacterium which exists at that time becomes two bacteria. No bacteria ever die. The colony goes on for a long, undefined period of time. Write a program that prints out the number of bacteria in the colony after each 20-minute period, starting from time zero. The program may also be considered to go on for a long, undefined period of time.

3.8   What is the printout of the following program?

1. BUD := 4
2. GOTO 6
3. MAXI := BUD + 8
4. GOTO 7
5. MAXI := MAXI + 1
6. GOTO 3
7. Print MAXI
8. END

*3.9   An undefined type of tree is growing in a hostile landscape. It grows according to the following rule. Each year between the first day of winter and the last day of summer the tree exactly doubles its weight. On the end of the last day of summer it stops growing until the first day of winter. On the first day of fall every year, a colony of termites begins eating the tree and consumes one-third of the tree's weight by the first day of winter. On the first day of winter, the termites stop eating the tree and go on vacation. Write a program that lists the weight of the tree on the first day of winter every year for an infinite number of years. You can assume any weight you wish for the weight of the tree at the start of its first year of life (just popping out of the seed).

*3.10   Assume we have a cube two feet on a side. There are six faces to this cube. The area of each face is the area of a square with two feet on each side. The total area of the surface of the cube will be the area of one face times the number of faces (6 faces). Now divide the cube so that the sides of the new cubes will be half as large as the sides of the original cube. This will produce a total of eight identical cubes. Each cube will have faces with one foot on a side. Calculate the total area. Once again, for all cubes, divide the edges by 2, creating eight cubes for each one which was there before. Again calculate the total area of the faces of the cubes.

Write a simple program to describe this process. At the end of each cycle the program should print out the total area of the faces of the cube. Using a hand calculator and a hand-written table, step through the values of the variables and the value of the total area for five division cycles.

You will note two things about this problem. First, the surface area increases in an almost explosive manner as the division process proceeds. What we are looking at is a model of the increase in surface area as particle size becomes smaller, while the total amount of material remains fixed. (No wonder a pound of coal dust has such explosive potential!) It is relatively difficult to guess at the surface area of a pound of finely ground coal dust. However, a computer simulation such as presented by this problem clears things up quite a bit.

The second thing one should notice is the relative difficulty in conceptualizing this problem. It is a bit tricky to get all the changes and calculations in the right place even when the algorithm is handed to us on a platter. Much later in this text, when our computing experience has grown and when we have better analysis tools, the problem will be assigned again. You will be surprised how really simple it is when approached properly.

CHAPTER FOUR

Flowcharting and Elementary Algorithm Development

WHEN ONE has been too long at a tough programming task or has been trying to search one's way through to the solution of a particularly elusive problem, certain types of hysteria unique to the computing profession may make themselves felt. Outrageous puns occur for no apparent reason. The class of word used as a variable may become very strange and even unsuitable for conventional mixed company. The whole process tends to reach a crescendo when the frustrating efforts are capped with success. My wife knows I've 'done it' when music (my claim, not hers) booms forth from the study:

> *I've got rhythm,*
> *AL-GO-RITHM!*
> *I've got rhythm,*
> *Who could ask for anything more?*

I must apologize for taking liberties with Gershwin's lyrics just to use that triumphant tune, but in combination they really say it all. They even say more than we think. An algorithm is a rule (usually a rule of calculation). It is named for a ninth century Islamic scholar (al-Khuwarizimi) who codified the idea of doing a series of steps in a standard pattern as a means of solving problems. In many cases, these steps were repetitive and the concept also related itself to the musical rules of repetition that we call rhythm.

In the original idea of the pattern of steps, it was not a requirement that one knew why the sequence worked; the important point was that this standard series of steps (the algorithm) always led to a correct result. Today a knowledge of the mechanism of the algorithm is essential, because the development of algorithms to enable computers to solve massive problems is at the center of computer science. Thus the technique of algorithm development comes early in the computer studies curriculum. You're going to have to develop experience at expressing procedures in abstract form to prepare yourself to combine them into the more complex algorithms that will make up the numerical and nonnumerical procedures in advanced computing problems.

An orderly approach to algorithm development can certainly be taught, but at some vaguely defined level we enter the realm of creativity. How can this be taught? What can be inspired within the student? The techniques for achieving this remain to be understood. In approaching this boundary, we hope to transmit to the student the ability for clear analysis. We present a multifaceted view of the problem that can lead him or her toward that result that can come only from within: an original, achievable analysis that will yield an efficient, satisfying solution of the problem.

First we are going to need a few logical tools and a simple way of indicating the order in which these steps must be carried out. We will use a flowchart representation at this early stage because it is easy to follow. We will also see that certain essential control structures will need to be included. But let's start with the simple ideas.

We have spoken generally of programs or algorithms. These are a series of steps, which when carried out in order will yield a predictable result corresponding to the answer of some question we have presented. This series of steps must have a beginning and an end. The beginning and end in each is marked by a **terminator** in the shape of an oval (Fig. 4.1). The one corresponding to the beginning is usually marked 'BEGIN' or 'START'; the one marking completion of the program is labeled 'END'. A rectangular block is used to represent a **process**, such as an assignment statement or a mathematical calculation (Fig. 4.2).

The next symbol we will need is some sign indicating that

Fig. 4.1   Terminations

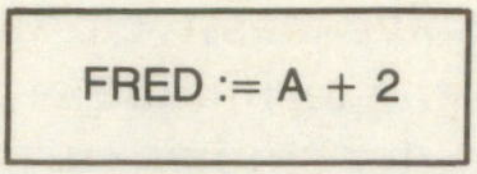

FRED := A + 2

Fig. 4.2   Process

values have been introduced into the program (input) or passed from the working part of the program to the external world (output). Input is normally something such as information from the keyboard, a card reader or a disk drive, while output is something like printed copy, the information presented on a screen or information submitted to the disk drive. Some years ago, the symbol for an input was the silhouette of a standard Hollerith card with a clipped corner. The symbol for output was the drawing of a scroll of paper with one ragged edge to indicate it had been torn from a printing device. While these rather quaint reminders of yesteryear have a nostalgic appeal, the present convention is to use a single symbol for both input and output. It is a parallelogram and represents a square of paper: hence it can be either input or output and it is called **input/output** (Fig. 4.3).

We now come to one of the most important symbols. This symbol is used to represent making a **decision**. It is in the shape of a diamond (Fig. 4.4). The program enters the top of the diamond. The body of the diamond contains a question such as, 'Is ABLE larger than MOXY?' If the answer is true and ABLE *is* larger than MOXY, then the line indicating the flow of program control exits the right-hand apex of the diamond. (Depending on the attitude of the programmer, the word 'true' may be written in small letters near the apex). On the other hand, if the statement is not

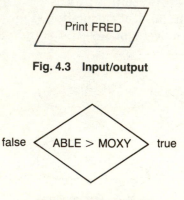

Print FRED

Fig. 4.3   Input/output

false < ABLE > MOXY > true

Fig. 4.4   A decision

true and ABLE is not larger than MOXY, then the line indicating the flow of the program will exit the diamond from the left-hand apex of the diamond. (Again, for similar reasons the word 'false' may be written in small letters near the left-hand apex).

Notice that we have skipped the fourth apex of the diamond. If, for convenience, we use a slightly different combination of vertices, we will use only three: one for entry of the program flow, one for exit of the program flow if the condition (question) is true and one for exit of the program flow if the condition (question) is false. *One* way in, *two* ways out for a total of *three* and *only three* egresses. Even though we have a diamond that is a four-pointed figure, we use only *three* points.

There is one small symbol left. It provides a place where the lines showing the flow of the program may intersect or pass easily to the next column or page. It is a small circle called a **connector** and is often identified by a letter or combination of letters (Fig. 4.5). Although this list seems short, it includes most of the symbols we will need. The list is summarized in Fig. 4.6.

R   O

Fig. 4.5   A connector

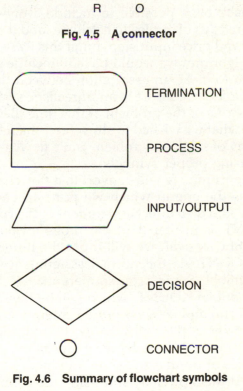

TERMINATION

PROCESS

INPUT/OUTPUT

DECISION

CONNECTOR

Fig. 4.6   Summary of flowchart symbols

Now that we have a set of symbols for describing algorithms in flowcharts, we will take some of the descriptions of calculations from the last chapter and write them as flowcharts. We have added the additional symbol DECISION and will use it to control processing in a much more detailed manner.

Consider one of the first trivial algorithms. We wish to determine the cost of a bag of Granny Smith apples (Chapter 3). We will write a flowchart of the way in which the calculation is made. Note that when we read a value into the program and indicate this with a parallelogram, we show the act of assigning this value to the appropriate variable as a separate process symbol. This practice will be discontinued after the first few diagrams, and the read and associated assignment statement will be combined in a single input symbol.

The reason is that in most languages, the act of reading a value in includes assignment. If we exclude assignment and write it separately, we must ask ourselves where the value has been stored between the time it has been read and the time it has been assigned. The flowchart for the cost of a bag of apples is shown in Figure 4.7.

It would have been possible to include a question asking if there were more bags of apples to calculate, and if so, to return to the apple type and price input step, but if this were to be a moderately realistic algorithm we would have to include some type of a look-up system to make an association between the apple name and its price. Unless we resort to an unrealistic system, a look-up is beyond the scope of the problem at this time. Besides, we have shown exactly what we wished to show (i.e., the relation between the written form of solving a problem and a flowchart of the problem solution using proper symbols).

The next algorithm we will convert to a flowchart is also from Chapter 3. It is the one in which we print an endless series of numbers. We could do a direct assignment of the constant 1 to the variable KOUNT as in Step 1 of the program, but in this case, following the BEGIN oval, we will input the number 1 and then assign it to KOUNT via the normal assignment statement and appropriate symbol. Some programmers may feel that 1 represents a fixed value of KOUNT, which will be the same each time the program is run and so need not be entered as an input from the outside. However, the ability to select the starting point of the calculation provides a greater degree of flexibility. A flowchart for an endless series of numbers is shown in Figure 4.8.

In looking at this flowchart and using the connecting lines to

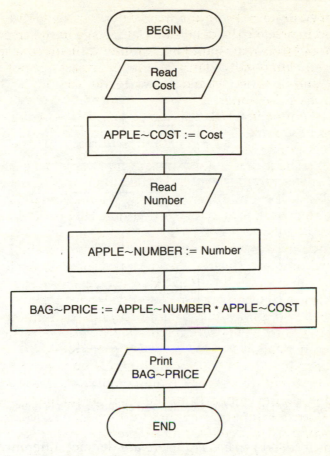

Fig. 4.7   Algorithm for computing the cost of a bag of apples

follow the course of the algorithm, we reach the statement block 'KOUNT := KOUNT + 1.' The line indicating the flow of the algorithm undergoes a compulsory change in direction, returning to the print statement and printing out the appropriate number before looping around once again. Whether we bother with an END oval in this case remains a matter of choice, since it will never be executed. We have produced a 'loop', and we will specifically refer to it as a loop. The loop structure will appear in a number of forms and is quite important, since it allows us to repeat operations and control their repetition.

We have produced a loop that prints out an endless series of integers. We have displayed the algorithm that accomplishes this in two symbolic forms: a graphic form called a *flowchart* and a

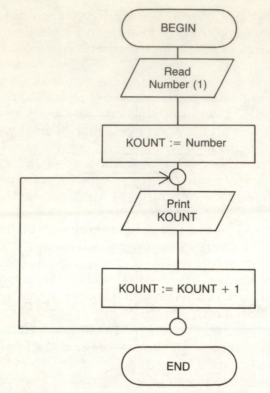

Fig. 4.8   Algorithm for generating an endless series of numbers

literal form called *pseudocode*. There are distinct differences in the properties of these forms that are important to their use in the design of algorithms.

In the flowchart we have the option of working in two dimensions. The line that indicates the flow of control in the chart may be moved around and between structures as we please. This versatility has several advantages and disadvantages.

We can organize an algorithm geometrically in a variety of ways. This gives us a lot of flexibility, but it can make it very hard to recognize structures that are functionally similar. On the other hand, since we are following lines to indicate the flow of control, it is not necessary to use a GOTO instruction followed by a statement line number and then go searching for the corresponding statement to try to integrate it into the algorithm as a whole. Properly designed, a flowchart can provide a clear description of the way an algorithm or a part of it functions. Improperly designed (as used to be the case more often than not) it is truly a can of worms. This dangerous dichotomy was recognized early in the development of computer language and algorithm design. The successful result of these investigations is presented in a later chapter.

Pseudocode is not a two-dimensional structure. You move linearly from one step to the next. If it is necessary to leave the line of linear succession, this is achieved by jumping to a new line in front of or behind the present position. Pseudocode is essentially a one-dimensional structure. If it is necessary to jump back and forth a lot in the course of running the algorithm, this could cause a great deal of confusion. This is often referred to as 'spaghetti coding' because of the difficulty in sorting out the true line of the algorithm.

A major cause of this jumping around was the 'unconditional jump' or GOTO. Every major language had the GOTO structure. It was used extensively and for the most part in a sloppy fashion to provide the kind of dimensional freedom inherent in flowcharting. It caused such confusion and disorder in the writing of conventional code that computer theorist Edsger Dijkstra wrote in his famous letter ('GOTO Statements Considered Harmful') that he advocated no or absolutely minimal usage of the GOTO structure. The cult of GOTO usage was so deeply established that Dijkstra's publication produced a storm of discussion. Though echoes still linger today, a great change may be attributed to the storm.

New versions of most languages developed a series of facilities that enabled the programmer to almost completely avoid GOTO and at the same time set programs up in highly organized 'modular' forms that made them much easier to compose, read and modify. The development of this modular form of programming and the recognition of the key structures necessary to make it work were also due to the investigations of Bohm and Jacopini. Before going on to the next chapter, where we will begin to use the structures that make modular programming possible, we will write a few more programs from variations of the algorithms with which we have begun to work.

Consider the problem of the counting algorithm from Chapter 3 (and Figure 4.8) which produces an endless (or at least very long) list of numbers. We can make use of the decision statement to cause it to stop where we wish. The flowchart in Figure 4.9 shows a form that will count to 98.

There is always the chance that you wish to count to some number other than 98, in which case it would be useful to use a different limit in the decision diamond. Nothing is wrong with

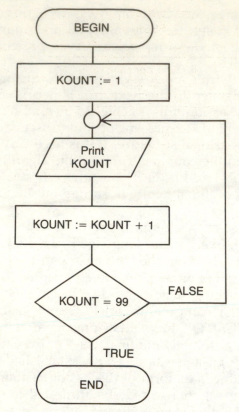

Fig. 4.9   A counting algorithm

using a variable that can be set to the desired limit by an appropriate pair of input and assignment statements. However, there is the problem of deciding which input is the starting position of the series and which input is the ending position. We must have the option of having the computer supply the outside world with information identifying inputs or outputs, or indicating important information about the state of the algorithm being processed. These pieces of information are called 'prompts' and communicate via an output statement using 'Print'. If we were printing out the contents of a variable, we would include the variable name. We are printing out a message, so we simply include the message itself and enclose it in quotation marks, so we will know it is a message. A simple example of this will be seen in Figure 4.10.

The student should write the output expected from this program, using 5 for the initial value and 17 for the final value. In those cases where the program puts out a prompt to be answered

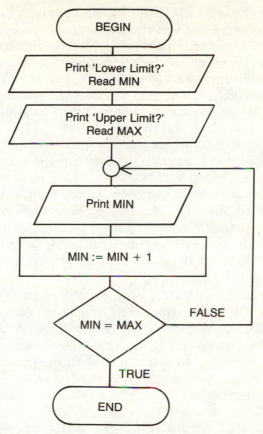

Fig. 4.10   Counting algorithm with variable MAX and MIN and prompts for input

by the student, the prompt should be written out just like any other program output, but the student's answers to the prompt (such as the numbers 5 and 17 in this case) should be underlined to show that they came from the student and not from the program. In this way we can see a clear dialogue between the operator and the computer.

In going through the increasing complications that present themselves as we develop this simple algorithm, the observant reader has noticed a problem just waiting to gum up the works. The algorithm of Figure 4.10 requires us to enter a small number with a variable name MIN to serve as the start of the counting process. The upper limit of the counting process will be a larger number that we enter and designate MAX. In the cycle of producing the elements of the series, we use a loop that adds 1 to MIN and redesignates MIN in the same manner in which KOUNT was treated in the algorithm of Figure 4.9. The difference is that in the present case we limit the length of the number series by comparing MIN as it is increased (the increment loop). When MIN has increased to the point where it is equal to MAX, the decision diamond causes the direction of program control to shift. MIN is not further incremented and the program ends.

Now suppose due to operator carelessness a number is entered for MIN that is actually larger than the number entered for MAX. The algorithm will not give us a limited series but an endless one, because MIN starts out larger than MAX and is increased by 1 each time. The stage is never reached where MIN is equal to MAX, so the loop never stops printing. Clearly, we must put in a test to see that MIN is smaller than MAX and if this is not the case, the program must ask for them to be entered again. This is shown in Figure 4.11.

The construction of tests within a program to ensure proper operator response is sometimes referred to as 'goof-proofing'. It used to be common to give the correction message a sarcastic or unpleasant tone. This is not often done today since we have come to realize how sensitive people are to machine criticism. Also, in the business environment where much of today's software is run, an impolite comment to call attention to an error is pointless. In the flowchart with test and correction module shown in Figure 4.11, the entry prompts are merely repeated until a correct relationship between MIN and MAX is achieved.

The last simple algorithm we will develop in this chapter will involve a physical rather than a mathematical problem. We are describing a machine our high-tech grandmother uses to peel apples for her apple pies. This will provide a somewhat more complicated flowchart than we have seen before and demonstrate one particularly unusual construction that will be with us in many future designs. As may be seen from the flowchart, the algorithm follows the BEGIN oval with an input symbol and the activity 'Reach into bucket.' This is followed by a decision diamond with the question 'Any apples?' If the answer is 'False', that is, there are no apples to peel, then note that the control line avoids all the rest of the program steps and outputs a prompt right at the end of the program which announces the machine is out of apples, and we go to the END oval.

On the other hand, if there are apples to be peeled, an apple is taken out, the selected apple is peeled and chopped in a normal

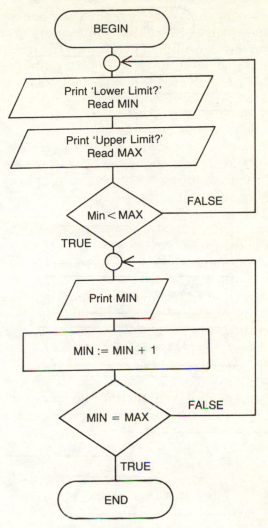

Fig. 4.11   Counting algorithm with a test for initial values

statement block, and the chopped apple is added to the pie mix in a standard output block. The flowchart for this program is shown in Figure 4.12a.

Although it is a bit early to be thinking this way, notice that we don't bother to descibe the peeling or chopping. We just handle the operation as a unified activity as if we were calling up a complete peeling operating or chopping operation. We are beginning to think in a modular form, where we call up a peeling or chopping module. Such thinking makes program design easy. We

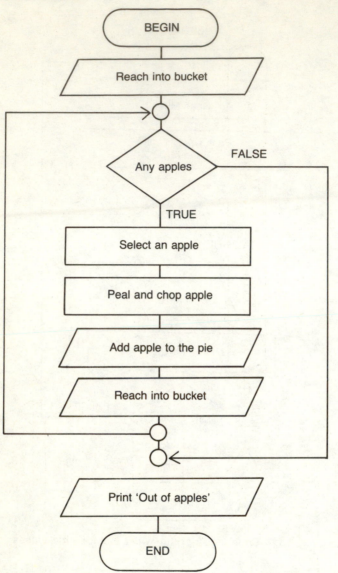

Fig. 4.12a   Algorithm for choosing, peeling and chopping apples

might just want to remove the core of the apple without peeling or chopping it. We would then eliminate the peel-and-chop module and replace it with a core-removal module. The details would be developed elsewhere and the flow of ideas we needed to develop the algorithm would be unbroken.

Now something a bit funny happens. We do a statement with

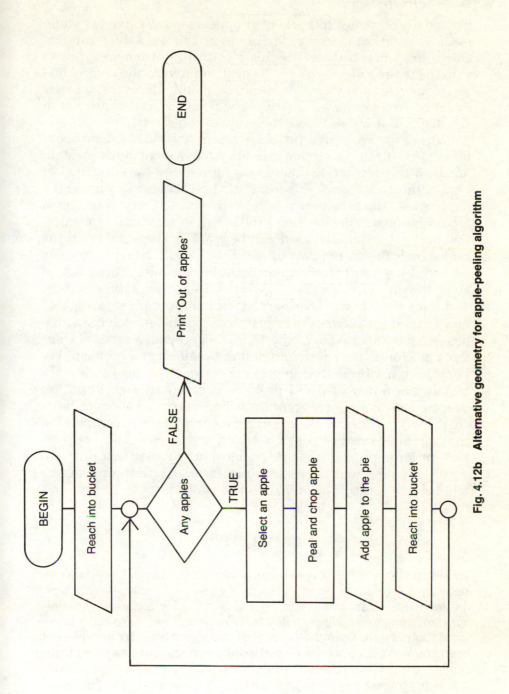

Fig. 4.12b Alternative geometry for apple-peeling algorithm

the activity 'Reach into bucket.' It appears exactly like the statement we used at the start of the program, but it is a different one. Our control line then leaves this block without making contact with the closing message or END oval and rejoins the control line via a connector just above the choice diamond. Of course, we may prefer to arrange the geometry of the flowchart differently, as in Fig. 4.12b, but we still have this duplication step.

During the years that program design was done by means of flowcharts, it was found that repetition loops were much easier to handle if the decision diamond was right at the start of a loop or right at the end of one. This form was best achieved by using the duplication structure shown here. The repeated step is usually a type of input step like reading a data card, in which case the question in the decision diamond will be whether the number on the card signals the end of data or that there is still data. In our case, our input step was to feel around in the bucket and get information about the presence of an apple, which was a physical type of data.

In this chapter we have learned a set of standard symbols that may be used to describe the logical steps in problem-solving activities. We have learned to connect these together in a series of steps that are a formalized description of the solution of a problem. We know that this formalized stepwise description of the solution of a mathematical or real-world problem is called an **algorithm**. We designed several simple algorithms and described them in flowchart form. Clearly, if the algorithms get a bit more complicated the manipulations of the symbols and their connecting lines will present large problems. Further, recognizing that two different arrangements actually represent the same algorithm or program will become difficult or perhaps impossible.

PROBLEMS

These problems involve constructing flowcharts as well as devising algorithms a bit more complicated than those of Chapter 3. Although the mechanisms are not particularly difficult, they are used throughout computing. You will probably feel like describing these activities in some form of simple English and then writing a flowchart to represent what you want to do. Since we will eventually be using pseudocode for composition, if the technique of drawing your flowchart from a crude sort of program in simple English works, by all means use it. However, you may note that the use of a flowchart will greatly simplify the presentation of procedures that sound a bit clumsy in ordinary English. Later, we will use a special type of English that will get around this problem while avoiding the difficulties in arranging the lines and blocks of a flow-chart.

Once again, the answers to all problems will be found at the end of the book. Problems 4.8 and 4.9 have not been designated challenge problems because they are simplified 'money-changing algorithms', and this type of thinking in different forms is common to many types of program.

*   *   *

4.1   Draw a simple flowchart that describes a program which prints out an infinite series of even numbers starting with 10. You need not include an input mechanism to start at 10. Just start at 10 by internal assignment using an assignment statement.

4.2   Draw a simple flowchart to describe a program that tests a number. If the number is equal to or less than 55, the program should print out the message 'Too small'. If the number is greater than 55, the program should print out the message 'Too large'. Do not worry about input. Just assume you start with a variable called BOX that has already been defined.

4.3   In problem 3.6 you wrote a program that caused the cost of a simple grocery list to be written. The list involved pounds of flour, boxes of eggs and quarts of milk. The cost of one pound of flour, one box of eggs and one quart of milk was given. To make the problem simple, you were told that the amounts were respectively one pound, one box and one quart. To save strain on the imaginary printing system, the program was only required to print out the sum. We are now ready for more complicated versions of the same thing. Modify the program so that it asks for the number of pounds of flour, the number of boxes of eggs and the number of quarts of milk. Based on these numbers and the costs given in the original problem, a bill in cents should be printed out. Draw a flowchart to show the structure of this program.

4.4   Draw a simple flowchart that describes a program which starts at 2 and prints all the numbers between 2 and 12, inclusive. It should then automatically begin at 2 again and repeat the print-out. This repetition process should be continued indefinitely.

4.5   Draw a simple flowchart that asks for two numbers and accepts them. The request should be something like 'First number please', followed by an input block that reads the number and assigns it to an appropriately named variable. This should be repeated for a second number. The two numbers should be compared and the larger number printed with an appropriate notice. In the event the two numbers are the same, a notice that they are the same should be printed out.

4.6   You have a deck of cards that are all greater than zero, except for the last card, which is negative. This last card is used to mark the end of the card deck. Design a flowchart that describes a program which reads each card in the deck. In the case of each card with a positive value it should multiply the value by 2 and print out the result. When the last card (the negative card) is read, it should print the message 'Out of data' and quit. The negative value should not be processed or printed out.

4.7   You work for a taxi company. At the end of each month, all the drivers turn in three punched cards arranged in order. The first is the number of miles the driver has driven, the second is the number of gallons of gasoline he or she has used. The third is the identification number of his/her taxi. The central office checks to see that each set of three cards is in the order listed above. Each set of three cards is then placed in one big deck. A card with a negative number is placed at the end of the deck.

Design a flowchart showing a program that will read each three-card block, calculate miles per gallon, print out the miles per gallon indicated by that card set, and label the miles per gallon with the number identifying the taxi that used the gasoline and made the trips. When the card that marks the end of the deck is read, an 'Out of data' message should be printed. Note that within each block of three cards the order of the cards is exactly as given above. Choose and assign variables as you wish.

*4.8   You are designing the change-making program for a machine to be used in a market in a simple society. This society has money that exists in only two forms: 'Globs' and 'Drips'. There are eight Drips in a Glob. The person using the machine enters the number of Drips that an article is worth. The machine calculates this value in Globs and Drips and prints out the result. The program should work in the following way. The program subtracts the value of one Glob from the total amount and repeats this until the result of the subtraction is less than one Glob, that is until the result is less than eight Drips. Each time it does a subtraction, it increments a counter that records the number of Globs. It then prints out the number of Globs and Drips equivalent to the number of Drips entered at the start of the program. You may not use division directly, because any operation other than addition, subtraction and assignment is against the moral precepts of this culture. Prepare a flowchart that describes this program.

*4.9   Just when you have the flowchart for Problem 4.8 ready, your marketing division informs you that the society for which you are designing the machine has made a great leap forward. They have invented a new coin called a 'Hunk'. Each Hunk is worth five Globs. Redesign the program and the associated flowchart to produce the value of a given number of Drips in Hunks, Globs and Drips.

*4.10   In problem 3.10 you designed a program that calculated the total area of a cube, then divided each of the edges of the cube in half, thus creating eight cubes with edges one-half of those of the original cube. The total surface area of all the faces of these cubes was calculated. Again the edges were cut in half, again producing eight cubes where one had been before. The total surface calculation was repeated and the edge division was repeated until division had occurred a total of five times.

Design a flowchart to describe the program that defines this process. In each cycle, it should print out the number of cubes and the total area. This printing process should include the first cycle, during which there is only one cube. The flowchart you produce should show a process that stops at 20 cycles.

CHAPTER FIVE

Flowcharting and Standard Flowchart Forms

THE EARLY period of algorithm and program design and description was characterized by attempts to find orderly approaches. The methods were primarily graphic, and although there were several different systems, the one we call flowcharting today was the most used. As we have already observed, flowcharting allowed the same algorithm to be written in many different forms that were often unrecognizable as being related. A second, similar problem was the undisciplined manner in which the flow lines traveled in all directions, resembling a bowl of spaghetti.

Some order was introduced by the work of Bohm and Jacopini, who showed that all flowcharts could be constructed from combinations of three simple standard structures. They also defined the constitution of these three basic units. The structures had been in use already, but the fact that they were the only ones needed had not been realized.

Before proceeding with an exact examination of the structure, operation and application of the standard forms, let us gain a limited understanding of the development of related ideas. The discovery of the standard forms did not become popular knowledge immediately. It was a later republication that established the beginning of their influence.

At the time that the importance of these standard forms began to be realized, the technique of program creation for larger programs was to produce a flowchart and then translate it into the programming language. The construction of flowcharts and conversion to a computer language was greatly improved by the introduction of the standard forms, but the basic problem of the flowchart remained. As one goes through the process of drawing and improving the chart, even small changes may involve the alteration of many flow lines and statement symbols.

The flowchart is two-dimensional. The kind of changes necessary during the creation process present difficulties. These difficulties are essentially mechanical and are associated with the two-dimensional structure. Improved theory was not likely to cause further significant advances in flowcharting.

Some programmers had been using crude forms of pseudocode to describe their programs in informal English. The initial descriptions were then refined to a more restricted form of English until conversion to a conventional programming language was relatively straightforward. As there was a lot of individual variation, usable standard forms were not defined.

The flowchart structures of Bohm and Jacopini provided patterns that developed into the standardized control structures used in pseudocode today. These structures are called **sequence, selection (IF–THEN–ELSE)** and **iteration (DOWHILE)**.

A number of parallel developments were also occurring. A major attempt had begun to produce working computer languages that organized themselves into sound logical structures on the basis of their own internal rules and statements. Although FORTRAN did not have control elements matching the three elementary ones, COBOL contained structures related to IF–THEN–ELSE and DOWHILE. PL/1, which is also a major programming language, was one of the early languages containing all control structures, as well as an overall architecture that ensured proper structure. The interaction of these efforts led to the development of certain principles of programming and of a more or less standardized type of pseudocode using the Bohm-Jacopini control structures.

One of these principles is the idea of working in modular structures. A modular structure is a block of commands that performs a function or small group of related functions in a larger module or in a program. It is designed so that there is only one entry and one exit, and its activities do not overlap those of other modules. A module itself may consist of smaller modules or be part of a larger module. This means that the computer program is built from a number of individual, independent parts, much in the manner of good electronic equipment. To make modifications or correct errors it is usually necessary only to change a module.

The modular concept also simplifies design of programs because the programmer sets up a series of activities to accomplish in a specific order. At the time of conception the programmer must concentrate only on the major modules needed to do this work and may leave the details to a later stage in the creative process. Though this may sound like a rather difficult concept, it is a powerful tool in building large programs. In fact it is not difficult, just a bit subtle. When we have used it, you will find it works in a straightforward manner.

We are immediately led into a closely related principle: top-down programming. This method owes much of its development to Niklaus Wirth, who later produced the languages Pascal and Modula-II. The idea is to take the task that one must perform and break it down into those subtasks that are its major components. Each subtask is then broken down in a similar manner. Further levels of degradation may be carried out. However, somewhere along the line it will become clear that the subtasks are at a level where they may be programmed in an obvious fashion and the process is complete. Clearly, the tasks and subtasks we have been talking about may be set up in a modular fashion. The combination of these two techniques in conjunction with modern pseudocode greatly simplifies the design of complex programs. It also ensures that they will be written in a logical order that is relatively easy to understand.

We have now looked at the major tools we will have to work with. They are flowcharts based on the Bohm-Jacopini structures, a pseudocode developed from the same elementary structures, modular construction of programs and top-down design. Flowcharting will be used to explain the operation of the control structures and the most used combinations derived from them. Flowcharts will also be used to document finished programs or algorithms. Pseudocode will be used for program design. Of course, it may be necessary to write the program several times with increasing detail to get to a final form in good pseudocode.

What about translation into the regular programming languages? There are still plenty of versions of the common languages that do not have the necessary structures built in. An appendix is included at the end of the text showing standard translations of the structures to BASIC and FORTRAN. Examples of more complex forms and programs from the text are also included. We suggest that the reader take the chapters in order and leave the translations until last.

Let us now examine each of the three Bohm-Jacopini forms, starting with the simplest. A sequence is just a series of simple statements linked together one after the other. It is normally presented as a series of three rectangular process blocks, but there is nothing special about the number 3. An example of sequence in which each block is simply a statement marked 'statement' is shown in Figure 5.1. Notice that there is only one way into the sequence and one way out. This is an important property and has been discussed in our treatment of modular structures. Since sequence is just a series of statements, it presents no problem of representation in any standard computer language.

The next structure is selection, or IF–THEN–ELSE. It consists of a choice diamond and two statement blocks assembled as in Figure 5.2. The flow of control enters the choice diamond at the top. The question or condition determines what happens next. If the condition is true or the answer to the question is true, control follows the line marked 'True' and a statement, which we call Statement A in the example, is executed. In the event the condition is false, Statement B is executed.

There are several characteristics to be noted about the selection structure. Only one of the two statements, Statement A or Statement B, will be executed. Further, one of the two statements *must* be executed. The control paths leaving Statement A and Statement B merge to form a single path that continues into the main line of the program. Once again, we have a modular structure with one way in and one way out. This modularization

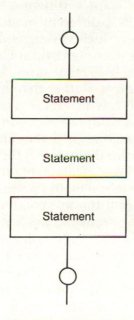

Fig. 5.1   A sequence

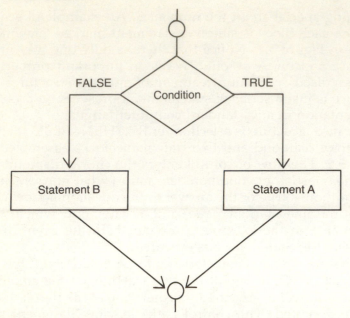

Fig. 5.2   Selection structure (IF–THEN–ELSE)

allows us to deal specifically with single selection or IF–THEN–ELSE situations. If we want a different set of conditions and choices, we just plug in a different module. It makes thinking about a choice situation much easier, and it makes updating a complex program or its documentation relatively simple.

A special case of the IF–THEN–ELSE structure occurs when there is only one alternative. Rather than have the ELSE arm of a selection contain a GOTO, which returns control to the main program, the structure is considered as having the form IF–THEN. The operation of this variation is diagrammed in Figure 5.3. The control line enters a choice diamond. If the test condition is true, the statement marked 'True' (Statement A) is run and the control line then recombines with the main program or algorithm control line. On the other hand, if the test condition is false, the line of control does not diverge from the main program.

Looping is one of the most common events in computing and one of the most powerful tools provided by the computer. We have already seen it at work in the earlier counting examples. The flow diagram of the Bohm-Jacopini structure used to produce a loop is shown in Figure 5.4. The loop is a subtle structure and should be studied carefully.

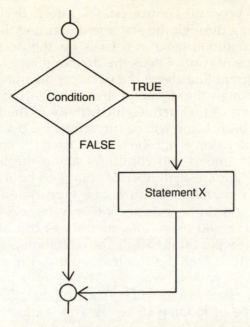

Fig. 5.3   Selection structure (IF–THEN)

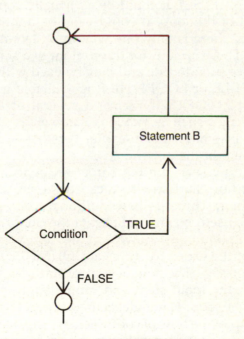

Fig. 5.4   A DOWHILE loop

The main program control passes into a decision diamond without passing through the statement defining the action of the loop. If the condition used as a basis for the decision diamond is true, the line of control exits the diamond and loops back into the main program line above the decision diamond where it will be carried through the diamond again. Note that the statement (here Statement B) that defines the activity of the loop is located on the return branch and will be run only if the decision condition is true. If the decision condition is false, then the control line exits the decision diamond and continues along the line it was originally on. There are a number of things to be noticed. First of all, we have a modular structure: one way in and one way out. Second, the path the loop takes will only be followed if the test condition is true and for as long as the test condition is true. In other words, it will be done while the condition is true, hence the name DOWHILE. Third, if the test is false, the action the loop performs *will not be done even once*. This sounds like an odd property to emphasize, but as will be shown later, this is in contrast to another type of looping structure and is quite important.

Look for a moment at the block marked Statement B. It could be a single statement like the assignment statement 'X := X + 1.' It could be a small group of statements like a sequence or selection (IF–THEN–ELSE). It could be a virtually complete program under control of the loop. It could even be another DOWHILE. Whatever it is, there is only one way into Statement B and only one way out. These options for the content of a statement are part of the design of pseudocode and may be used with any statement block. DOWHILE or LOOPWHILE is available in extended versions of BASIC, FORTRAN 77, and several of the FORTRAN-derived languages such as WATFIV, as well as Pascal and Ada. Its emulation by statements in earlier versions of FORTRAN and BASIC is shown in the appendices.

We have now seen the big three: sequence, selection, DOWHILE. Any flowchart structure can be constructed from combinations of them. There are two additional control structures that are sometimes used, but are not part of the Bohm-Jacopini group. Under certain conditions, however, they are very convenient.

The first of the extra structures is DOUNTIL. This structure is shown in Figure 5.5. The flow of control starts at the top as usual, follows down the main stem and immediately meets the statement run by the loop. Having executed the statement (Statement C in our example) the flow of control enters the decision diamond. If the test is true, control exits the loop and does not return. If the

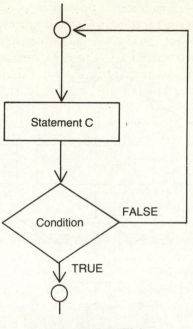

Fig. 5.5   A DOUNTIL loop

test result is false, the flow of control loops back and combines with the main control line above the statement to be run (Statement C). As is usual in all our fundamental structures, there is one way in and one way out.

At first glance DOUNTIL looks very much like DOWHILE, but there is a subtle difference. In DOUNTIL the looping statement is always run at least once. There is a good reason for this. The control line passes through the looping statement (Statement C) before it enters the decision diamond. Within the decision diamond, if the test is true control leaves the loop. Thus the loop does Statement C until the test has been made true and then stops looping. For this reason it is called DOUNTIL or LOOPUNTIL.

DOUNTIL structures are quite reliable, but there is one flaw. The statement controlled by the loop is always run once even when it should not be. This will become clearer when a few simple examples are worked. It is important that the student make a careful comparison of DOWHILE and DOUNTIL.

The second of the extra structures is CASE, shown in Figure 5.6. On the basis of a particular test made in the ingoing bowl-shaped symbol, one of a series of statements or process blocks is executed.

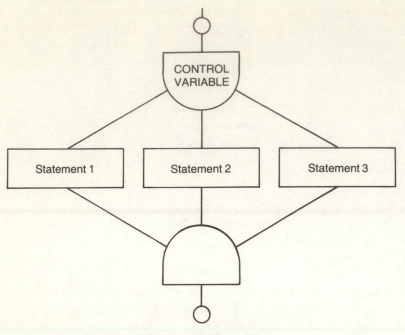

Fig. 5.6   CASE structure

The flow lines recombine after leaving the process blocks. An example would be testing a variable that might have integer values from 1 through 10. On the basis of the input variable value, one of ten different statement blocks would be executed. Early versions of many of the major languages had a command statement that worked very much like CASE.

Before going to pseudocode based on the three primary structures, we will build a few simple programs to see the structures in operation. The first step in producing a program or a flowchart is to describe the problem. Here is our problem description: A number is written on a card. Devise a program that prints out 'TOO BIG' if the number is larger than 100 and 'TOO SMALL' if the number is 100 or smaller. On completing the test it should print out the message 'ALL DONE'. In this case, the statement of the problem is actually a brief description of what the program will do. A good thing to do next is to list the input data and the output data separately. Then we know what we have to work with.

INPUT DATA: A single number on a card.
OUPUT DATA: Either a message 'TOO BIG' or a message 'TOO SMALL' followed in either case by a message 'ALL DONE'.

Next, following the top-down procedure, we must examine the activities to be performed and write them out in a series of logical steps. Mentally, we may wish to use the three standard steps of data processing as a guide. These steps are, as you will remember, input, process and output.

Our initial list of steps can be a bit sloppy, because we can always refine them by producing a better list of steps based on the first list. Nobody asks us to be perfect the first time. The important thing is to get something on paper that approximates what you want to do. Worry about improving it later. So our first list:

1. Read the number from the card.
2. Assign it to a variable called NUMBER.
3. Test NUMBER (greater than 100?).
4. Print result of test.
5. Print the sign-off message.

Now we can refine this a bit. Steps 1 and 2 are part of an input and assignment sequence. We can diagram this as a single input parallelogram in which NUMBER is assigned the number on the card. Of course, an INPUT parallelogram followed by a PROCESS rectangle with an assignment statement could be used, but this would present the question of how the number is being held between the time it was read in and the time it was assigned. The first procedure is less complicated, so we will use it. Now steps 3 and 4 are also related. We are looking at an IF–THEN–ELSE in which the decision diamond tests NUMBER and process blocks, that print out the applicable result messages. Finally, step 5 is just the signoff message. Rewriting the list of steps we have:

1. Read card value and assign to NUMBER.
2. Test NUMBER (NUMBER greater than 100?) and print out the answer.
3. Print the signoff.

A terminator oval is entered for a start, and the input/output parallelogram with a message defines the input and assignment of NUMBER. The decision diamond of a selection (IF–THEN–ELSE) unit asks, 'NUMBER greater than 100?' Each leg of the selection is an input/output parallelogram. One says 'Print "TOO LARGE"'; the other says 'Print "TOO SMALL"'. After control leaves the selection structure there is a final input/output parallelogram with the message 'Print "ALL DONE"'. The diagram is closed with another terminator oval containing END. The result is shown in Figure 5.7.

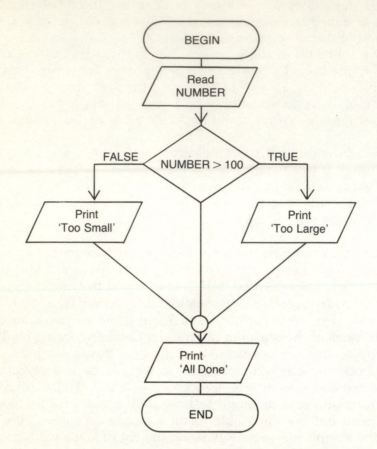

Fig. 5.7   Algorithm for reading and comparing a number from a card

For a second demonstration we will examine the program that counted up to 98 (Figure 4.9) and then stopped. This can be done in a general form in which we have two inputs, the starting point and the upper limit of the counting series. The first thing to do is to write a brief description of the problem.

DESCRIPTION: This program accepts two integers, the first smaller than the second. It then produces all the integers between them including the smallest, but excluding the largest.
INPUT DATA: The lower limit and the upper limit.
OUTPUT DATA: All the integers between the two limits including the lower one, but not the upper.

We are now ready to write a series of steps that define the general outline of the program.

PROCEDURE:

1. Input the limits.
2. Test the limits.
3. Calculate and print the numbers between the integers.
4. End the program.

We may now improve this result a bit. Follow the action by using Figure 5.8a. In the case of the input of the limits we will precede each actual input step by an output step that asks for the input we require (for example, the message 'Lower Limit?'). When we have the lower and upper limits, they must be tested to see that the upper limit is really greater than the lower limit. This could be done with a structure related to DOWHILE. As long as the incorrectness of the relation between the limits remains true (that is, as long as 'MAX <= MIN' remains true) the input system will loop. The warning message, 'Check Limits', would be on the DOWHILE repeat loop. The input instructions themselves would be on the portion of the DOWHILE preceding the decision block and so would always be run once, whether the loop repeated or not. The resulting flowchart is rather messy, but it works. The calculation step (MIN := MIN + 1) is included in the DOUNTIL structure. Notice that we have the 'Print' statement right at the start of the calculation, so that we print the minimum limit before reaching the step that causes it to be incremented. Finally, we reach an END oval to complete the program. The complete flowchart is shown in Figure 5.8a.

A second way to draw the flowchart is to consider the input step:

Print 'Upper Limit?'
Read MAX
Print 'Lower Limit?'
Read MIN

and the test step:

MAX <= MIN

as a single unit. This discussion may be followed using Figure 5.8b. We would continue to go through the input step again and

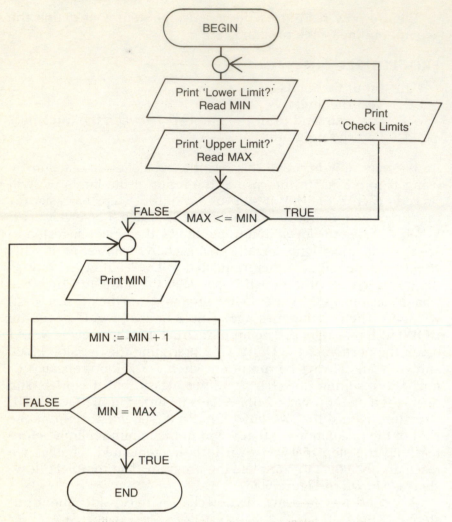

Fig. 5.8a   Algorithm for generating a list of integers between given limits

again, as long as the relationship between the upper limit and lower limits was incorrect. This would require a DOWHILE structure with the input sequence as the repeating element. This is not too bad, but it muddles the modules and makes the insertion of the warning message virtually impossible. The calculation step could also be a DOWHILE loop in which the loop continued as long as the lower limit, which is being incremented each time, remains less than the upper limit. Remember once again that the print statement must come first, so that the initial value will print

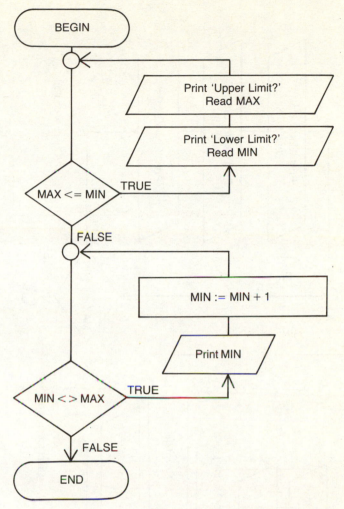

Fig. 5.8b   Integer-generating algorithm, with an initial test

out. This version is also closed with an END oval. The complete flowchart is shown in Figure 5.8b.

A third way to draw the flowchart shown in Figure 5.8c retains modularity nicely, but involves writing the input sequence twice. In the first part, which is the input module marked 'Entry Module', we have a straight sequence structure consisting of input/output blocks which writes the prompts to the screen asking for the proper limits. Next we have the test sequence, designated 'Check Module', which is a DOWHILE with a condition saying that as long as the relationship between the limits is incorrect, the loop should be run. In the loop the first thing one meets is the warning

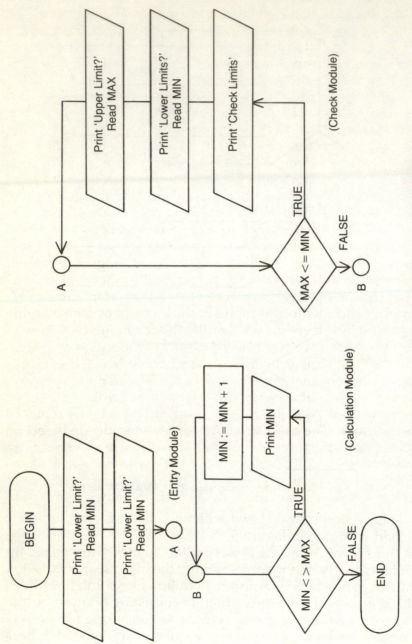

Fig. 5.8c   Final modular version of integer-generating algorithm

message, followed by a duplicate of the input sequence. Since this test module is a DOWHILE, looping and hence display of the warning and reentry messages will occur only if the test condition is true. The calculation in the calculation module for the series of numbers is next and is run with a DOWHILE exactly as it was run in the second version. Then we are ready for an END oval. The entire flowchart is shown in Figure 5.8c.

Of the three versions of this program, the preferred one is the third (Figure 5.8c). Here, all the modules are well defined and fit together logically. There is no overlapping of tasks as in the first flowchart problem or in the first version of this problem. The modularity is so well defined that we may separate the individual modules by connector symbols. Here, this is done to emphasize the success of our analysis and the resulting modularity. Normally, the modules would be connected in the usual fashion. The only drawback is that we had to write the input sequence twice.

Statement duplication will be avoidable once we have the ability to call subroutines. A subroutine is a short program fragment that is 'called' and put to work automatically whenever it is required. Thus in the input sequence of step 1 and step 2 above, we can replace each of the two copies of the input steps with a calling statement which merely asks that the input routine be run.

In this chapter we have examined the organization and function of the three basic structures of flowcharting. Using these three structures in combination, any program can be diagrammed. We have kept in mind that modifying a flowchart involves changing quite a few lines. As a design tool, flowcharting is better replaced by pseudocode. The basic structures of pseudocode are based on the three basic structures of flowcharting. We have also seen from the way these various structures have been presented in flowcharts that flowcharting is excellent for understanding what is going on and for documenting the results of a program after the design process has been completed.

In the next chapter the control structures which until now have been seen as flow diagrams will be converted to pseudocode. Additional features will be added to create a complete pseudocode language. Problem analysis and program development will be presented as procedures with well-defined steps.

PROBLEMS

Most of the examples in this set can be solved with structured flowcharts that are more or less straightforward modifications of structures already presented in the text and illustrations of Chapter 5. The answers to problems 5.3, 5.5, 5.6, 5.7 and 5.10 will be found at the end of the book. Problems 5.8 and 5.9 have been designated challenge problems. However, you should note that modifications and refinements of these challenge problems will be presented as exercises in future chapters.

*   *   *

5.1 Using the DOWHILE loop structure, design a flowchart that shows a program that counts backward from 10 down to and including 0. It should print out each value including both 10 and 0. When the backward count is complete, it should finish by writing the word 'Pop'.

5.2 Using the DOUNTIL loop structure, design a program that does exactly the same job as done in Problem 5.1 by the DOWHILE structure. In addition, make a list of all differences in the flowcharts of problems 5.1 and 5.2. This includes the choice of limits, relational symbols used, and order of the print and incrementing steps in the loop. This order is relative to the top and bottom of the page, not to the execution order.

5.3 Assume you have a deck of cards, each of which contains a number that is positive or negative, but not zero. This deck may have any number of cards. The number on the last card will be zero (0). This zero card will mark the end of the deck. Write a flowchart illustrating a program in which each card is read. When the end card is reached, the message 'End of Data' should be printed out and the value of the card (0) should not be printed.

If the content of the card is a number that is not zero, the value of the number should be written and another card read. This structure must be written as a DOWHILE loop. Remember to include the 'priming' read step just before the loop begins, as well as a read step within the loop. The read and value-assignment steps may be combined, as has been discussed earlier in the text.

5.4 Repeat the exercise in Problem 5.3. However, this time write the flowchart as a DOUNTIL instead of a DOWHILE. How can you prevent the zero from being printed out?

5.5 Assume you have a single variable with the value already assigned. The value may be either a positive number or a negative number, but it may not be zero. Draw a flowchart of a simple program that tests the variable and prints the words 'Negative' or 'Positive', depending on whether the number is negative or positive.

5.6   In Problem 5.3 a flowchart was designed which read a set of cards and printed out the contents. This program was structured as a DOWHILE. The statement executed on the return loop of the control involved a 'Print' to print out the values of the numbers on the cards as the cards were read. Replace this print statement with the selection or IF–THEN–ELSE module designed in Problem 5.5. The entire program should now read a set of cards and print 'Negative' or 'Positive' for each of the cards read. It should read, recognize, but not print the zero (0) card that marks the end of the deck of cards. When this is reached, the message 'End of Data' should be printed out.

5.7   In Problem 4.9 you designed a program that accepted a value in a coinage called 'Drips' and expressed it in a combination of coins called 'Drips', 'Globs' and 'Hunks'. Construct a flowchart of this device using DOWHILE loops. You should be able to do this by using two DOWHILE loops arranged one after the other. Of course, there will be other steps, but it is not necessary to include one DOWHILE loop inside another.

*5.8   You are concerned with a machine that sneaks up on walls. (This is an unlikely machine, but there are a lot of unlikely things in the universe, so why not?) The machine works in the following way. After it has been assigned to a wall, it moves halfway to the wall. Then it moves one-half of the remaining distance between itself and the wall. It then repeats this behavior as many times as is required. You are asked to write a program that will predict certain aspects of the behavior of the machine.

The program asks for the starting distance between the machine and the wall. It then asks you how many jumps you wish to take. It then prints out the distance between the wall and the machine at the end of the number of jumps that is entered. All measurements may be considered to be in feet. You need not convert anything to inches. When it has completed its tasks, it prints 'Thankyou' and quits. Prepare a flowchart of the program describing this machine. A DOWHILE loop might be useful, although this can be run just as easily with a DOUNTIL.

*5.9   In Problem 5.8 you designed a flowchart describing the behavior of the wall machine. Prepare a table listing each of the variables you use in the machine. You should show the value of all these variables at the time of printout of each cycle. You need not write out the complete set of variables at each step because the flowchart does not include step numbers. As input values, use a machine-to-wall distance of 5,280 feet and instruct the system to take seven jumps. You may use a pocket calculator.

5.10   When we say that a number is divisible by 3, we mean that when the number is divided by 3 the quotient is a whole number with no fractional parts. Another way to express this is to say that if we take the number in its positive form and subtract 3 from it a sufficient number of times, we will reach exactly zero (0). We will never pass through a condition where there is a residue of 1 or 2. Design a flowchart describing a program that tests a positive whole number or integer to establish whether it is evenly divisible by 3. The program should ask for a positive integer to test. After the subtraction step controlled by an appropriate loop and condition, the program should test the residue and provide a printout stating whether the original number was or was not evenly divisible by 3. You will probably need two control structures, but they need not be nested.

CHAPTER SIX

The Details of Pseudocode and Program Solution Layout

Beginning work in any computer language involves the old problem of which came first, the chicken or the egg. The computer version of this dilemma is whether to learn the advanced structure of a language more or less completely before beginning to write serious programs or to write a simplified version of the language first, then produce a number of sloppy programs and refine things later to really good form. In either event the initial activities will involve confusion, extensive later revision, or both. We have tried to work with the best of both worlds by doing several limited problems in reasonably well-structured flowcharts and discussing the difficulties of understanding them in a rational fashion. Now that we have an idea of how things go, the time has come to refine and extend our ideas. Knowing the role that structure will play and the uses we will make of flowcharting, we are ready to approach pseudocode.

Not everything will be formal. Without turning this text into an encyclopedia, there is no way to consider all of the operations we will need. These operations will be the tasks the computer actually does, like 'Read' or 'Print' or 'Assignment (:=)', and include arithmetic operations such as addition, subtraction, multiplication and division.

We will discuss each of the above operations briefly to get an idea of usable forms, what they mean, and how much we may vary them. They will be classified as input, process and output according to function. The input operation will usually be 'Read'. We will begin the word with a capital letter. It is conceivable that we will refer to a specific device like a card reader or a disk drive or a particular file. This additional information can be added in a flexible manner (for example, 'Read from disk drive #1.'). If the source is not defined in the programming problem description, or there is only one source to read from, then 'Read' says it all. Each number read will be assigned to some variable. We could read a data number and then in the next line assign it to a variable. In this case it is not clear in what type of intermediate storage the data is stored between read and assignment. Since we will only read one number at a time, it is just as easy and much more straightforward to include the variable assignment in the read statement. Thus, we can say something like:

Read data, assign to STRUTH

or

Read data (STRUTH)

or

Read into STRUTH

or

Read (STRUTH)

or

Read disk #1 (STRUTH)

All of these forms are brief and say what we want to say. Each one is an example of pseudocode, as we are not governed by the restrictions that limit a real software situation.

'Print' will serve nicely for output. If there is a question about where, then you can say 'to screen', 'to line printer', or in the event you are sending the results to some sort of storage such as a disk file or a tape file, you might say 'Print to disk file'. In the case of sending the information to a file or something like a disk you may prefer 'Write'; it's perfectly acceptable. Forms might be:

Print STRUTH

or

Print STRUTH to screen

or

Print (STRUTH)

or

Write STRUTH to disk file

One other important aspect of 'Print' is that information can be sent to the screen or written on a printer which will provide instruction for an operator, or give an indication of program status. Such an output is called a 'prompt'. In this case the information will be printed between quotation marks. Examples are:

Print 'Enter lower limit'

or

Print 'No more data'

or

Print 'Integers only!'

or

Print 'Loading complete'

The process section will be considered last. In this case the operations will be included in statements of one form or another. Some of these will be statements assigning constant values to variables; some will be computations.

The operations themselves are the assignment operator ':=' and the arithmetic operators '+', '−', '*' and '/'. The function of the assignment operator and the hierarchy of the arithmetic operators have already been discussed. Parentheses '()' are also included in the process section. Examples of application of these operations in statements included in the process section are:

FRAP := 35.65

or

$$ACCK := ACCK - 1$$

or

$$SMERD := 3/A + FLEX - (27.635 * DRIP - DROP)$$

That covers the operations for input, process and output. Have we missed anything? Undoubtedly we have missed something that will turn up in some particular program. Perhaps we are building a program that will run in a device interfaced to a signal light. Then an output step might be 'Turn on orange light.' Or an input step might be to 'Set a switch.' If you need an operation for some particular reason, work it out in a simple fashion. The main concerns are simplicity and clarity.

We now have the 'control functions', which introduce formality into our work (don't worry, you already know them). The three main ones are sequence, selection (IF–THEN–ELSE) and DO-WHILE. Two more that may be useful are DOUNTIL and CASE. We only have to produce them in a written form. We will use them in a more formal fashion so that our program is easily readable and is divided into modules.

Let's look at the easiest one first. This is SEQUENCE. We almost never bother to put it in. A SEQUENCE is a series of statements. We will see this as a series of operations in a program. There is no need to mark them off further. A sequence might be:

Print 'Enter an integer larger than 10'
Read the integer into SUDS
MOP := 5 * SUDS

Normally, as we will see below, the control structure divides the operations within it from the rest of the program. However, in the case of a sequence, this is not necessary. Therefore, although we refer to a sequence of statements or operations, we do not use a sequence block to mark off a section of the pseudocode program.

Selection is a different matter. This is a control structure within which something happens. Not only are 'IF', 'THEN' and 'ELSE' written; they are written in a special form and with a system of indentations. Furthermore, the end of the selection block must be defined. This requires a statement called ENDIF. The IF part of this structure will contain a *condition*, such as 'MEATBALL is greater than MITT.' A condition may be written out in words or may include symbols for equal to (=), greater than (>), less than (<), greater than or equal to (>=), less than or equal to (<=) and unequal to (<>). These symbols are called 'relational operators' because they describe relations between variables and constants or variables and other variables. Notice that the equals sign (=) is a member of this set, but the assignment operator (:=) is not.

The IF begins at the normal line position. The THEN is beneath the IF and indented. The ELSE, if there is one, is directly below the THEN. The ENDIF is still lower down and is exactly below the IF to which it belongs. We will look at two selection blocks, one containing an ELSE and one without an ELSE. The first block is:

```
IF MEATBALL is greater than MITT
    THEN KOUNT := KOUNT + 1
    ELSE NEBISH := 5
ENDIF
```

The second block is:

```
IF A is equal to 5
    THEN Print K
ENDIF
```

These modules are diagrammed in Figures 6.1a and 6.1b, respectively.

DOWHILE is equally straightforward. However, again, we have the problem of identifying the statements that should be contained in the DOWHILE module. For this reason we have an ENDDO statement. The sample shows a simple module that prints out the numbers from DOG to A. The starting point is not defined because we are only interested in the DOWHILE. Note that the statements within the structure are indented.

```
DOWHILE A is larger than DOG
    Print DOG
    DOG := DOG + 1
ENDDO
```

This is diagrammed in Figure 6.2.

We will now consider two additional control structures. DO-UNTIL is quite straightforward. It is set up just like DOWHILE, but operates according to slightly different rules, as we have

IF MEATBALL is greater than MITT
    THEN KOUNT := KOUNT + 1
    ELSE NEBISH := 5
ENDIF

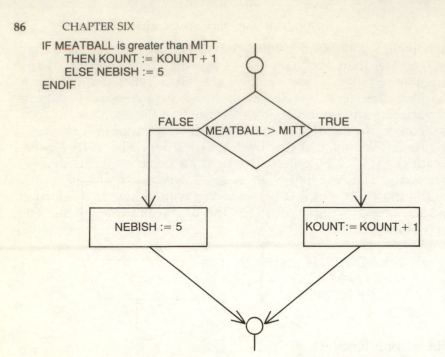

FALSE   MEATBALL > MITT   TRUE

NEBISH := 5

KOUNT:= KOUNT + 1

Fig. 6.1a   Selection, IF−THEN−ELSE, as pseudocode and flowchart

IF A is equal to 5
    PRINT K
ENDIF

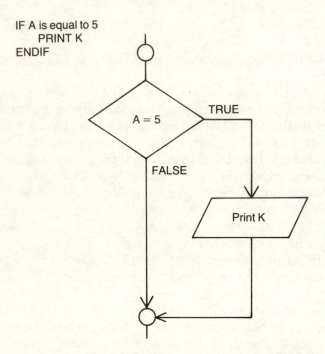

A = 5   TRUE

FALSE

Print K

Fig. 6.1b   Selection, IF−THEN, as pseudocode and flowchart

DOWHILE A is larger than DOG
    Print DOG
    DOG := DOG + 1
ENDDO

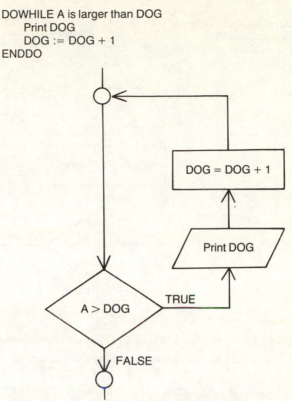

Fig. 6.2   DOWHILE as pseudocode and flowchart

seen. The same indent pattern is used. The end of the module is marked with ENDDO.

DOUNTIL DROPS is larger than 15
    Print DROPS
    DROPS := DROPS + 1
ENDDO

The flowchart is shown in Figure 6.3.

CASE is not really a major part of structuring, but it is useful in that it may be used to replace a series of IF–THEN–ELSE statements. The variable used in CASE is treated in a preceding part of the program so that it is an integer. This variable is then introduced at the opening statement of CASE. Depending on the value of the variable, a particular statement within CASE is executed. We will assume that the variable to be used is called FUMBLE. It

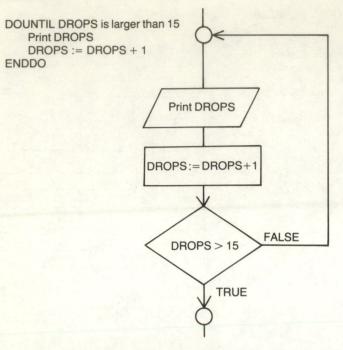

```
DOUNTIL DROPS is larger than 15
    Print DROPS
    DROPS := DROPS + 1
ENDDO
```

Fig. 6.3   DOUNTIL as pseudocode and flowchart

has been set up in an earlier part of the program so that it has integer values between 1 and 4. In this example CASE will be used to convert from a number to a written version of the number. Because of its special structure, the layout of CASE must be written carefully to prevent confusion.

```
CASE OPEN (FUMBLE)
    CASE 1
        Print 'first'
    CASE 2
        Print 'second'
    CASE 3
        Print 'third'
    CASE 4
        Print 'fourth'
ENDCASE
```

Obviously, CASE provides a method to translate from one set of symbols to another. The flowchart is shown in Figure 6.4.

We now know the control structures and the types of opera-

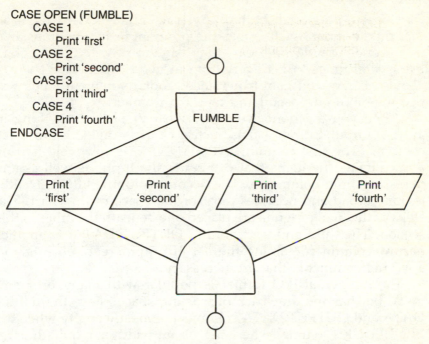

```
CASE OPEN (FUMBLE)
    CASE 1
        Print 'first'
    CASE 2
        Print 'second'
    CASE 3
        Print 'third'
    CASE 4
        Print 'fourth'
ENDCASE
```

Fig. 6.4   **CASE as pseudocode and flowchart**

tions they control. It is time to consider how we will set up the formalities of program development. The first thing to do is to write a brief description of what the program will do. We may mark this as DESCRIPTION. The next step is to list all the input data required. This can be labeled INPUT DATA. Next we will list all the output data required. This will be labeled OUTPUT DATA. The next step is to make a list of the main sections of the program. This list is placed under the heading PROCEDURE.

You can get a guide to the order of operations in the procedure by remembering that the first part will be the way things are entered into the machine. This will be the 'input' section. The second will be the part where the actual calculations are done. This is the 'processing' section. The final part is where things are read out to the environment. This is the 'output' section. There is no need to actually write the words *input*, *process* and *output*. However, thinking this way makes writing the program easier. In this case we have not capitalized the words input, process or output because we are referring to sections within the procedure that should be considered, but will not be formally designated in the written structure of the program.

This first program list can be in normal English. Once it is seen that the informal list describes the program it may be translated into proper pseudocode. One may have to rewrite the program list several times to get everything in good order. Don't worry about this. As you gain experience, your refinement steps will become more purposeful and fewer in number.

When you are done, you may wish to place everything in an IPO (input/output chart). Such a chart is divided into three columns. The first column, INPUT DATA, is relatively narrow and contains the items that constitute the input as well as any necessary brief comments. The second column, PROCEDURE, is quite broad and occupies most of the space of the chart. The steps of the final program are placed one beneath the other in this section. The third and last column, OUTPUT DATA, is another narrow column containing the list of output requirements and any brief comments that are necessary.

The horizontal IPO format is popular with many programmers, but has the drawback of wasting space, since the INPUT DATA and OUTPUT DATA columns are mostly empty while the PROCEDURE column, where maximum width is required, is restricted. We will use a slightly different vertical format. Both forms of IPO diagram are shown in Figure 6.5.

Within the program itself, line numbering may present a problem. Since we will almost totally avoid the use of GOTO, line numbering as a way to address a statement is not necessary. It is

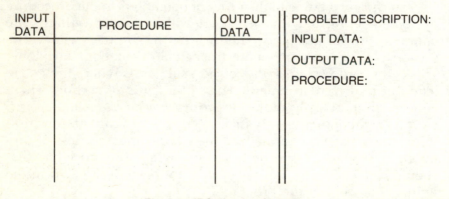

Fig. 6.5   IPO diagram formats

quite possible to write a program totally without line numbers, but this may make it hard for people to discuss a particular location. The most straightforward way is to supply a line number to each individual statement occurring outside a control structure and for the initial line within each control structure. The statements within a control structure are not numbered because, at least in the initial programs, there will be only a few statements.

In programs with more complicated structures, the line numbering may have to be more complex. In this case, the initial rules we have described are extended. Individual statements outside a control structure acquire a line number. The top line of a control structure is given a line number. Individual structures within a numbered control statement are given a number by stating the number of the top line of the structure, adding a period and appending a number corresponding to the position of the individual statement within the control structure in question. Numerous examples will be shown in the text. In using a numbering system, the important criteria are that it be simple and clarify the program structure.

In looking at examples, let us begin with the 'number on card' problem diagrammed in Figure 5.7.

DESCRIPTION: Read a number from a single card. If it is greater than 100, write 'TOO BIG'; otherwise write 'TOO SMALL'. Sign off by writing 'ALL DONE'.

INPUT DATA: A single number on a single card.

OUTPUT DATA: Either 'TOO BIG' or 'TOO SMALL' and, in any case, 'ALL DONE'.

PROCEDURE:

    1.   Read card value, assign to NUMBER
    2.   IF NUMBER greater than 100
          THEN
               Print 'TOO BIG'
          ELSE
               Print 'TOO SMALL'
          ENDIF
    3.   Print 'ALL DONE'
    4.   END

Since we have already done the preliminary programs for PROCEDURE, we have just gone to the final form and included it in the vertical style of problem layout. If you have a wide sheet of paper, you can write up the second form in which INPUT DATA, PROCEDURE and OUTPUT DATA are spaced across the top of the table. In the above example, a statement number has not been assigned to ENDIF. If you feel more comfortable giving ENDIF a number, by all means do so.

We have also included an END statement to mark the close of the program. Many of the regular programming languages have an END statement as the last statement in the program. In some cases it is compulsory, in others it is not. Good pseudocode includes an END, even though one rarely sees the beginning of the pseudocode marked with a START (as would be the case in a flowchart).

Finally, we will write a pseudocode program for the final programming example of Chapter 5, which prints a series of numbers between defined limits. The third variation as diagrammed in Figure 5.8c will be used because it will be the most meaningful in future work, despite the fact that it involves a redundant sequence resulting from our present lack of certain devices in our toolkit.

DESCRIPTION: The program accepts two integers, which serve as lower and upper limits. It then tests them to see that they are properly related and requests correction if necessary. Finally, all integers including the lower limit and up to the upper limit are written out.

INPUT DATA: Two integers; one as lower limit, one as upper limit.

OUTPUT DATA: Two prompts to identify lower and upper limits. The series of all integers lying between lower and upper limits and including lower limt.

PROCEDURE:

    1.   Print to screen, 'Enter lower limit'
    2.   Read number from screen, place in LOWER LIMIT.
    3.   Print to screen, 'Enter upper limit'
    4.   Read number from screen, place in UPPER LIMIT.
    5.   DOWHILE UPPER LIMIT <= LOWER LIMIT
    5.1.   Print to screen, 'Lower limit must be less than upper limit'
    5.2.   Print to screen, 'Enter lower limit'
    5.3.   Read number from screen, place in LOWER LIMIT.
    5.4.   Print to screen, 'Enter upper limit'
    5.5.   Read number from screen, place in UPPER LIMIT.

5.6.   ENDDO
6.   DOWHILE LOWER LIMIT < UPPER LIMIT
6.1.   Print LOWER LIMIT
6.2.   LOWER LIMIT := LOWER LIMIT + 1
6.3.   ENDDO
7.   END

In this program we have numbered the statements within the first DOWHILE (5) because they are relatively numerous. The steps within the second DOWHILE (6) have also been numbered, even though this module is short. This was just done for consistency and could have been omitted. The input sequence (steps 1 through 4) has been repeated within the test module (step 5.1 through 5.6) because this results in a program with the best overall top-down and modular structure. Without this construction we would have had to use a GOTO to get us back to the beginning of the input sequence. This overlong alternative has been used since later in the text we will introduce the use of subroutines and will then be able to define and call standard routines, which will make such compositions optimal.

Note, once again, that when a read or assignment statement is part of the control condition of a DOWHILE loop, its initial value must be defined before the DOWHILE loop is entered. Without this proviso, the initial application of the DOWHILE test will have nothing to work on. Needless to say, the variable or variables critical to the test must be altered during execution of the loop, otherwise there will be no way to exit the loop.

Let's examine the variation of this problem as shown in Figure 5.7. This variation extends and generalizes the selection process. In this case, we might make the input several numbers on a series of cards and use the selection process in Figure 5.7 to determine which of them is greater than 100. The input cards include one card for each number to be tested. An additional card is marked in some way so that we know that this card itself is not data and that it represents the last card in the series.

Two concerns should be noted as we consider such a construction at this point in our development. First, to properly set up the program using the control structures, one control module must be nested inside another control structure. Although there is nothing really wrong with this, I prefer to delay formal consideration of this type of structure until we gain more experience. Still, initial exposure to this structure at this time follows my dictum of using previews and is thus not really forbidden, even now.

Second, the other way of handling the problem requires the use of GOTO, when with the development of our ability to handle the Bohm-Jacopini structures properly, such an application of GOTO will be undesirable.

Now that the complaints have been filed, the only sensible thing to do is to set up the program both ways: once with nested control structures and once with GOTO. The same description, input data and output data sections will serve for both versions.

DESCRIPTION: This program reads a number from one card of a deck of cards. If the number is data, it is tested to see whether it is greater than 100, an appropriate message is printed out and the next card is read. If the number is not data, the closing statement is printed and program activity ceases.

INPUT DATA: A deck of cards with a single positive number on each card. The end card of the deck contains '−1', which is not data.

OUTPUT DATA: A message that names the number and says it is too large, or a message that names the number and says it is too small. When there is no more data, a message, 'OUT OF DATA'.

PROCEDURE:

1. Read the number and assign it to a variable.
2. Test the variable to see that it is data. If it is, process it. If it is not, write the closing message and quit.
3. If the number is data, test it to see whether it is less than 100 and print the appropriate message.
4. When there is no more data, print the closing statement, 'NO MORE DATA'.

It is not absolutely clear how to get this crude presentation in English into reasonably good pseudocode, but we know what the pseudocode commands will do and we can try it out. We know from the simple version of this in Chapter 5 that the actual size test is probably best formulated as selection (IF–THEN–ELSE). We know from other programs that a test of data presented to the machine may run as a selection or as DOWHILE. We will try to write the next refinement using only a selection. In one case, we will use as many GOTOs as we need. In another version we will limit the GOTOs as much as possible. Let us consider a first refinement in which we use all the GOTOs we need.

PROCEDURE:

1.   Read a card and place the value in NUMBER
2.   IF NUMBER < 0
2.1.   THEN
2.2.   GOTO Step 5
2.3.   ENDIF
3.   IF NUMBER < 100
3.1.   THEN
3.2.   Print NUMBER, 'TOO SMALL'
3.3.   ELSE
3.4.   Print NUMBER, 'TOO LARGE'
3.5.   ENDIF
4.   GOTO Step 1
5.   PRINT 'OUT OF DATA'
6.   END

The flowchart of this extravaganza is in Figure 6.6a.

It is not too difficult to eliminate one GOTO, but one remains until we use a more sophisticated structure. In the second variation we write the program with the elimination of the GOTO in the selection block beginning at step 2. However, in eliminating this GOTO we are forced to locate the END statement (2.4) in an awkward location. This modification emphasizes the need for structure nesting if we wish to reduce GOTO usage without producing some rather grotesque alternatives.

PROCEDURE:

1.   Read a card and place the value in NUMBER
2.   IF NUMBER < 0
2.1.   THEN
2.2.   Print 'OUT OF DATA'
2.3.   END
2.4.   ENDIF
3.   IF NUMBER < 100
3.1.   THEN
3.2.   Print NUMBER, 'IS TOO SMALL'
3.3.   ELSE
3.4.   Print NUMBER, 'IS TOO LARGE'
3.5.   ENDIF
4.   GOTO Step 1

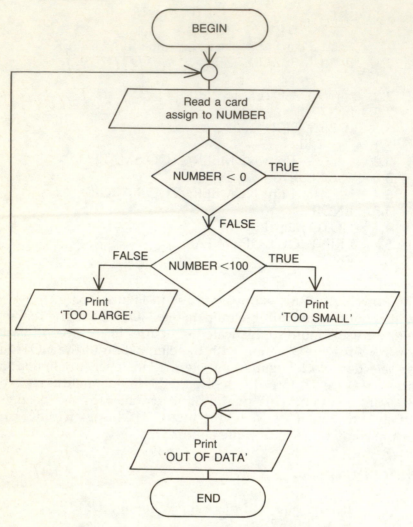

Fig. 6.6a   Card-reading algorithm with unlimited GOTOs

This is diagrammed in Figure 6.6b.

Finally, let's put together a program that makes proper use of the Bohm-Jacopini control structures, even though one may have to be nested inside another. We have not tried to eliminate the GOTO statements, but they are gone. Notice in the last procedure that the 'Read card' statement (Step 1) must be done once before entering the DOWHILE loop, so that the DOWHILE condition will have something to test. Notice also that it is present again (Step 2.2) just before the DOWHILE is exited. This is to

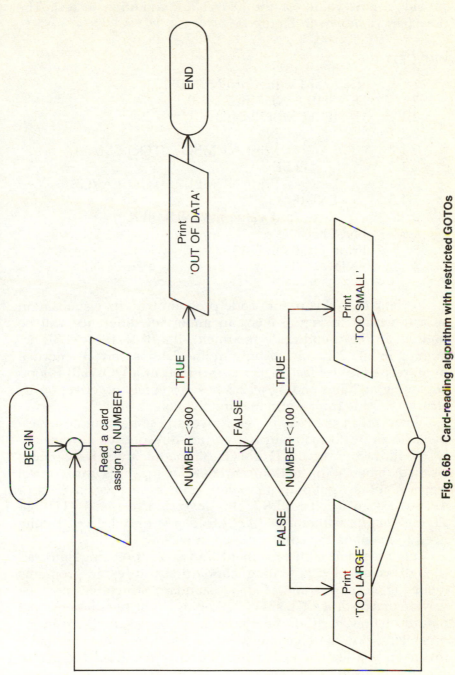

Fig. 6.6b   Card-reading algorithm with restricted GOTOs

provide a new value for the DOWHILE condition to test. The flowchart is shown in Figure 6.6c.

PROCEDURE:

1.	Read card value into NUMBER
2.	DOWHILE NUMBER >= 0
2.1.	IF NUMBER < 100
2.1.1.	THEN
2.1.2.	Print NUMBER, 'TOO SMALL'
2.1.3.	ELSE
2.1.4.	Print NUMBER, 'TOO LARGE'
2.1.5.	ENDIF
2.2.	Read card value into NUMBER
2.3.	ENDDO
3.	Print 'OUT OF DATA'
4.	END

In comparing this pseudocode program with its visualization as a flowchart in Figure 6.6c, an important difference will be noticed. In the pseudocode treatment, the IF–THEN–ELSE beginning in line 2.1 and finishing in line 2.1.5 is perfectly normal in all respects. The fact that it is included in a DOWHILE loop beginning at 2 and ending at 2.3 has absolutely no effect on its structure, aside from additional indentation.

However, in the case of the flowchart, something odd happens. In order to maintain the correct direction of flow in the DOWHILE loop, the IF–THEN–ELSE module must have its decision diamond at the 'bottom' and develop upwards until control leaves it at the input/output parallelogram, where we have 'Read a card, assign to NUMBER.' This inversion of the IF–THEN–ELSE structure within a DOWHILE loop is forced on us by the need to maintain the correct direction of flow.

This inversion is inconvenient and a bit confusing since although we are always writing standard structures, in programs involving nesting, some of these standard structures must be written upside down. This is forced on us by the two-dimensional nature of flowcharts. In combination with the difficulty in reorganizing flowchart geometry when changes must be made, inversion is a limitation that has seriously restricted the use of flowcharts in program design. This difficulty will be further examined at the end of Chapter 8.

In this chapter we have introduced the properties of pseudo-

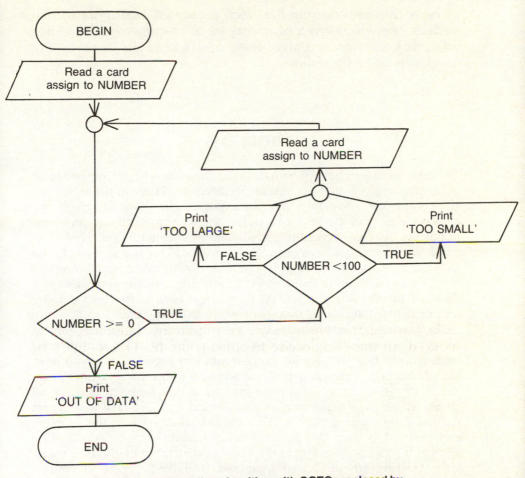

Fig. 6.6c Card-reading algorithm with GOTOs replaced by Bohm-Jacopini control structures

code in a more formal fashion. In particular, the way in which the control structures must be written and indented has been handled in some detail. Two possible layouts of the problem description, input data, output data and procedure have been presented. Simple problems already treated by flowcharting have been treated by pseudocode. The problems have been extended in a manner requiring the use of GOTO or the 'nesting' of control structures. Although the nesting of control structures has not been formally presented, the use of this technique provides a preview of its detailed discussion and demonstrates the importance of control structures in reducing the number of GOTOs and the corresponding danger of 'spaghetti programming'.

Now that pseudocode has been presented in a more formal manner, we will use the next chapter to examine the difference between programs and algorithms and will begin to study the development of algorithms.

PROBLEMS

The experience you have acquired, in combination with the refined tools for logical analysis that constitute pseudocode, increase the efficiency and confidence with which you can approach algorithm design. If you have done most of the problems so far, there are probably no problems in this set that really constitute challenge problems for you. However, problems 6.1 and 6.2 have been so designated. This is due more to the fact that they are related to earlier problems with that designation than that they are difficult in themselves. At any rate, I would skip them and do other problems in the set. When you get back to them after doing four or five of the others, they will seem relatively easy.

In attacking problems that have been treated in an earlier problem set, or which are closely related to earlier problems, it is useful to start from scratch. By this I do not suggest that you forget all that you have already learned. Your programs that were used to solve an earlier problem have given you great insight into what that problem is really all about. What I do mean is that you should not just take a program written earlier and update it. You should go directly to the problem and examine it from the perspective of structured pseudocode. This gives you an understanding of the value of structured methods in translating the problem into a well-organized, readable program. Of course, the first simple English program you wrote for the problem may serve as the first programming attempt, which can eventually be refined into the final pseudocode masterpiece. Complete pseudocode programs corresponding to the even-numbered exercises of this section will be found at the end of the book.

*   *   *

*6.1   Consider the machine that sneaks up on walls. This was described as a flowchart in Problem 5.8. Using a DOWHILE structure, pseudocode and a complete problem layout that includes description, input data, output data and procedure, produce a wall-machine program that accepts the starting distance between the wall and the machine, and which puts out the number of jumps required to go from the first distance to a distance that is less than or equal to the final specified distance.

*6.2   Construct a second wall-machine program, also using DOWHILE. This program accepts the starting distance from the wall and the number of jumps to take. It puts out the final distance between the machine and the wall.

6.3   Write a pseudocode fragment that tests to see whether the variable GNU has the value 10. If it has the value 10, the variable DOOR takes on the value 2; if the value of GNU is not 10, the value of DOOR becomes 200.

6.4   Consider a deck of cards, each containing a nonzero number. The number zero is used to indicate the end of data. Prepare a short pseudocode program that reads the value of each card and, if it is a data card, prints it out. If it is the end-of-data card, the program should print out the message 'Time to Retire' and stop.

6.5   Write a program that tests a variable called MUD. If MUD has a value 8, the program should print the word 'ate'. If MUD does not have the value 8, the word 'hungry' should be printed out. It should then print the word 'Finished' in either case and stop. You do not have to include a method of assigning a value to MUD. Just consider it as already assigned at an earlier time. The program activity must be exactly as described. The words 'ate' and 'hungry' should never be printed at the same time. Obviously, you will use the IF–THEN–ELSE version of SELECT.

Write a second program just like the first one, but use only the IF–THEN version of SELECT. *Hint:* You can't do it with one IF–THEN, but . . .

Do not use any control structure other than IF–THEN in this second program!

6.6   In Problem 4.9 you wrote a program in simple English to describe a change-making process for three coins called Drips, Globs and Hunks. In Problem 5.7 you wrote a flowchart of the problem using the standard devices of structured flowcharting. Now write another program to describe the process. This time, write the program in pseudocode using DOWHILE.

6.7   Look again at Problem 4.8. This was the change-making process that operated only on two coins, Drips and Globs. Rewrite the program in pseudocode with the following changes. In this new version, the machine checks at the end of the change-calculating run to see if the value of Globs required is greater than 10. After printing out the number of Globs and Drips as previously, it also prints out an appropriate message from the treasury department. If the number of Globs required is larger than 10, a message is printed out informing the user that he or she will need a witch doctor's approval to complete the transaction. If the change involves 10 or fewer Globs, a message approving the transaction is printed out automatically.

6.8   Write a pseudocode program that accepts values for each of two variables. It then interchanges the values contained in the variables. When this has been completed, it writes the message, 'Swap Completed'. When you have written the program, write a trace diagram that starts with the reading and assignment of two values, 20 and 45, one to each variable. The trace then follows the program through to its end, showing the values of all variables at each step in order to establish that at the end of the program, the initial contents of the variables have been interchanged.

6.9   Write a pseudocode structure that deals with two variables. One is called HOLDER; the other is called BIGGEST. This structure should compare HOLDER and BIGGEST. If HOLDER is larger than BIGGEST, it should assign the value contained in HOLDER to BIGGEST. At the end of the cycle it should print out the value of BIGGEST with a comment stating that this is the larger number.

6.10   Write a pseudocode structure that tests a variable called FLASHER. If the value of FLASHER is 8, the word 'RED' is printed and the value of FLASHER is changed to 10. If the value of FLASHER is not 8, the word 'GREEN' is printed and the value of FLASHER is changed to 8. When you have written this structure and tested it to be sure that it works, insert it inside an appropriate loop structure that will cause the test and printout to be repeated ten times in such a way that the first word printed is 'GREEN'. The program should print either the word 'GREEN' or the word 'RED', it should print the words out alternately and it should print a total of 10 words.

CHAPTER SEVEN

Development of Algorithms

T HE RENOWNED biochemist Professor Ephriam Racker once said that if you wanted to make an important point you should present it carefully and precisely once – and then present it again and again and again. Well, we have presented the concept of algorithm once and I see no reason, in light of Professor Racker's words, why we should not present the idea again.

An algorithm is a rule of calculation. It may be repetitive, but it need not be. An algorithm and a program are not really the same thing. The method of calculation is embedded in the program. To turn an algorithm into a program we usually have to add input steps, output steps, and perhaps some type of testing or verification steps. We may have to bundle several algorithms together in one program. Sometimes when the input procedure represents a complicated series of inputs and tests, it is considered an algorithm, but, in general, the algorithm is found in the processing part of a program.

In setting up a program, we use a 'top-down' procedure in which the program is broken down into simpler steps, which are broken down in turn until we have a level of complexity we can deal with easily. Further, we try to set up the individual tasks of the program in 'modular' form, where each task is reasonably complete and more or less independent of other tasks.

The actual development of the algorithm is often done in a similar way. However, the top-down type of analysis is a bit trickier, because in writing a program we usually know the logic connecting the various parts. In developing an algorithm, it is just this logic which we must discover.

As one attempts to advance in mathematical sophistication, one is continually taught and reminded that the fundamental gadget in the mathematician's toolkit is the ability to ask the right question, or to rephrase a given problem in just the right way. While most of us will not become outstanding mathematicians, there is no law preventing us from using the tools that the great mathematicians use. These are magic in that we can borrow them without paying rent, and the more we use them the sharper they become. 'Asking the right questions' is one of those generalities like 'moving in the right cirlces' or 'playing your cards right'. The idea is fine, but its application is elusive. In this text we will consider several well-known problems of modest complexity and work our way toward a proper algorithm to solve them. Our treatment will be a bit informal, since the idea is to let you see how someone else's brain works toward a solution. We will also review the idea of substituting symbols for numbers and the manipulation of these symbols.

The first algorithm we will work with was developed by Sir Isaac Newton as a way to calculate square roots. This type of algorithm is a good example of computer technique, because it demonstrates how one guesses at a solution to a problem and then uses each guess to define a better guess until one has as close an approximation to the true solution as one desires. It is also simple enough to be understood by beginning students. In later chapters we will examine other types of algorithms and see if we can get a feel for a pattern of thinking that will lead toward creative problem solving.

In developing an algorithm we must gain a thorough understanding of the materials with which we operate. When we achieve this understanding the crude outlines of the algorithm will often appear to just drop into our lap, and we need only do a series of refinements to achieve an exact algorithm and proper pseudocode. Developing this kind of understanding is not easy, but a lot of effort and practice can produce results.

Consider some positive target number N whose square root R is known. If we divide our target number N by its square root R, the quotient Q is:

$$Q = N/R$$

and further:

$$R = Q$$

because that is the meaning of 'square root'.

When studying the relation between N and its square root, let us guess a number G that might be close to the square root of N. For the sake of argument, suppose that this guess, G, is a bit larger than the real root R. We do almost the same division problem as before. We divide the target number N by the guess G to get a test quotient T:

$$T = N/G$$

Since our guessed number G is a bit larger than the true square root R, the N/G that is the test quotient T must be a bit *smaller* than the quotient N/R, which we called Q.

The person who is not used to symbols should run through this a couple of times on paper and even explain it to him/herself out loud to get the feel of the ideas. Don't be shy. You will only be using some of the tricks for understanding complex ideas that the professional mathematician uses.

Another idea the professional mathematician uses is to insert some numbers and check that his/her symbolic or generalized ideas are correct. We will take a perfect square for a test of the ideas because it is easier. So for our number N we will take 64. We know that the square root of 64 is eight. So we can say that $R = 8$. We must now evaluate the quotient Q of the root R and the number N. Of course, we find that N/R is the same as 64/8, which is 8. So we have said in numbers that $Q = N/R$ and $Q = 64/8$, and we find that Q also has the value of 8, just as we said in our previous symbolic analysis.

Continuing with a numerical example, we now pretend that we really do not know that the square root of 64 is 8, but must use our method to calculate it. We want a number we can use as a guess. That's right, we are just going to make a guess at the value of the square root of 64. Suppose we guess 9.4. Thus:

$$G = 9.4$$

Then we have G a bit larger than R, which is eight times the square root of N (64). This is exactly the situation we had in our symbolic analysis.

We must now calculate the test quotient T by dividing the target number N by the guess G. This gives N/G, which is the same as 64/9.4, which is the same as 6.8085, which is slightly less than the real square root, 8, and slightly less than the guess, which is 9.4. If you understand this idea, go on to the next paragraph; if not, try out the same ideas with different values for the guess G, which may be either larger or smaller than the true root R.

Let us move toward the algorithm in a way that seems simple, but is really rather sophisticated mathematics. If we make a random guess G at the square root and wish to guess again, can we in some way make a better guess by using the value of the first guess? This is an extremely important idea. If we could make a guess and use some property of it to make a better guess, we could get as close as we wished to that true root R, whatever it is. We are like some gigantic snake which, having gotten hold of an elephant's trunk, grabs more and more until it swallows the elephant whole.

We must *refine* the guess. To see how this works, let us draw a simple graph of the problem.

```
        6           7           8           9           10
        :...........:...........:...........:...........:
                    ^           ^           ^
             6.8085           (8)         9.4
               (T)                         (G)
```

The numbers above the line are the scale of our graph. The numbers below the line are the numbers we are working with. Although 8 is the true root, we are pretending we don't know it. Just the same, note that the guess G and its corresponding test quotient T bracket the real root. We see that if our first guess is too high for the square root of the test number, then the quotient of the target number and the first guess will be too low. Do not get the idea that the true root will be exactly midway between any pair of values G and T. It is near the middle of the space between them, but not exactly so.

Now to continue the guessing game. It is clear that the average of this particular guess G and its associated test quotient T will be closer to the real root than either G or T. If we were to use this average to define a new guess, we could use this new guess to define a new test quotient, and then the average of this new guess and this new test quotient could be used to define a still better guess, and so on, until we are as close to the true square root as we wish.

Let's go back to our original guess G (9.4) and the corresponding test quotient T (6.8085). Our better guess will be somewhere between this G and the corresponding test quotient T.

An easy way to get a number that lies between these numbers is to take their average. This will be our better guess. We could call this better guess G_1. Since we are now working toward an algorithm to be run on computers and written in pseudocode, we will convert from equal sign notation to assignment operator notation. Then:

$$G_1 := (G + T)/2$$

Evaluating the right-hand side:

$$:= (9.4 + 6.8085)/2$$
$$:= (16.2085)/2$$
$$:= 8.104$$

For the sake of clarity, we have used a new variable called G_1, but, of course, since this problem has a structure similar to that of the counting problems of earlier chapters, we can use this procedure to redefine the guess G. In this case, our statement would read

$$G := (G + T)/2$$

This involves remembering that we are working with the assignment operator as shown, and not with the equals sign.

To get the new test quotient T we could divide the target number N by the better guess, which again we will call G. So the test quotient T, which is really the new value of T, is

$$T := N/G$$
$$T := 64/8.104$$
$$:= 7.897$$

Note that our new and better guess G and its associated test quotient T have the values 8.104 and 7.897 respectively, and that this pair of values once again brackets the true value of the square root ($R = 8$), which we are pretending that we do not know.

Immediately we can see that the second guess ($G := 8.104$) is much better than the first ($G := 9.4$). We can see this intuitively, but we can also get a quantitative idea of why this is true. Remember, that if the number R is the true square root of the number N, then the quotient $Q := N/R$ will be equal to the perfect root R. This is because $N := R * R$, which is another way of defining the square root of a number. Looking at the distance between the perfect root and the quotient Q, we see that if the difference is called D, then

$$D := R - Q$$

and

$$D := 0$$

Let us now follow the difference between our initial guess and its associated test quotient, and our better guess and its associated test quotient. Here we will work with the 'equals' relationship rather than the 'assignment' relationship. In the first case, the difference between G and T is

$$9.4 - 6.8085 = 2.591$$

In the second case, the difference between G and T is

$$8.104 - 7.897 = 0.207$$

Certainly it looks like our improved guess was closer, and we could keep improving things in the same manner until our much-improved guess and its corresponding test quotient had a difference that was as small as we wanted.

We are now in a position to produce an algorithm in words, then refine it to pseudocode and reduce this to whatever language we please. Our course, we should remember that we have an algorithm here, and that to make a complete program we must at some point embed it in a set of input-output statements so it may communicate with the outside world. But we can leave that for now and concentrate on the problem of presenting the algorithm in words.

Given the number for which we need a square root:

1. Make a guess at the root.
2. Take this guess and make a test quotient.
3. Take the average of the guess and the associated test quotient.
4. Use the answer to define a new guess.
5. Using this new guess, return to Step 1 and go through the steps in series again.

But this goes on forever! How do we stop? We must define some standard of accuracy that will tell us to stop when it is met.

We know that in the case of a perfect square root, the difference between the perfect square root R and its associated quotient Q is zero. So we set a tolerance that must be met by the difference between the current guess G and its associated test quotient T. For simplicity we will represent this difference by D. When the difference between the current improved guess and its associated test quotient is smaller than this value D, we quit and print out the value of the current guess. We should add a further refinement, since we do not know whether the improved guess G or its associated test quotient T will have the larger value, we use the absolute value of the difference between these two numbers. That is, if you do the subtraction and get a negative number, you just ignore the minus sign and treat the number as if it were positive.

There is one more small problem: what will be the first guess for the square root? The number used for the first guess should be simple, obvious and easy for the computer to do automatically. We want as little need for operator intervention as possible. Reexamination of the description shows that we really can use any number as the initial guess. Then why not use 1? It sounds outrageous, but why not? It will work and will be easy to program. The corresponding test quotient is the target number N divided by 1, which equals the target number itself.

Having developed the algorithm, we would normally test it on several sets of data having known results. In this case, running through the whole procedure again and examining the results will improve our understanding of the process.

We will use the algorithm to extract the square root of 225. We will set the tolerance at 0.001. (Naturally, we know that the square root of 225 is 15, but we won't tell the program.) To follow the progress of the program, the values of successive pairs of the guess, the test quotient and the absolute value of the difference between them will be listed.

Guess	Test quotient	Difference
1	225	224
113	1.99115	111.00884
57.49557	3.91334	53.58223
30.70445	7.32792	23.37653
19.01619	11.83202	7.18417
15.4241	14.58755	0.83655
15.0058	14.99417	0.01166
15.00001	14.999989	0.000002

We have achieved the result in 7 loops after making our initial guess. You should follow this result on a desk calculator. Note that in all the differences, we were interested in the magnitude of the difference, not its sign; thus we actually use absolute value.

We are ready to write a program using the algorithm by going through the general procedure to write a pseudocode program. First, we will write a one- or two-sentence summary of what the program is intended to do. Then we will list the input and the output we desire. We should then be in a position to write out a program in rather restricted English. The next step will be to write the program in pseudocode and present it along with the necessary input and output in an IPO diagram. So let's do it.

DESCRIPTION: The program should accept a target number and a tolerance. It should calculate an approximation of the square root of the target number that is within the tolerance of the true square root. The printout should be the target number, the calculated root and the tolerance.

INPUT DATA: The target number, the tolerance

OUTPUT DATA: The target number, the tolerance, the calculated square root

PROCEDURE:

1. Print 'Enter the target number'
2. Read the number and place in NUMBER
3. Print 'Enter the tolerance'
4. Read the tolerance and place in DELTA
5. GUESS := 1
6. TEST := NUMBER
7. DOWHILE ABS(TEST − GUESS) >= DELTA
        GUESS := (GUESS + TEST)/2
        TEST := NUMBER/GUESS
    ENDDO
8. Print GUESS, 'is the square root of', NUMBER, 'within a tolerance of', DELTA
9. END

The flowchart of this program is shown in Figure 7.1. Notice that the program naturally divides itself into modules for input, constant initialization, calculation and output.

In this chapter the details in developing an algorithm have been presented. In doing this we have examined the technique by which variables may be used instead of numbers in stating the

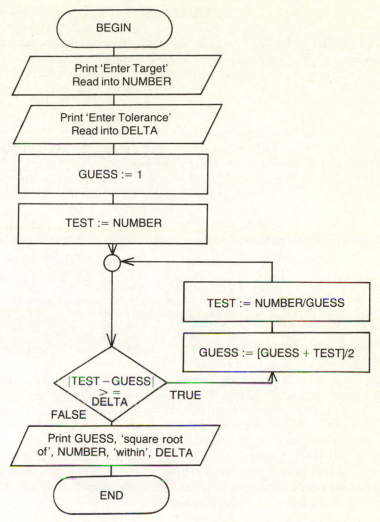

Fig. 7.1   Final algorithm generated from pseudocode program

ideas used to develop an algorithm. We have also shown how calculation with selected numbers may be used to help in algorithm development and checking. The difference between algorithms and programs has been explored.

The present chapter, as well as the preceding chapter, has shown the efficiency of nesting one control structure inside of another. In the next chapter the nesting of control structures will be examined more formally.

PROBLEMS

When I studied problem solving I often felt frustrated, because my mathematics and physical sciences texts lacked a sufficient number of problems that were challenging and related to previous problems, but not impossible. Chapter 7 is an extension and consolidation of our algorithm development technology. The problems are similarly designed. Problems 7.4 and 7.7 have been designated as challenge problems more because the final programs are a bit long than because they are really complicated. No new ideas have been presented. The even-numbered problems are answered at the end of the book.

*   *   *

7.1   The wall machine has been modified to chase a particular type of jumping beetle. We will call this type of wall machine a 'frog'. This beetle only jumps when it sees the frog jump. When the frog jumps, it jumps 75% of the distance between the unmoving beetle and itself, as defined just before its own jump. Of course, when the frog has started its jump, the jumping beetle notices this and jumps. The distance the beetle jumps is 25% of the distance between the frog and the beetle as defined just before the frog started its jump. They both jump along the same straight line with the frog chasing the beetle.

Construct a pseudocode program that asks for and accepts the initial distance between the frog and the beetle and asks for and accepts the desired final distance separating the frog and the beetle. It should output the number of jumps required to achieve this result and then print the message, 'Next beetle, please.'

When you have constructed the program, assume that the frog is 50 feet from the beetle and you wish it to move to within 1 foot of the beetle. Construct a table listing the values of all variables at the completion of each jumping cycle.

7.2   Compound-interest calculation is a common activity of computers in business. We will imagine a bank in which the interest is calculated and compounded once a year. That is, once a year the interest is calculated and then this interest is added to the old principle to get the new principle.

Devise a pseudocode program that accepts the size of the initial deposit, the rate of interest in percent and the number of years the account is to run. It should print out the value of the account for each year after the interest has been calculated and added to the principle, the amount of interest paid as a result of the most recent interest calculation, the total of all interest paid into the account so far and a number that designates the most recent year (1, 2, etc).

Using a hand calculator, show the expected printout for an account with an initial deposit of $2,000 and 6% interest that runs for a total of 5 years.

7.3   Problem 6.10 was a two-color flasher program. Using similar technology, write a flasher program that flashes the words 'BLUE', 'GREEN' and 'ORANGE'. The printout should start with 'ORANGE'. *Hint*: You may wish to use a series of IF–THEN structures rather than a combination of IF–THEN–ELSE structures.

***7.4**   In some particular country, an income tax law works as follows. On all income up to, but not greater than $1,500, a tax of 10% of the actual amount is paid. On income greater than $1,500 but not greater than $5,000, the tax is 15%. On all income greater than $5,000 but not greater than $10,000, the tax is 22%. On all income greater than $10,000 but less than $20,000, the tax is 27%. Because of the economics of the country, no one ever earns more than $20,000.

What this means is that if a person has an income of $1,200, the tax is 10% of $1,200. If the person has an income of $7,250, the tax is 10% of the first $1,500, plus 15% of the amount of income between $1,500 and $5,000 (in this case a tax base of $3,500) plus 22% of all the money that lies between $5,000 and $10,000 (in this case a tax base of $2,250).

Devise a pseudocode program that accepts a given amount of money that is less than $20,000 and calculates the tax on it. It need only deal with one income at a time. That is, you need not include a loop that causes it to check a deck of cards or ask for another income. It should print out the total income, the tax calculated and the remainder along with the identifying prompts. Use the program to write the tax calculated for an income of $2,200 and an income of $1,100.

7.5   Devise a pseudocode program that accepts a positive integer. It then counts from this integer down to zero and immediately, without further operator intervention, counts back up from zero to this integer. Each of the values produced by the counting process should be printed out in order of production. Zero and the number entered should be included in the printout.

7.6   Prepare a pseudocode program that reads two numbers in turn. The first number is assigned to a variable called BIGGEST. The second number is assigned to a variable called NORMAL. The program then tests the numbers to see if BIGGEST actually has the larger value. If it does not have the larger value, the values of the variables are interchanged. The program then prints the contents of BIGGEST and notes that this is the larger number. It then prints the contents of NORMAL and notes that this is the smaller number.

*7.7   Consider a modified form of the taxi company problem (Problem 4.7). In this problem, each taxi driver turned in three cards showing the miles driven, gasoline used and taxi identification number. From this information, the program calculated the average gas mileage for each taxi and printed this information out with the taxi number. The end card of the data deck had a negative number.

Repeat this program in pseudocode form, but include a running total of the mileage and a running total of the gasoline used. The printout should contain the miles per gallon of gasoline for each taxi along with its identification number. In addition, the total miles driven, the total gallons of gasoline used and the average gasoline consumption in miles per gallon for the taxi fleet as a whole should be calculated and printed out at the end of the list of gasoline consumption for the individual taxis.

7.8   Write a pseudocode program to describe a lock mechanism. In this device, the person wishing to open the lock is instructed to enter a number. If the entered number matches the standard code number built into the program, a message is printed indicating that the lock is open. You should write two versions of the program.

The first version should be based on a simple number comparison program with no attempt to model the mechanism of the lock. In the second version, the correct number should cause an intermediate variable that you might call LATCH, to be increased in value by one. The message indicating that opening has occurred can be based on checking whether LATCH has the value 0 or 1.

Remember to have a constant within the program that contains the correct test number and which can be changed by rewriting the program. The technology used in the second method looks rather complicated, but in some cases it might be useful.

7.9   In some situations, locking mechanisms require keys or codes entered by two persons. Prepare a pseudocode program that models a two-key lock with the following properties. The program first requests the supervisor's key number. It accepts this and then asks for the operator's key number. If both are correct, an 'unlock message' is written. This program should be written without nesting control structures. No intermediate message acknowledging or denying the correctness of the supervisor's key should be printed. Nested control structures may be avoided if a 'latching' system is used as in Problem 7.8. In this case, each correct answer should increment the latch, and the final test should determine whether the latch has been incremented twice.

7.10 Prepare a pseudocode version of the two-key lock problem using IF–THEN–ELSE and nested structuring. After the supervisor's key has been inserted, if it is not correct, a notice stating that the supervisor's key does not fit should be printed and the program should go to the final message. If the correct supervisor's key has been inserted, the correctness should be acknowledged and the operator's key should be requested. If the operator's key is incorrect, notice should be given and the program should go to the final message. If the operator's key is correct, a message should declare the system unlocked and the program should proceed to the final message. The final message should state that the key-testing procedure is complete without indicating whether the key combinations were correct.

CHAPTER EIGHT

Nested Control Structures

THE ABILITY to handle a number of control conditions at once is one of the most important attributes of computers. Actually, the computer does not handle all multiple conditions simultaneously. Programming languages permit the development of networks of relations. The way in which variables fit into each level of the network determines the way in which the succeeding level of conditions will be presented. This technique sounds a bit complicated, and frankly, it is. However, if one is programming in a structured way using modular techniques and top-down design, the development of a set of interrelated conditions to solve a particular problem can be straightforward. The whole process resembles the old game of Twenty Questions wherein the answer to a given question, whether it is positive or negative, immediately sets up the next question.

When we talked about modules in a general way, we discussed modules inserted inside other modules. If both the outside and inside modules are control structures, then to execute an activity that lies inside the innermost control structure we must satisify multiple conditions. Pseudocode provides tools to make such developments easy. One can easily imagine that the complicated connections between the various systems would come to resemble a can of worms. This gave rise to the term 'spaghetti code' before the worm can comparison had currency. The point of structured flowcharting and structured coding is that it keeps programs nice and tidy.

Let us consider an example inspired by a famous comment on life: 'If we had ham, we'd have ham and eggs – if we had eggs.' Following the process of recasting the question, we will substitute 'breakfast' for 'ham and eggs'. Further, we should probably quantify things so we can handle them more easily. Retaining the original order of statements, we have: 'If we have three slices of ham, we will have one breakfast – if we have two eggs.' This is

116

not as literary, but it is a more exact description of the real world and may be immediately turned into a programming description.

DESCRIPTION: This program tests to see if we have two or more eggs at the same time as we have three or more slices of ham. If this is the case, it indicates that we may have breakfast; if not, it indicates that we may not have breakfast.

INPUT DATA: Two numbers. The first is the number of slices of ham, the second is the number of eggs.

OUTPUT DATA: One of two messages. The first is 'No Breakfast Today'. The second is 'Breakfast Will Be Served Today'.

PROCEDURE:

1. Initiation (assign values to constants and limits)
2. Input variable values (Ham and Eggs)
3. Test variables versus limits
4. Print out appropriate result
5. End the program.

Now the procedure will be revised. Notice that in designing the selection module, we test to see if the number of ham slices is equal to or greater than the limit, and on the basis of this we either print out the notice that breakfast can't happen or we go into a second selection system that compares the number of eggs with the limit. Whatever the situation was with the ham, if the number of eggs does not equal or exceed the limit, then a 'No Breakfast' notice is printed. On the other hand, if the number of eggs does equal or exceeds the limit, we know that the test could not have occurred unless the number of ham slices had reached the limit, so both variables are equal to or in excess of their respective limits. Under this condition, a message will be written indicating that the breakfast may be prepared.

PROCEDURE:

1. HAMLIM := 3
2. EGGLIM := 2
3. Read first number and assign to HAMSLICE
4. Read second number and assign to EGGS
5. IF HAMSLICE >= HAMLIM
5.1   THEN
5.2   IF EGGS >= EGGLIM
5.2.1.   THEN
5.2.2.   Print 'Breakfast Will Be Served Today'

```
5.2.3.                ELSE
5.2.4.                     Print 'No Breakfast Today'
5.2.5.           ENDIF
5.3.      ELSE
5.4.           Print 'No Breakfast Today'
5.5.  ENDIF
6.    END
```

Figure 8.1 shows a flowchart of this program. In examining this program, there are a number of points worth noting. The condition limits are handled in a special way. Instead of building them in as numerical constants in each statement where they are used, they are given variable names. The actual assignment of values to these variables is done all at once in the initiation portion of the program. Utilizing this process is a good idea for any constants in the program. If we need to change the values of the constants, they can be changed all at once at the start of the program, and we do not have to search through the program to change numerical values inside statement lines. This procedure is particularly important in longer programs, which may use a given constant many times in the course of execution.

The indenting system has been looked at before, but is now treated again. Within selection, the IF starts things off and the IF line contains the condition. The attached THEN clause has the THEN indented to the right relative to the IF it belongs to. Whatever activity is connected with this THEN (a Print, a Read, another IF or what have you), it begins on the next line below this THEN and is also indented to the right. We see this structure in lines 5, 5.1, 5.2, and 5.2.1.

The THEN clause beginning at 5.1 ushers in a new selection module, starting with IF and a new condition at 5.2. It is not until we have completed all the details of this selection (5.2) and any other modules that may lie within it, that we may return to consideration of the ELSE associated with the THEN at 5.1. The ELSE occurs at 5.3 and is exactly aligned with the THEN clause at 5.1. (This matching indentation is a bit tiresome to write at first, but it pays dividends when we have to quickly scan the structure of a program or module. It soon becomes second nature to write in this fashion.) Back at the ELSE clause in line 5.3, we see that it controls a print clause at 5.4 and that this print clause is indented. The selection module that started with an IF at 5 is finished with a matching ENDIF statement at 5.5, which exactly aligns with the indentation of the initial IF.

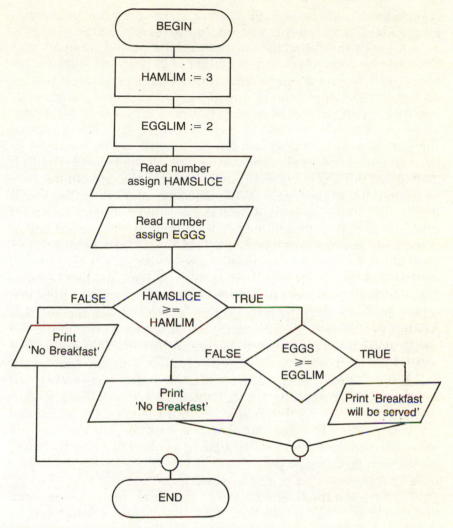

Fig. 8.1 Modules reflecting nested structures

The same type of structure occurs with the selection beginning with IF at 5.2. The associated THEN is found at 5.2.1, indented relative to the IF at 5.2. This THEN clause controls a print statement found at 5.2.2, which is indented relative to the controlling THEN. We follow on to an ELSE at 5.2.3, which exactly matches in indentation the THEN at 5.2.1. The structure of line 5.2.4 is just like the print line of 5.2.2. We need not discuss this ELSE at 5.2.3 further, except to say that this module is closed with an ENDIF at 5.2.5, which is indented to match the IF at 5.2, which is the IF marking the beginning of this selection module. This is a bit complicated, and one should perhaps go over it a few times until all the ideas drop into place.

Although the discussion of the various nested modules was detailed, we were never in any danger of getting lost, because we had a well-designed numbering system. Let's see how it works. At the start, each statement line is numbered as an integer ending with an apparently unnecessary decimal point. At statement line 5 we begin a selection control structure. The initial part of the statement line number will remain 5, with further additions to the right of the decimal point until we reach the control structure statement (in this case ENDIF), which marks the close of the control structure starting at 5. While the line number of the initial line of the control statement (5) has the same number of decimal places as the line number just preceeding it (4), the second line of the control structure, in this case a THEN, will be designated by a line number (5.1) with one more decimal space.

The line immediately following this will have the line number 5.2. This line (5.2) could be any statement, but happens to be the initial line (IF) of a second selection control structure. For this reason, the next line number after 5.2 picks up an additional decimal place and line number, becoming 5.2.1 and marking the second line of a further embedded selection structure that began at 5.2. We do not have any additional control structures embedded in the selection beginning at 5.2. Thus the interior of this selection is numbered from 5.2.1 to 5.2.5, without the need for additional decimal places. The line number 5.2.5 marks the end of this embedded control structure and labels an ENDIF, which corresponds to and is aligned with the IF at 5.2, which marks the beginning of this particular selection structure.

We have left the deepest level of structures and are now on a line that is part of the selection block that began at 5 and had its THEN at 5.1. The line we are on is the ELSE corresponding to that THEN (5.1). Since the ELSE is not buried deeper, it will have a line label with the same decimal structure as THEN (5.1). Because 5.2 has already been used as a label, this will be 5.3. The numbering will continue to 5.5, which marks the ENDIF corresponding to and aligned with the initial IF of this selection, which started with the IF at 5. The next line, which happens to be the program END, is no longer a part of the control structure running from 5 to 5.5, so we drop a decimal place and continue with the line count to give a line number of 6.

Now look at the column of line labels as a whole. There is one control structure in which all of the labels start with 5, and as long as we are in that control structure the first number of the label is 5. Within that structure we pick up a second control structure. As long as we are within this second control structure, the number after the first decimal place of the label is 2. Thus all of the lines within this structure will have the initial numbering 5.2. We can see the extent of control structures by the organization of the line labels. Notice that the number of decimal places is not changed by statements such as Print or Read or by assignment statements. We must enter a control structure before the line numbering decimal change will take place. When a statement like the print statement of line 5.2.2 runs out of space and has to be continued on the next line, the next line is obviously part of the print statement as a whole. For this reason a physical line below 5.2.2 would not get any line label. It doesn't need one because it is part of 5.2.2.

You've done it. You have waded through two rather turgid descriptions; the first describes the organization of nested control structures, and the second a line numbering system that contributes to easy recognition of the nesting organization. Take a breather; then if you have any areas of uncertainty, work through the material again until you are reasonably certain of it. You may need to note line numbers or work with pencil and paper to get it down. By all means do so. This is tricky, but mastering these concepts is important, because they are not only fundamental to the development of complex programs but are also extremely powerful tools for simplifying the creation and understanding of such programs. Don't get the idea this technology is terribly intellectual or abstract. It certainly was for the people who developed it, but we have inherited the toolkit complete and ready to run with instructions in every box.

We will write two more programs without bothering with such detailed analysis. We will then close the chapter by examining the rules in a more formal fashion.

DOWHILE loops are often used to control input from automatic card readers or similar devices. As long as the input is recognizable as data, the program housed in the DOWHILE will run. A special value related to the DOWHILE condition serves as a marker or flag to signal the end of the data. The program that ran Newton's square root method will be modified to accept sets of data.

DESCRIPTION: The program should accept a series of number pairs considered to be on cards. The first number of the pair is the target number, the second a tolerance. It should calculate an approximation of the square root of the target number that is within the tolerance of the true square root. The printout should be the target number, the calculated root and the tolerance. The end-of-data card contains a target number of zero. When the program is out of data it should write a message, 'End of Data'.

INPUT DATA: The target number, the tolerance, an end-of-data indicator

OUTPUT DATA: The target number, the tolerance, the calculated square root, an end-of-data message

PROCEDURE:

1.	Read a card, assign first value to NUMBER, second to DELTA
2.	DOWHILE NUMBER ⟨ ⟩ 0
2.1.	GUESS := 1
2.2.	TEST := NUMBER
2.3.	DOWHILE ABS(TEST − GUESS) >= DELTA
2.3.1.	GUESS := (GUESS + TEST)/2
2.3.2.	TEST := NUMBER/GUESS
2.3.3.	ENDDO
2.4.	Print GUESS, 'is the square root of', NUMBER, 'within a tolerance of', DELTA
2.5.	Read a card, assign first value to NUMBER, second to DELTA
2.6.	ENDDO
3.	Print 'End of Data'
4.	END

The structure of this program is shown in Figure 8.2a. Line label numbers and indentation follow those shown in the first program. Line spacing is normally up to the programmer. As can be seen from a comparison of the two programs, the indentation and special line numbers serve to keep modules and control structures well defined.

The above structure is similar to the simple version of the Newton square root method, but additions were necessary. The major change involves the basic square root program. An additional DOWHILE has a condition that says the contents of the control structure will repeat as long as the contents of the target number variable are not zero (0). The zero value is used as a flag

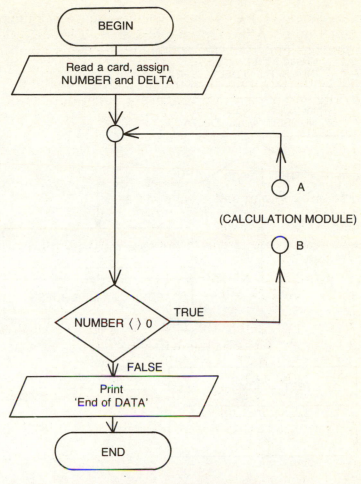

Fig. 8.2a   Data entry module

to indicate the end of input data. This is a typical DOWHILE input control structure and, therefore, needs something for the DOWHILE to work on the first time it is entered. Thus, a data reading unit is placed at line 1 while the DOWHILE starts at line 2. The last activity before leaving this DOWHILE with ENDDO at 2.6 is a read statement at 2.5 identical to the one at 1. When this DOWHILE is exited, there can be no more data, so a print statement at line 3 provides the 'End of Data' message. The inner DOWHILE, which starts at 2.3, is essentially identical to the DOWHILE of the simplified Newton's method program. The initialization steps are at 2.1 and 2.2. These steps must be inside the input control DOWHILE loop, since they must be rerun

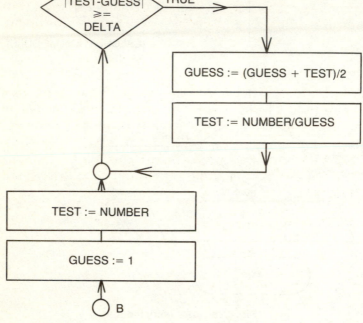

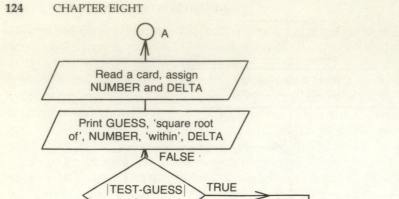

Fig. 8.2b   Calculation module

each time new values are introduced for NUMBER and DELTA. In addition, we want them to be in front of the calculation loop beginning at 2.3 since, if they were inside this loop, the calculations would never end because TEST would be reset to NUMBER and GUESS to 1 at every repeat cycle. As with all pseudocode programs, it is important to check the program using inputs with known values.

The flowchart of this program (Figure 8.2b) displays the same inversion problem discussed at the end of Chapter 6 with regard to the problem diagrammed in Figure 6.6c. It is clear that as programs become more complex and control structures more nested, the use of flowcharts in program design becomes seriously limited.

The last program in this chapter will be a system with multiple selection steps to allow a choice between four alternatives. It is presented to show that proper indenting and line numbers keep things straight in more complex situations. If one were producing this program for a job instead of a demonstration, the structure CASE might be used.

Our problem concerns designing a program to control a machine that stamps the rider classification on monthly public transport passes. If the customer's age is 5 or under, it is a free ride; if older than 5 but 14 or younger, it is half fare; if older than 14, but 65 or younger, it is full fare; and people over 65 travel for one-quarter fare.

DESCRIPTION: The program accepts customers' age in years. The ages are divided into four groups: Free (5 or younger), Half-fare (6 to 14 inclusive), Full-fare (15 to 65 inclusive), and Quarter-fare (over 65). A message is produced depending on age.

INPUT DATA: A single number (customer's age)

OUTPUT DATA: Free, half-fare, full-fare, or quarter-fare

PROCEDURE:

1.	Read a number and assign to AGE
2.	IF AGE <= 5
2.1.	THEN
2.2.	Print 'Free'
2.3.	ELSE
2.4.	IF AGE <= 14
2.4.1.	THEN
2.4.2.	Print 'Half'
2.4.3.	ELSE
2.4.4.	IF AGE <= 65
2.4.4.1.	THEN
2.4.4.2.	Print 'Full'
2.4.4.3.	ELSE
2.4.4.4.	Print 'Quarter'
2.4.4.5.	ENDIF
2.4.5.	ENDIF
2.5.	ENDIF
3.	END

Figure 8.3 shows the flowchart.

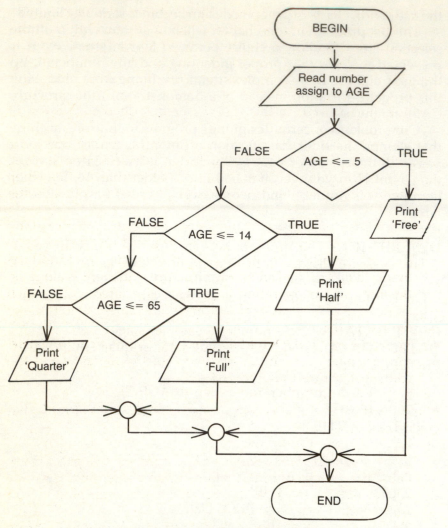

Fig. 8.3   Nested selection steps

In this case, little can be added to the comments on indenting and numbering made earlier in this chapter. A few remarks, however, are in order about the logic of the design. Note that the conditions which control the IF statements are set up to eliminate the region involving ages of 5 years or less. Then this region can be ignored and the region 14 years or less is eliminated. The region of 5 years and less is not included in the 14-year region because it has already been removed. Run a few sample numbers and you will get a better understanding of how the program works.

In closing the chapter, we will look at the rules of indenting and numbering in a more formal fashion. Remember that this code does not have to pass through a syntax or structure test in a machine. The reason we write it as it is written is to simplify writing new programs and interpreting programs that have already been written.

Indenting as used in this text can be described as follows:

1. Statement lines are located one directly below the other.
2. In the event that the preceding line is a control statement (IF, DOWHILE, THEN, ELSE, etc.) from a control structure, then the line being written is indented relative to the control statement lying one line above it.
3. The individual control statements of a control structure are written on separate lines. The first or initial line includes the decision condition. In the case of intermediate structure statements like ELSE or THEN, the structure statement is alone on the line and any operating statements associated with it, such as Read, Print, or assignment are immediately below it, indented to the right.
4. The markers (ENDDO, ENDIF, etc.) that end a control structure are aligned with the first word of the initial line of the control structure they terminate.

Numbering is not quite as complicated. Here is a set of rules that cover most cases:

1. Every statement line will have a line number, except for those lines that are direct continuations of an earlier line.
2. All line labels will end with a decimal point. Examples: 1., 10., 10.3.2., etc.
3. If a line number follows the line number marking the first line in a control structure, then this new line will have one additional number to the right of the last decimal point in the first line marker, and line counting shall continue with this new number.
4. If a line number labels the end marker of a control block (ENDIF, ENDDO), the line following it will lose the right-most decimal marker and number and resume counting with the remaining right-most number.

Both of these sets of rules may look a little confusion. The easiest way to handle them is to look at the indentation and line numbering as it occurs in the text. When you have repeatedly reviewed the comparison between the text examples and the rules, you will find that it is the description of the rules that is complicated and not the rules themselves.

Further, please note that these are suggestions, not absolute rules. The patterns of indentation and numbering used in this text provide reasonably clear assistance in top-down design and modular construction. Other patterns exist, but all the patterns are similar in many of their details.

In this chapter the technique of nesting control structures has been examined. These methods have been applied to examples in which the algorithms depended on the use of multiple decisions or conditions. An indentation procedure introduced to facilitate program documentation has been expanded to include applications to nested structures. Similarly, numbering procedures introduced in an earlier chapter were also extended to deal with nested control structures.

Although many facilities that we have mastered will be expanded in future chapters, our use of flowcharts as a routine tool in this text has virtually come to an end. In Chapter 6 we saw the beginning of 'inversion' problems associated with nested control structures. A second example of this was seen in this chapter in connection with the problem diagrammed in Figure 8.2. As programs become more complicated and convoluted, the flowchart will cause more troubles than it solves, while pseudocode will read more and more like a familiar narrative. For this reason, in the following chapters the use of flowcharts is reduced. However, any time a mechanism or algorithm proves particularly difficult, flowchart analysis is a useful tool. Even if the overall chart is a failure, the attempt to organize it will often provide the necessary insight.

PROBLEMS

By this time you are so used to handling pseudocode that the algorithms needed in this set of exercises should present few problems. Careful examination of the text examples in Chapter 8 will reveal a nesting pattern that may be easily modified to fit the needs of these problems. However, Problems 8.2, 8.8 and 8.10 are a bit tricky and have been designated as challenge problems. Answers to the odd-numbered problems will be found at the end of the book.

*   *   *

8.1   Prepare a pseudocode program that reads cards. Each card contains a positive value, except the end-of-data card, which contains a negative number. The end-of-data card is not data and should not be used in the calculation. When a card is read, the program should print a series of eleven numbers that begins at the number read and continues to a number equal to the number read plus 10. The program should then perform the same procedure on the next data card. Of course, if there is no more data it should print out the message 'End of Data'.

*8.2   Problem 7.4 was an income tax problem. Using the same tax table calculation, change the pseudocode program in the following ways: It should read a set of cards. The cards contain three nonzero numbers. The first is the taxpayer's reference number. It is like our social security number, but does not have the hyphens (it is just one large number). The second number is the income of the person with that number. The third number is either 1 or 2. If it is 1, the person is single and his/her income is completely subject to tax. If the number is 2, the person is married and $500 is deducted from his/her income before the income tax is calculated. On the end-of-data card, all numbers are zero. Thus a zero indication in any number on a card is enough to signal the end of data. You are free to use whichever variable you wish to mark the end of data.

       The printout of the program is the tax identification number for the person, his or her total income without deductions or tax removed, the word 'married' or 'single' to indicate his or her family status, and the total tax he or she must pay. When the end of data is reached, the program should print out 'End of Data'.

8.3   Design a pseudocode program that accepts two numbers and prints them out in order from smaller to larger.

8.4   Each card of a deck of cards contains a single nonzero number. The end-of-data card contains a zero. Design a pseudocode program that reads all the cards in the deck. When all the cards have been read, it indicates that it is out of data and states the value of the greatest card in the deck.

       Hint: You will need two variables in the program. One variable holds the value of the card being read, and one contains the largest card value read in the entire reading process at the end of each read-and-test cycle.

8.5   Each card of a deck of cards contains a single number that is either positive or negative. There is one card containing zero, which marks the end of the deck. Design a program that reads all the cards in the deck, and prepares running totals of both the number of positive cards and the number of negative cards. When all the cards have been read the program should state whether there are more positive or negative cards. Naturally, in the event that there is the same number of positive cards as negative cards, an appropriate message should also be printed.

8.6   In an unnamed country the power plants are sensitive to the external temperature, that is, to the temperature of the country around them. This is because of the design of their cooling systems. If the external temperature is greater than 105 degrees Fahrenheit, then if either the pressure is higher than 400 pounds per square inch or the boiler temperature is higher than 325 degrees Fahrenheit, the system is in danger and a notice should be written out. Design a pseudocode program that describes a test unit that accepts three numbers. The first is outside temperature, the second is inside pressure and the third is inside temperature. These values should be tested for safety against the standard temperatures and pressures. Appropriate messages indicating acceptable performance or danger should be printed out. The program should be designed so that the standard values can be easily changed.

8.7   You have a seconds counter that increments itself automatically once each second. When the counter reaches 59, the next time it increments it converts its internal holding value to zero. Of course it keeps on incrementing itself. Each time the seconds counter changes from 59 back to zero, a counter that counts minutes is incremented.

When the minutes counter reaches 59, the next time it is incremented the internal holding value for minutes is reset to zero. Each time the minutes counter is reset to zero, it increments an hours counter that resets when it is incremented beyond 11. Each time the seconds counter is incremented, the value of seconds, minutes and hours on the internal counters is printed. To keep the system running beyond 12 hours you will need some kind of control loop surrounding everything. This might be set to run for ten periods of 12 hours. At the end of this time, the message 'Wind me up again, please!' might be written.

Write a pseudocode program that describes the operation of this clock. Test it for such critical times as 59 seconds; 59 minutes and 59 seconds; and 11 hours, 59 minutes and 59 seconds.

*8.8   You have the usual deck of cards containing nonzero numbers with an end-of-data card containing a zero. Each time the system reads a number, it tests to see if the number is the same as either of the two previous numbers it has read in the two previous card-reading steps. If this is the case it increments a counter. Of course, there may be hundreds of cards in the deck, but each card read is tested against the two cards read previously to it. At the end of data, a message is printed indicating the number of times that two cards located within three cards of each other were the same.

You will have to design some special routines to handle the situation that arises when the system is just beginning to read and when the system comes to an end. At these times, the three holding variables containing the contents of three cards will not be entirely filled with fresh data.

Write a pseudocode program that describes such a system. Test the system by running a seven-card deck that includes several duplicates within the limits of the duplication definition.

8.9 The pseudocode program you are called upon to design in this example reads three numbers, arranges them in order from greatest to smallest and then prints them out twice. The first printout is in the order that they were entered and the second is in their order after being placed in order of descending value. This is not a particularly easy problem to do on your own. A bit of experimentation, though time-consuming, will eventually get you onto a workable design.

Hints: You will probably want two sets of three variables. The first set is to hold the numbers as entered; the second is to hold the numbers after rearrangement.

It is easy to select one number that is larger than the other two or smaller than the other two. If this works, then it is easy to select one of the three entered numbers that is different from those already selected.

Another approach is to observe that once you have selected the largest of the three, the problem of selecting the middle value reduces to determining the larger of two values – a process you already know how to accomplish.

*8.10 You now have enough information to solve the house number task (Problem 1.4) in a more or less routine fashion. As you will remember, the house number was on a card that was given to you on the bus. This can be treated as normal input. You might think of it as a number that is entered into some kind of machine that will give you instructions as you proceed with the quest. Reading numbers from the houses can also be normal read-type inputs. The two end-locations of the street can be considered to be empty lots with a real-estate agent's sign that has a telephone number 000000, which you read in and test for just like an address.

Escaping from a reading loop if you find the right house could be done with GOTO, but this is sloppy. A better way is to set the loop test variable to 000000 which, as it is the real-estate sign, will probably be the test limit. Instructions the program gives to the user include which way to turn when you get off the bus, whether to turn around if the house numbers you are reading are increasing or decreasing in the wrong direction, whether to take a doorknob, and several others, including some you may invent yourself. Remember to build a paper street model and test the program a couple of times. This is a rather tough problem, but it is interesting to see that a relatively simple program can be used to solve a complicated problem in the real world once we learn how to handle ideas in a logical fashion. Good luck!

CHAPTER NINE

Boolean Algebra and Nested Control Structures

O NE OF the most pleasant aspects of working with computers and programming is the magic involved. Of course, this is obvious in the case of the hardware. Having a microcomputer on your desk is like having an Aladdin's lamp. You turn it on and bring it up instead of rubbing it, but the genie is right there, ready to provide conversation, the latest stock market quotations, an exciting game with pictures, or calculations that have meaning in the world around us.

The magic spells are a bit harder. Many of us have a subconscious belief in magic. If only we knew the right combination of words and diagrams we could make things happen the way we want them to. The spells, incantations, and cabalistic signs that we find in old legends or fantasy fiction invariably have a marvelously exotic appearance and invariably don't work. It's frustrating.

Yet in programs and program theory we have our incantations. We even have a special algebra that describes ideas and logic, not just numbers. This special algebra is named after a nineteenth century English mathematician. The algebra of George Boole, Boolean algebra, really works. To describe how it works we will use 'truth tables', and to visualize the elements of this mathematics we will use Venn diagrams.

The point in using Boolean algebra and Boolean operators is that they enable us to decide questions that involve several relations occurring simultaneously. Their value in programming is that they provide an alternative to nested control modules. This permits us to write simpler program structures, and at the same time to have greater flexibility in program design.

Boolean operators and simple Boolean algebra are introduced at the pseudocode level for two reasons. First, all major computing languages have them. Second, they take a bit of getting used to if one is to handle them well. When one is learning a computer language there is usually little enough time to concentrate on using Boolean operators well, and in addition there are many other new ideas to distract the student.

We will work with the three main Boolean operators, AND, OR and NOT. We will also learn a smattering of Boolean algebra so that we can understand how the operators interact with each other.

Let us consider a Boolean operator in a real sentence in English:

If an animal has four legs AND square teeth, then the animal is a horse.

This statement can be expanded in a way that will present a somewhat better idea of the Boolean AND relation:

If it is *true* that (the animal has four legs) AND it is *true* that (the animal has square teeth) then it is *true* that (the animal is a horse).

How must these conditions be met? If both conditions (animal has four legs) and (animal has square teeth) are simultaneously true, then the combined condition produced by connecting them with AND is true. Since this combined condition is true, the animal in question is a horse.

If anyone is disturbed by the biology, remember that you were warned that dealing with the real world in programs could get complicated. If either of the conditions connected by AND is false, then the combined condition is false and the animal is not a horse. Further, if both conditions are false at the same time, the combined condition is also false, which means the animal is not a horse.

In Figure 9.1 a Venn diagram describing the situation is displayed. The outside square encloses an area that contains all the types of animals that exist. The right-hand circle inside the square contains all the animals with square teeth. The left-hand circle contains all the animals with four legs. In that space common to both circles (where the two circles intersect) is an area containing all the animals that have both square teeth and four legs. This area is shaded. All the animals within this shaded area are horses, according to our definition.

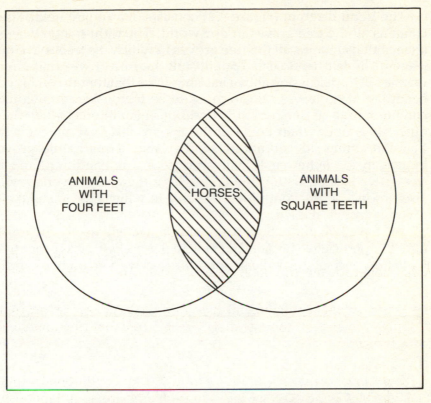

Fig. 9.1   Venn diagram of a Boolean AND statement

The second Boolean operator we will consider is OR. Again, we can consider an interesting problem from the real world:

If there is no grass under the trees OR the trees have no leaves, then we won't have a picnic in that grove of trees.

This may be recast in the same form as the last example:

If it is *true* that (there is no grass under the trees) OR if it is *true* that (the trees have no leaves) then it is *true* that (we won't have a picnic in that grove of trees).

Here it is a bit easier to decide whether we will have a picnic. Obviously, if both conditions are true the picnic will be called off. Further, if only one (and it can be either one) of the conditions is true, there will be no picnic. In the case of OR it is only when both conditions are false that the compound condition is false.

The Venn diagram (Figure 9.2) consists of a square field. This contains all the tree groves in our world. The right-hand circle is an area that contains all the tree groves in which the trees have no leaves. The left-hand circle contains all the tree groves that have no grass. The discussion above has shown us that for the combined condition of no leaves OR no grass to be true, either individual condition may be true, or both conditions may be true simultaneously. It is only when both conditions are false simultaneously that the combined condition will be false. Thus a tree grove located inside either circle will produce a true condition, and a tree grove located within the area where the circles overlap will also produce a true condition. The area in which the overall condition is true is shaded.

We have two of the Boolean operators we will need. The third one is superficially simpler, but is actually tricky to use properly. Until now each of the Boolean operators has worked on two condi-

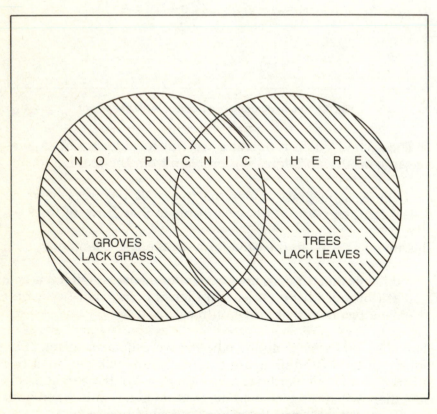

N O P I C N I C H E R E

GROVES
LACK GRASS

TREES
LACK LEAVES

Fig. 9.2 Venn diagram of a Boolean OR statement

tions. That is, we have had to feed in two pieces of information before we could make a decision. Feeding in only one condition would do us no good because the operators in question, AND and OR, must connect two entities. A more formal way of stating this is that AND and OR each require two **arguments**.

The third operator is NOT. It only uses one argument. Let's try another example:

If it is NOT raining then we will go to the grocery store.

This will be divided with parentheses to show what we really mean.

If NOT (raining) is *true* then it is *true* that (we will go to the grocery store).

This structure is disturbing because we do not use a double negative in English, so analysis of negative operators does not seem natural to us. If (raining) is *true* then NOT (raining) must be *false*. On the other hand, if no rain is falling from the sky, then (raining) is *false*, so NOT (raining) must be *true*. The idea behind the NOT operator is so simple that it appears difficult unit we get used to it.

The Venn diagram is also rather subtle, as we see in Figure 9.3. Here, the square represents all the places in our world where it may be raining. Of course, when we say 'may be raining', we are also talking about places where there is no rain. The circle in the center of the square is an area representing *all* the places where it *is* raining. All the places where it is not raining will be outside the circle. This area, the area outside the circle, is shaded. This is the NOT of whatever the circle represents. In this case it is the NOT (raining) area. You will probably want to run through this idea several more times. The Boolean operator NOT involves such a fundamental idea that it is hard to get an exact grip on it in English.

There are other Boolean operators used in computer languages, but the examples we have chosen are enough to do any job and will be found in almost all computer languages.

We have used examples from a 'real' world to describe Boolean operators because it is the easiest place to begin. A few numerical examples will now be considered to show how these interesting operators can be used in programs that do numerical calculations. Instead of conditions establishing the shape of teeth, the existence

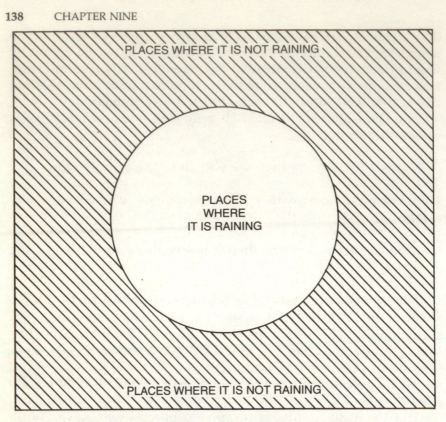

Fig. 9.3   Venn diagram of a Boolean NOT statement

of grass or whether rain is falling, we will have to consider numerical conditions. This can best be done by describing relations
between numerical variables and constants.

We have already discussed a set of operators that can be used
for such comparisons. These are the operators that describe the
relations between numbers. They are < (less than), > (greater
than), = (equal to), <= (less than or equal to), >= (greater than or
equal to), and ⟨ ⟩ (not equal to). We have used these to define the
conditions that determine the activity of control structures like
selection (IF–THEN–ELSE) or DOWHILE. When we used them
for that purpose, we had only one condition. Now we will use
compound conditions. At first, compound numerical conditions
may seem somewhat abstract, but after we have worked with
them for a while, they will become as natural as the real-world
conditions we have already examined.

One of the standard kinds of restrictions is to say that something will happen while a variable lies between two numerical

limits. Let's use the numerical variable A. Remember, there is nothing special about this variable, we could have used MOXY or UGH4. These are all variables. We just decided to use A. Whatever is going to happen is going to happen while A lies between 10 and 95 but is not equal to either 10 or 95. Writing this as a mathematical condition, we would say that:

$$10 < A < 95$$

The mathematical way of writing this is included because the range of limits may often be presented to you in this form. This expression is an example of great mathematics, but lousy semantics in almost any computer language you can name. How can we explain this to a computer? What we mean by the condition $10 < A < 95$ is that A will be larger than 10 and at the same time A will be less than 95. Once we are sure what we are talking about, the compound control condition can be written with the aid of Boolean operators as:

$$(A > 10) \text{ AND } (A < 95)$$

This Boolean expression says exactly what we want said. There is one aspect of the structure worth careful explanation. The relation expressions are enclosed in parentheses. Technically, this is not necessary in so simple an expression; however, the exact precedence relation within Boolean expressions varies slightly from one computer language to another. One is always safe with parentheses because they define what is to be done first. Parenthetical expressions will be used throughout this text because they are unambiguous.

Another common type of limitation is to have a range of numbers that must not be used. Consider some procedure that will occur only if the variable SLUG is equal to or larger than 28 or equal to or smaller than 3. The control condition may be written in at least two forms. First, consider the straightforward way resulting from the above description of the expression. The ranges of values that are and are not legal are shown in Figure 9.4. Examine the range of values where the procedure is allowed. These two ranges (SLUG <= 3 and SLUG >= 28) are separated from each other by a continuous range of values, 3 < SLUG < 28, where the procedure is not allowed. The direct approach consists of a condition describing regions where the procedure will work. It is important to remember that the relations SLUG <= 3 and

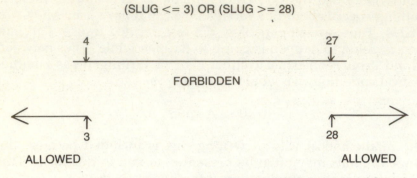

Fig. 9.4   Example of legal and illegal ranges

SLUG >= 28 cannot occur simultaneously. Once this is clear, the control expression written with Boolean operators is obviously

$$(SLUG <= 3) \text{ OR } (SLUG >= 28)$$

Similarly, when we realize that the middle region is continuous and forbidden, we can write the other obvious form of the control statement:

$$NOT \, ((SLUG > 3) \text{ AND } (SLUG < 28))$$

Note the use of parentheses here. Each comparison statement is isolated by the innermost sets of parentheses to ensure that these expressions are evaluated first. Next, a set of parentheses isolates the AND expression in combination with the two comparison expressions. Thus, after the comparison expressions are evaluated, they are combined using AND, and this expression is evaluated. This AND expression defines the region where the procedure will not run. However, we are interested in the region where the procedure will run. The NOT version of this combined expression is exactly what we want because this says that if the value of SLUG is not in the region defined by the combined structure, then the NOT expression will be *true*.

Since this NOT expression constitutes the test for the conditional control statement that governs the procedure we are studying, then the procedure will run.

As a partial review of the Boolean operators and their applications, let us evaluate the above two expressions for several values of SLUG. First, the direct statement:

(SLUG <= 3) OR (SLUG >= 28)

If the value of SLUG is 40, then we substitute 40 for each occurrence of SLUG and evaluate the relational statements as either TRUE or FALSE. This evaluation is done before any other evaluation because it is within the innermost set of parenthesis. The above expression becomes

(40 <= 3) OR (40 >= 29)

Which becomes

(FALSE) OR (TRUE)

Under the rules for evaluating OR Booleans, the value of the overall expression is

TRUE

Which means the procedure under control will run. Now a much quicker evaluation for the same expression with a different value; SLUG := 8:

(SLUG <= 3) OR (SLUG >= 28)
(8 <= 3) OR (8 >= 28)
(FALSE) OR (FALSE)
FALSE

We will use the same values of SLUG for a rapid evaluation of the indirect form written with NOT.

SLUG := 40
NOT ((SLUG > 3) AND (SLUG < 28))
NOT ((40 > 3) AND (40 < 28))
NOT ((TRUE) AND (FALSE))
NOT (FALSE)
TRUE

Thus, for SLUG:= 40 the control test says the procedure should run.

SLUG := 8
> NOT ((SLUG > 3) AND (SLUG < 28))
> NOT ((8 > 3) AND (8 < 28))
> NOT ((TRUE) AND (TRUE))
> NOT (TRUE)
> FALSE

Thus, for SLUG:= 8 the control test says the procedure should not run.

In evaluating Boolean expressions for a particular value(s) of the variable(s), it is important to do just one level of simplification at a time. Similarly, when designing the control expressions, careful use of parentheses is essential to produce a clear, unambiguous expression defining the intended control limits. We will again review the structure of Boolean relations in detail when we consider truth tables. In the meantime, we will prepare solutions for a programming problem in two ways.

In the first method, we will use nested control structures like the ones we introduced in the last chapter. Notice that as we develop more sophisticated abilities with control structures, the problems we can solve easily become more numerous and more realistic.

We are designing a program to control the warning devices on a simple reactor or steam turbine. A thermometer and a pressure gauge regularly supply information about temperature and pressure. If the temperature is over 400 degrees Fahrenheit and the pressure is over 350 pounds per square inch, both at the same time, a dangerous condition exists. The thermometer reports only on the Fahrenheit scale and the pressure gauge reports only in terms of pounds per square inch. Thus we need think only in terms of numbers and not assign particular units to them in the program. We are not exactly describing the form in which a temperature–pressure number pair are held in the measurement machine, but since we don't have to worry too much about limitations of our imaginary hardware, we assume that they can be handled by read statements. In the first program nested selection will be used.

DESCRIPTION: Read in numbers corresponding to temperature and pressure of a reactor, if both simultaneously exceed the safety limits, then print a warning notice on the record sheet. If the danger condition does not exist, print 'Within Limits'.

INPUT DATA: Two numbers: the first a temperature (Fahrenheit); the second a pressure (pounds per square inch)

OUTPUT DATA: Either a danger message, or a report that the measurements are in order

PROCEDURE:

1. Initialize program (assign limit values)
2. Read in the data values
3. Test data values
4. Print the results
5. Finish the program

We now revise the procedure block and set it up in pseudocode.

PROCEDURE:

1.	TEMPLIM := 400
2.	PRESLIM := 350
3.	Read first number, assign to TEMP
4.	Read second number, assign to PRES
5.	IF TEMP <= TEMPLIM
5.1.	THEN
5.2.	Print 'Within Limits'
5.3.	ELSE
5.4.	IF PRES <= PRESLIM
5.4.1.	THEN
5.4.2.	Print 'Within Limits'
5.4.3.	ELSE
5.4.4.	Print 'DANGER'
5.4.5.	ENDIF
5.5.	ENDIF
6.	END

The flowchart of this program is shown in Figure 9.5.

This is a well-structured program. Note the rather formal use of line numbers and decimals to label modules and their internal steps. As mentioned earlier, once you get used to working with these, they are a real help in quickly analyzing the modular structure. Now we will rewrite the detailed pseudocode using Boolean operators where possible. Needless to say, it will not be necessary to rewrite the first crude version of the procedure.

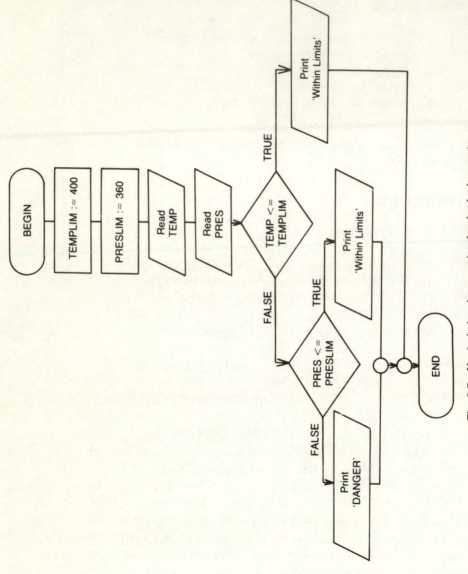

Fig. 9.5 Nested structures not using logical operators

PROCEDURE:

1.   TEMPLIM := 400
2.   PRESLIM := 350
3.   Read first number, assign to TEMP
4.   Read second number, assign to PRES
5.   IF (TEMP > TEMPLIM) AND (PRES > PRESLIM)
5.1.   THEN
5.2.   Print 'DANGER'
5.3.   ELSE
5.4.   Print 'Within Limits'
5.5.   ENDIF
6.   END

The flowchart is shown in Figure 9.6.

Two improvements stand out in this design. The program is less complex because we have eliminated the sequence that was nested. Also, the meaning of the program is immediately obvious because of the Boolean structure, which states very clearly that the decisive condition is that both limits will be exceeded simultaneously. This is easier to set up and easier to interpret if you have to go back and change things a few weeks later. As usual, you should build both designs and run a few values to desk-check the program.

The safety device used is a good place to start the second example. Here we will change the danger condition. If either or both of the limits are exceeded, the danger message must be printed. Notice that the initial rough outline procedure will be exactly the same as in the first example, because we did not define the nature of the test step until the actual pseudocode was written.

DESCRIPTION: Read in numbers corresponding to temperature and pressure of a reactor. If either exceeds the safety limits, then print a warning notice on the record sheet. If the danger condition does not exist, print 'Within Limits'.

INPUT DATA: Two numbers: the first a temperature (Fahrenheit); the second a pressure (pounds per square inch)

OUTPUT DATA: Either a danger message, or a report that the measurements are in order

PROCEDURE:

1.   Initialize program (assign limit values)
2.   Read in the data values
3.   Test data values

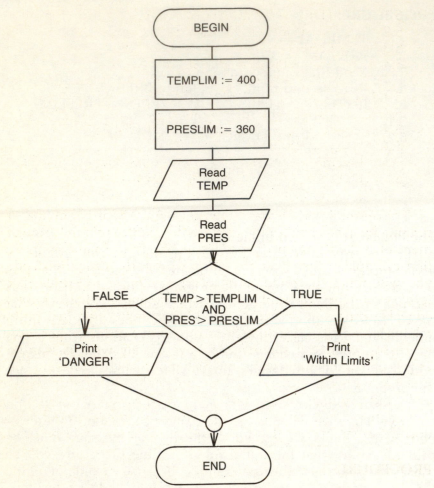

Fig. 9.6   Program rewritten with Boolean operators

4.   Print the results
5.   Finish the program

Refined into proper pseudocode, the PROCEDURE becomes:

PROCEDURE:

1.   TEMPLIM := 400
2.   PRESLIM := 350
3.   Read first number, assign to TEMP
4.   Read second number, assign to PRES
5.   IF TEMP > TEMPLIM

```
5.1.        THEN
5.2.              Print 'DANGER'
5.3.        ELSE
5.4.              IF PRES > PRESLIM
5.4.1.                  THEN
5.4.2.                        Print 'DANGER'
5.4.3.                  ELSE
5.4.4.                        Print 'WITHIN LIMITS'
5.4.5.                  ENDIF
5.5.   ENDIF
6.     END
```

Try running various data pairs through this program and arranging the nested conditions differently. Notice that the arrangement of nested sequence modules is exactly the same as in the first example. When you are writing properly structured code, you will notice that modular structures often show similar patterns, even when the problems seem to be unrelated. The knowledgeable programmer with a good library will often just pull a relatively complex structure from the library of his or her word processor, change it slightly and have exactly what is wanted. This is one of the many ways in which modular structures, in conjunction with top-down programming, not only produce better code, but produce it faster.

Again, we will refine the rough procedure into a proper pseudocode structure, but this time Boolean operators will be used.

PROCEDURE:

```
1.     TEMPLIM := 400
2.     PRESLIM := 350
3.     Read first number, assign to TEMP
4.     Read second number, assign to PRES
5.     IF (TEMP > TEMPLIM) OR (PRES > PRESLIM)
5.1.        THEN
5.2.              Print 'DANGER'
5.3.        ELSE
5.4.              Print 'Within Limits'
5.5.   ENDIF
6.     END
```

When we compare the two programs derived using Boolean operators, it is clear that all we needed to do to go from one to the other was to change the Boolean statement. This is because the condition defining the test was completely contained in the Boolean statement, and did not depend on the nature and arrangement of the THEN or ELSE clauses or of that part of the test contained in a second nested IF statement. There is no guarantee that things will always be this simple, but it is surprising how often they are, provided one is writing properly structured code.

Having completed the examination of two applications of Boolean operators, we are ready to review these operators and examine their properties as displayed in truth tables. Until now, we have considered the conditions connected by Boolean operators to be such comparisons as DILP < 8.5 or Z >= K. The condition consisted of a variable and a constant or another variable connected by a relational operator. By introducing values for the variables, we were able to determine whether the relation was true or false. Based on this, the condition was then assigned the value 'true' or 'false', and several such variables were combined using Boolean operators and the laws of Boolean algebra. The compound condition could then be evaluated to a single value of true or false. The truth or falsity of this compound condition determined the operation of a control structure such as selection or DOWHILE.

The simple conditions defined by variables and constants and relational operators will now be replaced by a single variable letter *A*, *B*, etc. These variables may take on only the value of true or false. They are generally of little use in providing conditions for decision processes using control structures such as DOWHILE or selection, but they are excellent for running combinatorial studies to determine the properties of Boolean statements. We shall use them only to simplify the building of the truth tables.

These tables for AND, OR and NOT are shown in Figures 9.7a, 9.7b and 9.7c, respectively. They consist of a horizontal axis on which is found each of the variables involved, usually just *A* and *B*, followed by the relation in question. Below each of the variables is written the values it can have; either T or F. One reads across to the column titled with the combination relation and enters the value (either T or F) corresponding to the effect of the variable values in each row. This is an easy way to define the effect of the values of Boolean variables on particular Boolean statements. It is not restricted to the operators we have used and may be applied with any number of variables.

This chapter has provided a brief overview of the simpler Boolean operators and Boolean algebra. The construction and

A	B	(A AND B)
F	F	F
T	F	F
F	T	F
T	T	T

Fig. 9.7a Boolean AND operator

A	B	(A OR B)
F	F	F
T	F	T
F	T	T
T	T	T

Fig. 9.7b Boolean OR operator

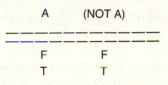
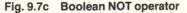

A	(NOT A)
F	F
T	T

Fig. 9.7c Boolean NOT operator

evaluation of compound conditions has been examined, as well as applications of Boolean technology to algorithm and program development. By the time the student has carefully worked through the examples presented in the text and the problems at the end of the chapter, he/she will find a powerful tool at his/her command to simplify algorithm development and the presentation of structured programs.

PROBLEMS

Virtually all computer languages allow the use of Boolean operators, although these may be designated as 'logical' operators. Unfortunately, in the press of learning the other details of a new language, specific explanation and application of these essential operators are slighted.

The following examples give the student an introduction to both the convenience and limitations of Boolean techniques. Problems 9.9 and 9.10 are a little difficult and have been designated challenge problems. Because these methods are new to many beginning students, all the problems are answered at the end of the book

*   *   *

9.1 A control condition may be defined by stating that the system will operate when a key variable, BIRK, is greater than or equal to 7 or less than or equal to 15. Write this control condition as a Boolean statement that avoids the NOT operator. Evaluate the expression in terms of 'TRUE' and 'FALSE' for BIRK := 5 and for BIRK := 22.

For the second part of this problem, write this control condition as a Boolean statement that makes direct use of the NOT operator. Evaluate the expression in terms of 'TRUE' and 'FALSE' for BIRK := 4 and for BIRK := −3.

9.2 A control condition may be defined by stating that the system will not operate when a key variable, KRONCH, is greater than 8 and less than 45. Write this control condition as a Boolean statement that avoids the NOT operator. Evaluate the expression in terms of 'TRUE' and 'FALSE' for KRONCH := 78 and for KRONCH := 16.

Write this control condition as a Boolean statement that makes direct use of the NOT operator. Evaluate the expression in terms of 'TRUE' and 'FALSE' for KRONCH := −3 and for KRONCH := 30.

9.3 We have our usual deck of cards. In this case, each card may contain positive or negative nonzero values. The end card will contain a value of zero. You wish to locate a particular number, which may or may not be in the deck. You will thus continue a read loop until you have read zero into the test variable or you have read the sought-for number into the test variable. When you leave the read loop, the test variable will contain either the end-of-data code or the target value. An appropriate test will cause a printout indicating successful discovery of the desired value or that the desired value is not in the deck.

Design a pseudocode program to conduct the above test. Use a Boolean expression to define the reading loop conditions. Do not use nested control structures. The value you are going to search for may be entered directly in the program.

9.4 Write the truth table of the Boolian expression,

(NOT (A) AND NOT (B))

You will need headings for A, B, NOT (A), NOT (B) and the final function itself.

9.5   In Problem 8.6, we considered a power plant in which the safety requirements included reference to the external temperature. If the external temperature exceeded a critical value, then either excessive internal temperature or excessive internal pressure caused a dangerous condition. Rewrite the program describing the test system using Boolean statements to replace nested structures wherever possible.

As a second program in the same problem, change the danger conditions to indicate that when the external temperature exceeds the critical temperature, both the internal temperature and the internal pressure must exceed their critical values during the same measuring period before a danger condition is indicated. Again, use Boolean expressions wherever possible to avoid nested structures. Notice how much easier it is to change the control conditions of selection systems when one is using Boolean structures instead of nesting multiple selection structures.

9.6   Write a truth table for the following Boolean expression:

NOT (NOT (A) OR NOT (B))

You will need headings for A, B, NOT (A), NOT (B), the expression (NOT (A) OR NOT (B)) and the final expression being examined.

Do the patterns of truth elements for the final expression and the columns for A and B suggest a Boolean expression you already know?

9.7   In Problem 8, you were called upon to design a program that accepted three numbers, arranged them in order from greatest to smallest and printed out the three numbers in the order in which they were entered as well as the order they acquired after rearrangement. Prepare a similar program making use of Boolean expressions. Although you had a successful design using nested control structures, you may find that the properties of Boolean operators are such that it is better to start from scratch in designing this new program rather than merely translating the earlier program involving nested structures.

9.8   Once again, return to the problems of Chapter 8. In Problem 8.7, you designed a clock that printed out hours, minutes and seconds. Although the number of loops to be nested was rather large, the program was not especially difficult once the trick of handling the nested structures was learned.

Attempt to repeat the design using Boolean structures as often as possible to replace loop nesting. Do you feel that Boolean technology is optimal for a network with multiple counters?

*9.9   You have a single card. This card contains three values. Each of these is either 0 (zero) or 5. The three values on the cards may be arranged as follows:

0,0,0

or

0,0,5

or

0,5,0

or

0,5,5

When you read the card, the three values are assigned respectively to variables called ADOOR, BDOOR and CDOOR. The card might be thought of as a room. Each of the three values on the card might refer to the existence of a door associated with the room the card represents.

We assume the 0 (zero) to stand for a door that actually exists and a 5 to stand for a door that could exist but does not actually exist then we have three types of rooms (one room of a type that has three doors, two rooms of a type that has two doors and one room of a type that has one door). You can see these rooms are related to the room that might be found in the house of Problem 1.9.

Write a program that reads a card. It should assign the values of the card to ADOOR, BDOOR and CDOOR respectively. It should then increment the value of ADOOR by 1 and print the message 'Entering Room'. Notice that in all of the arrangements of 0 and 5 we have used, the first of the three numbers is always zero, implying that each of the rooms has at least one door.

The program should now examine the variables BDOOR and

CDOOR. Of course, if they are both 5 then no other door exists. The program prints the message 'This is a closet, I leave the way I entered.' It should then increment ADOOR again to show that it has passed through this doorway again. In this case there is no more to be done, so the program quits.

If either BDOOR or CDOOR is zero, it should increment whichever value is zero to show that it went through that doorway and print the message, 'Leaving by the only other door'.

If both BDOOR and CDOOR are zero, it should increment one of them (the choice or the method to make the choice is up to you), and then print the message 'Leaving by one of the two other doors'. Needless to say, it should increment one of the two zero-value variables to show which doorway it passed through.

In all events, after printing out the appropriate message and incrementing the appropriate variable, it should shut down with the final comment 'What next?'

*9.10   You have two decks of cards. They may be designated the A deck and the B deck. Each card contains a single positive integer, except in the case of the end card of each deck, which contains 0 (zero). The cards in each deck are ordered, starting with the highest number at the beginning of the deck and the lowest number just before the end-of-data card in each deck. The numbers are ordered, but they are not necessarily sequential. That is, a given value is not necessarily related to the value immediately before or after it by a difference of 1. Another way of saying this is that there may be gaps in the sequence of cards in either or both decks. The decks may or may not have the same number of cards. A particular number may or may not appear in either or both decks. No number will occur twice in the same deck.

You may assume you are working with a computer that can read cards in either deck, at the choice of the program. Your task is to print an ordered list of the combined numbers in the two decks. The end-of-data cards should not be printed out. No number should appear more than once, even though it is found in each of the two decks. The order of numbers in the final list should be as in the two decks, that is, from largest number to smallest number. When the final printout is complete, a message should be printed stating that the 'data-merge' routine is complete.

Some of you will be able to handle this without help, but here are a few general remarks that may be useful. The initial read-in step should read one card from each deck. After assignment to appropriate variables, they should be compared and the larger printed. As soon as a card in one of the two holding variables is printed, it should be replaced by having a new value read into it.

This kind of a hint may seem like giving the problem away, but I am sure that if you carefully imagined a type of machine to do the work described in the initial specifications, you would come up with this hint anyway. I just want to hurry the process along.

Some mechanism must be devised to prevent a number that occurs in both decks from being printed more than once. The simplest way to do this might be to check to see if the numbers in the holding variables associated with each deck are the same. When the same number is held in both variables, one of these might be destroyed rather than printed out. You should satisfy yourself that this routine will eliminate duplication. Another possible approach is to move the number selected for printout to the first of two additional holding variables after each selection cycle. At the same time, the number from the first of these two additional holding variables would be moved to the second intermediate holding variable and the number in the second holding variable would be printed out. Then at some intermediate point in each cycle of comparison, the contents of the two intermediate variables could be checked and duplication eliminated.

A final problem will be the nature of the program's response when one of the two decks reaches its end-of-data card. There are several solutions. Once one deck is empty, the remaining cards of the other deck can be printed out in order without the necessity of comparison between decks. Essentially, one way to handle the problem is to invalidate or short-circuit the comparison process within the loop that reads both decks and at the same time stop the reading process of the empty deck. Another method is to go to a new reading loop that reads only the deck having cards left and prints these out directly. The mechanism selected will depend on one's individual programming preferences and the results of experiment. This is a tough exercise, but it is a realistic one.

CHAPTER TEN

Arrays and Array Processing

WE HAVE all heard sports commentators on TV remarking that computing has come to football coaching. The hysteria that prompts programmers to produce outrageous variable names sometimes causes them to have strange visions. One of mine concerns a football team run by the type of computer-conscious coach mentioned above. He has all his plays worked out by player number, and he has a set of football jerseys numbered 1 to 11. At the start of the training season when he must decide on his team organization, he lines up his many candidates, takes the first eleven in order and hands each one a jersey beginning at 1 and going to 11. The players in the jerseys then run through a few plays and the coach evaluates the plays in terms of how the numbered jerseys move. Then he has the players take the jerseys off, loads the jerseys with 11 new players in order and repeats the process. He may also swap players between jerseys, but everything is always done in terms of the jersey numbers and these match the football play layouts. This probably isn't very realistic. Besides questions from the local board of health, there is the problem of how a player, when he dons jersey number 5, will know exactly what jersey number 5 is supposed to do on the play diagram. This is bad football, but it is great programming.

Substituting variables for constants enables us to manipulate large numbers of separate values with the same program. We don't have to know the value of a particular constant and rewrite the program for that constant; we simply assign the constant to a variable and the program does the rest. However, each time we need to use a particular variable, we must refer to that specific variable by name. There should be a way we can designate a class of variables and then manipulate the variables with the program in the same generalized way in which we can manipulate constants. There is a method. This is to use a type of variable called an **array**.

Consider the variable A1. There is nothing special about this variable. The number 1 is part of the name, but the number 1 may not be manipulated or changed by the program. How do we designate an array variable? We will move into this rather carefully. Consider a set of variables A(1), A(2), A(3), A(4), A(5). Suppose we generalize these a bit further, so that we have a set of variables A(I) in which I may take on any value between 1 and 5 inclusive. The variable I, which is a part of the array variable A(I), may be thought of as a kind of pointer. If a value between 1 and 5 is assigned to this pointer I, we have designated a particular member of the set of variables A(1) through A(5).

Any particular element of the array may be addressed by including the pointer number in the parenthesis. In this case, the array element in question behaves like any individual variable and does not show any special properties related to its membership in an array. If further analogies are required, we could think in terms of numbered buckets, but the most constructive thing we can do is to consider the operation of a simple array.

How do we know that an array of variables exists in a program? Simple – we **declare** the array and its size at the start of the program. This is normally in the initiation phase. In pseudocode, array declaration is necessary only for the sake of neatness. Even though there is no mechanical or logical reason, declaration will always be done. In programming with a language that runs on a machine, the declaration is necessary to set aside automatically a certain amount of main storage to hold the array. This reservation process is required because arrays involve a specific storage strategy that simplifies the use of the sequential pointers.

The first program we will consider loads five numbers into a five-element array. It then goes through the array and selects the largest number. When you are studying this, think of it in terms of two programs following one after the other. First work through the loading module until you understand it. Then the part that selects the largest number will be easy to understand.

DESCRIPTION: Program accepts five numbers, stores them in an array, selects the largest and prints it out.
INPUT DATA: Five numbers
OUTPUT DATA: The largest of the five numbers
PROCEDURE:

1. Initialize program
2. Load five numbers into an array
3. Determine largest number in array
4. Print out largest number

Now, expanding this rough outline:

PROCEDURE:

1.	DECLARE RACK (5)
2.	I := 1
3.	DOWHILE 1 <= 5
3.1.	Read a number, assign to RACK (I)
3.2.	I := I + 1
3.3.	ENDDO
4.	BIGGEST := RACK (1)
5.	POINT := 1
6.	DOWHILE POINT <= 5
6.1.	IF RACK (POINT) >BIGGEST
6.1.1.	THEN
6.1.2.	BIGGEST := RACK (POINT)
6.1.3.	ENDIF
6.2.	POINT := POINT + 1
6.3.	ENDDO
7.	Print 'The largest number is', BIGGEST
8.	END

The program we have just written has a number of interesting features. Speaking in generalities one can say that four clear-cut modules show up. The first is the initiation module. In this case it is quite short and only sets up the array.

The second module begins at line 2, with the assignment of the value 1 to the pointer variable I. This variable I is going to be used to point to the various members of the array. There is nothing special about our choice of I. Any variable name could have been used as pointer variable. The assignment of 1 to the variable I is just the same initial priming step we always have to include when setting up a DOWHILE structure. Line 3 is the initial line of a DOWHILE loop with the condition that the system will loop as long as I remains smaller than or equal to 5. This number (5) refers to the number of elements in the array RACK (), which was declared in step 1.

We are now inside the DOWHILE loop, so the next line has another decimal place and is 3.1. This line tells us to read a number from our input and assign it to the element of the array that has the pointer I. Of course, on the first time through the loop, the pointer will have the value 1 because that is how it was assigned. Line 3.2 is next and causes the value of the pointer to increase by 1. If the value of the pointer is less than or equal to 5, the

DOWHILE loop will start again at its beginning, line 3, with the pointer equal to 2. Another value will be read from the input device and this time is assigned to array element RACK (2).

The whole process will repeat itself until the incrementing step in line 3.2 produces a value of I that is larger than 5. Then the loop will be exited at the ENDDO at 3.3, instead of being turned back to the initial DOWHILE line. We have watched the operation of this data input module in some detail to review the looping techniques. Future discussions of looping will not be so detailed.

The third module selects the largest number that has been loaded into the array. The strategy used is interesting and will be used in one form or another throughout your development as a programmer. We take a value and say that it is the biggest of a list of numbers. We say it is, even though we know it may not be. Then we test it against one number in the list. If this number we said was biggest is bigger than the number we tested, then we do not change the value we consider to be biggest; we go ahead and test another number in the list. Again, if our chosen biggest number is bigger, we do not change it.

If our choice was a lucky one, we might go through the entire list of numbers, always with our initial choice greater than the other members in the list. Then it would indeed be the biggest and our search would end. Suppose at one of the test steps, the number we said was the biggest is actually smaller than the list member we test it against. Don't worry. Replace the number we said was biggest with the list member, which was really bigger, and go on with the list. In short, if it isn't the biggest, make it the biggest. This is a neat kind of thinking mechanism, and you will find yourself using it again and again in computing and in life in general.

Now that the mechanism of the module has been examined, we can take a brief look at its organization. It is a nesting of two control structures, as can be seen by examining the indentation and/or the line numbers. The outermost shell is just a DOWHILE based on incrementing the array pointer. Note that this time we have used a different pointer variable name – we have called it POINT. We could have called it UGH, or Z, or DOGMEAT, as long as we maintained the same name through the body of the loop in which this name was assigned. Of course, we have the usual initial feeding or priming step for this loop, just as we have had before. All that this outer loop does is to guarantee that we test each of the array elements in order.

One more activity of special importance is accomplished. In

line 4 an initial value is assigned to BIGGEST, so that the test routine will have something to test the first time it is used. Any number could have been assigned. We took a value from the list of numbers contained in the array because the problem asked for the largest number contained in that list.

If we had taken any number to start, there would have been two problems. First, how would we have chosen the number? Second, if the number we used was not in the list, and it turned out to be larger than any number in the list, it would be printed out as the largest number in the list and this would not be correct. For this reason, a number in the list was chosen. The obvious choice was the first number, that held in RACK (1). Further, note that since the contents of element number 1 of the array have been chosen, the DOWHILE need only do its repeat cycle between POINTER values of 2 through 5 instead of 1 through 5, as it is written.

The test itself is run by an IF–THEN block nested in the DO-WHILE. This is IF–THEN instead of IF–THEN–ELSE, because the ELSE clause is not needed. In the event the THEN clause is not activated, the program simply exits the IF–THEN at ENDIF, and control is returned to the contents of the DOWHILE loop, which increments the pointer and checks to see if it exceeds the limiting condition (POINT <= (5)).

When this third module is completed, the variable BIGGEST is, indeed, loaded with the biggest number in the array, and this value may be passed to the output module which, in this case, is a simple print statement with a message line to identify the value it prints out.

This is a relatively simple program, but it is somewhat long and involves a reasonable amount of numerical manipulation. It presents a good opportunity to use a trace diagram. All that a trace diagram does is to record the values of the variables as the program is run, one step at a time. We have already used it to follow the development of an answer in Newton's square root method. The diagram lists the step number, the statement number being run, the state of the variables and any printouts produced. The numbers waiting to be read are 13, 4, 44, 62, 10, in that order.

Step	Statement	I	POINT	ARRAY	(1)	(2)	(3)	(4)	(5)	BIGGEST
1	1.	0	0		0	0	0	0	0	0
2	2.	1	0		0	0	0	0	0	0

3	3.	1	0	0	0	0	0	0	0
4	3.1.	1	0	13	0	0	0	0	0
5	3.2.	2	0	13	0	0	0	0	0
6	3.3.	2	0	13	0	0	0	0	0
7	3.	2	0	13	0	0	0	0	0
8	3.1.	2	0	13	4	0	0	0	0
9	3.2.	3	0	13	4	0	0	0	0
10	3.3.	3	0	13	4	0	0	0	0
11	3.	3	0	13	4	0	0	0	0
12	3.1.	3	0	13	4	44	0	0	0
13	3.2.	4	0	13	4	44	0	0	0
14	3.3.	4	0	13	4	44	0	0	0
15	3.	4	0	13	4	44	0	0	0
16	3.1.	4	0	13	4	44	62	0	0
17	3.2.	5	0	13	4	44	62	0	0
18	3.3.	5	0	13	4	44	62	0	0
19	3.	5	0	13	4	44	62	0	0
20	3.1.	5	0	13	4	44	62	10	0
21	3.2.	6	0	13	4	44	62	10	0
22	3.3.	6	0	13	4	44	62	10	0

We have filled the array, left the first module and entered the second.

23	4.	6	0	13	4	44	62	10	13
24	5.	6	1	13	4	44	62	10	13
25	6.	6	1	13	4	44	62	10	13
26	6.1.	6	1	13	4	44	62	10	13
27	6.1.3.	6	1	13	4	44	62	10	13
28	6.2.	6	2	13	4	44	62	10	13
29	6.3.	6	2	13	4	44	62	10	13
30	6.	6	2	13	4	44	62	10	13
31	6.1.	6	2	13	4	44	62	10	13
32	6.1.3.	6	2	13	4	44	62	10	13
33	6.2.	6	3	13	4	44	62	10	13
34	6.3.	6	3	13	4	44	62	10	13
35	6.	6	3	13	4	44	62	10	13
36	6.1.	6	3	13	4	44	62	10	13
37	6.1.1.	6	3	13	4	44	62	10	13

POINT now has a value of 3. The next member of the array to be compared will be ARRAY (3), which, having a value of 44, will cause BIGGEST to take on a value of 44.

38	6.1.2.	6	3	13	4	44	62	10	44
39	6.1.3.	6	3	13	4	44	62	10	44
40	6.2.	6	4	13	4	44	62	10	44
41	6.3.	6	4	13	4	44	62	10	44
42	6.	6	4	13	4	44	62	10	44
43	6.1.	6	4	13	4	44	62	10	44
44	6.1.1.	6	4	13	4	44	62	10	44

POINT has taken on a value of 4, which has brought ARRAY (4) into position for comparison with BIGGEST. Since ARRAY (4) has a value of 62 and BIGGEST has a value of 44, the value of BIGGEST will be changed to 62.

45	6.1.2.	6	4	13	4	44	62	10	62
46	6.1.3.	6	4	13	4	44	62	10	62
47	6.2.	6	5	13	4	44	62	10	62
48	6.3.	6	5	13	4	44	62	10	62
49	6.	6	5	13	4	44	62	10	62
50	6.1.	6	5	13	4	44	62	10	62
51	6.1.3.	6	5	13	4	44	62	10	62
52	6.2.	6	6	13	4	44	62	10	62
53	6.3.	6	6	13	4	44	62	10	62
54	7.								

The largest number is 62

| 55 | 8. | 6 | 6 | 13 | 4 | 44 | 62 | 10 | 62 |

That was a monster! However, if you go through it carefully you will see how the various changes interrelate and how the control structures cause the program to change direction. Another point worth noting is how the pattern of line labels gives a clue to the way in which things are repeating.

Searching lists of numbers or names is one of the most common uses of computers, particularly in business. Anyone who has tried to find a particular playing card in a shuffled deck realizes that it is much easier to search an ordered list than an unordered list. The lists that computers must often deal with may have thousands or tens of thousands of elements. For this reason sorting algorithms, which produce ordered lists, have been a major area of computer research. In this text we will deal with two of the simpler sorting algorithms, which illustrate useful programming strategies.

The simplest algorithm I know of for ordering a list of numbers comes directly from the program we wrote for finding the largest number in a list of numbers. Suppose we have a list of numbers and wish to put it in order, with the largest first and the smallest last. Finding the number that will be the first element of the ordered list is not so hard. The disordered list is searched for its largest member. This number is then placed at the beginning of a list that will become the ordered list. Now we are stuck. If the largest-element algorithm is run on the disordered list, it will just come up with the same number we already have. However, suppose that when the largest member of the disordered list is located and copied out, it is then replaced in the disordered list with something that the ordering algorithm cannot see. Then the largest-element algorithm could be run again on the disordered list. It would come up with a number that is the largest number after the absolutely largest number is removed. This, of course, is the second largest number. It is copied into the second position in the ordered list. Meanwhile, back in the disordered list, the second largest number is also replaced by something invisible to the largest-element algorithm and the whole process is repeated. There are a few procedures in the overall process that are unclear, but it looks like we are on to a good thing.

Let's look at the problem of replacement in more detail. To select the largest element in a list, we went through all the elements in the list. Even though the variable that was designated to hold the largest element might contain that value early in the isolation process, we could not be sure that this was the largest element until the search of the list was complete. However, all's well that ends well. At the end of the process we have the value of the largest element in our holding variable (BIGGEST, perhaps), and all that is necessary is to go back to this element in the disordered list and replace it with that element that is invisible to the largest-element algorithm. But here is a problem! The value of the largest element is known, but its location is not. We are thinking of things held in an array, of course. We know the value of the largest element but we do not know its pointer. If one has gotten used to thinking in terms of pointers, there is a pretty good way around this. If one has not gotten used to thinking in terms of pointers, then this slight modification gets one on the right track.

In the largest-element algorithm, the statement that set things up for the search was the assignment of the first element in the array to a variable which would eventually hold the largest element in the array. This statement was:

BIGGEST := RACK (1)

If the thinking were done in terms of the element of RACK ( ) that held the largest number, and since it is the location, and hence the pointer to that location, which is unknown, the statement could be redesigned to read:

BIGPOINT := 1

This is a precise way of saying that RACK (BIGPOINT) has the same value as RACK (1), and we are talking about the pointer that points to the largest element rather than the largest element. It is the same thing, but we get more information from the search. Using this pointer method of thinking, we will end up with the location of the largest element as well as its value. In redesigning the search section, the DOWHILE loop that permits examination of one element of RACK ( ) after another may be left the same. The examination itself must be done in terms of the pointer so we change it to read:

IF RACK (POINT) > RACK (BIGPOINT)
  THEN
    BIGPOINT := POINT

Notice that, just as before, the values of the elements are used to decide if a change should be made, but the change itself is made in terms of the appropriate pointer instead of directly in terms of an element.

We now have an algorithm that will select the biggest element of an array and provide its location. If we were going to replace the value of the biggest element with a value that will not interfere with the selection procedure, we would do so right after this biggest-element-selection algorithm has checked all five elements of the array. For example, if we had restricted the numbers under examination to numbers larger than zero (0), the number selected in each pass might be replaced by 0.

Progress is being made! We now know how to find the largest number in the array, how to determine its location, and how to replace the largest number with a marker of some sort that the biggest-element-selection algorithm will ignore in future searches.

The only remaining task is to tuck the values isolated by the biggest-element selection algorithm into the appropriate spaces in a second array that will contain the list in order. It is clear that for this we will have to go through the process of selecting the biggest element five times, once for each element that must be put in order in the second array. Five times? Well, perhaps not. After all, when we have gone through the selection process four times, there will be only one element left in the small array. We just need to find it and quit. Ah, there's the rub! We have to find it. Of course, the selection process would find it for us. Otherwise, we will have to go to another module that will locate the last number by identifying it as the only element that is not a replacement marker. It is probably just as well to let the selection process run five times. However, be aware that we could save a few search steps by going to a module that would run through the disordered array, and as soon as it found an entry that was not the replacement marker would take the nonmarker element, pass it to the last place in the ordered array and quit.

We wish to do the entire largest-element-search algorithm five times and each time, move the largest element found to the next open position of a second array. To ensure that we won't find the same element each time, after each element is found and transferred, its position in the old array is replaced with a marker that will not interfere with the search process. To be sure that each element going into the ordered array will go to a new position, we increment the pointer of this second array as soon as we have assigned a value to an element.

This has been a rather long and complicated discussion. However, it is important to work out all the details as we design algorithms. We start out with a simple idea that looks like it will do the job, and then work our way through the various details to ensure that we understand the algorithm well enough to write it in pseudocode. We can now proceed to the formalities.

DESCRIPTION: Take a list of five positive numbers and put it in order, with the largest first and the smallest last.

INPUT DATA: Five numbers larger than zero

OUTPUT DATA: The same five numbers ordered from largest to smallest

PROCEDURE:

1. Initialize the program (two arrays).
2. Load first array with five numbers larger than 0.
3. Search the first array for the largest value it contains.
4. Load this value into the first open position of the second array (the act of loading a value will close this position).

5.   Replace this value in the old array by 0.
6.   Increment a counter that also serves as the pointer to the second array.
7.   If the value of this pointer is 5 or smaller, go back to step 2; otherwise, continue to step 8.
8.   Print out all five numbers of the new array, starting with the first array element.
9.   End the program.

Note that as the loops become more complicated, it gets harder to describe what is happening in a concise form using ordinary English. It should also be observed that flowchart presentation also becomes complicated. At this stage, conversion to pseudocode represents a true refinement, but because the code is not as syntax-limited as a language that must be run on a machine, it is easier to concentrate on structure.

The programs are beginning to become complex. In programming with conventional computer languages, it is normal to include comment lines arranged in such a way that the translation system will ignore them. The line is begun with a particular reserved word or letter to indicate that it is a comment. A second way of handling this is to include a comment embedded in a specific line. Since our standard protocol includes a description, titling and description is not necessary, but embedded comments may help simplify analysis of looping structures. These comments will be enclosed in ⟨ ⟩ written only in bold lowercase letters to differentiate them from the actual code structure. Their only purpose is to help the person reading the program. Keep comments brief when you use them.

Assume that the five numbers to be loaded are 5.38, 2, 8.763, 6.7, and 3.95.

```
1.     DECLARE BOX (5)
2.     DECLARE FRAME (5)
3.     MARK := 0                    ⟨end initiation module⟩
4.     K := 1                       ⟨feeder for dowhile⟩
5.     DOWHILE K <= 5               ⟨begin loading module⟩
5.1.      Read a number, assign value to BOX (K)
5.2.      K := K + 1
5.3.   ENDDO                        ⟨end loading module⟩
6.     KOUNT := 1                   ⟨feeder for dowhile⟩
7.     DOWHILE KOUNT <= 5           ⟨begin sort module⟩
7.1.      LARGST := 1
```

```
7.2.          ZIP := 1
7.3.          DOWHILE ZIP <= 5              ⟨begin select – max⟩
7.3.1.            IF BOX (LARGST) < BOX (ZIP)
7.3.1.1.            THEN
7.3.1.2.                LARGST := ZIP
7.3.1.3.            ENDIF
7.3.2.            ZIP := ZIP + 1
7.3.3.          ENDDO                        ⟨end select – max⟩
7.4.          FRAME (KOUNT) := BOX (LARGST)⟨move max⟩
7.5.          BOX (LARGST) := MARK     ⟨zero replaces max⟩
7.6.          KOUNT := KOUNT + 1
7.7.  ENDDO                                  ⟨end sort module⟩
8.    I := 1
9.    DOWHILE I <= 5                         ⟨begin print module⟩
9.1.      Print FRAME (I)
9.2.      I := I + 1
9.3.  ENDDO
10.   END                                    ⟨end print module⟩
```

To see how the separation occurs, we will show the two arrays, BOX ( ) and FRAME ( ), in parallel as the sort proceeds. They will be examined starting just after BOX ( ) is loaded.

Pass	Pointer	1	2	3	4	5
0	BOX ( )	5.38	2	8.763	6.7	3.95
	FRAME ( )	0	0	0	0	0
1	BOX ( )	5.38	2	0	6.7	3.95
	FRAME ( )	8.763	0	0	0	0
2	BOX ( )	5.38	2	0	0	3.95
	FRAME ( )	8.763	6.7	0	0	0
3	BOX ( )	0	2	0	0	3.95
	FRAME ( )	8.763	6.7	5.38	0	0
4	BOX ( )	0	2	0	0	0
	FRAME ( )	8.763	6.7	5.38	3.95	0
5	BOX ( )	0	0	0	0	0
	FRAME ( )	8.763	6.7	5.38	3.95	2

The sorting program we have just examined is relatively slow and uses a lot of memory because it requires two storage spaces for each piece of data treated. However, it is a good learning tool and useful in simple sorting situations where time and memory size are not critical.

In this chapter we have introduced the concept of the array. These arrays have had a single pointer or subscript and may be thought of as a special kind of list in which each member has an index number or a pointer. This pointer is special in that it may interact directly with programming and control statements. These single pointer arrays are called one-dimensional arrays. An algorithm that uses arrays and nested control structures for the selection of the largest element in a list has been studied. This largest-element selection algorithm has been used as the basis for development of a rather primitive sorting algorithm.

In the next chapter we will extend the idea of an array to two pointers and provide a special statement that will simplify pointer manipulation and loop design.

PROBLEMS

Manipulating one-dimensional arrays and designing clever ways to make use of them in solving problems is a major part of computer programming. Unfortunately, this usually is completely new to the student, since operations involving manipulation of subscripts or pointers come relatively late in mathematics.

The problems in this section present a range of types, extending from the conventional ones that keep cropping up to several applications that may stimulate the imagination without drowning you in detail. Although Problems 10.5, 10.6, 10.9 and 10.10 are considered challenge problems, I hope you will at least give them limited consideration even if you are a bit pressed for time. At this stage, all the experience you can get at manipulating arrays is worth a little extra effort. The even-numbered problems are answered at the end of the book.

*   *   *

10.1   Devise a pseudocode program that describes a routine that selects the smallest element of an array. Assume you will load the array by reading 20 cards.

10.2   In the sort used as a demonstration program in this chapter, after an array element was selected for transfer to the ordered array, its position in the original array was taken by a value that the selection process could not 'see'. Since the demonstration example restricted itself to numbers larger than 0 (zero), the number 0 was used as this invisible value.

A more generalized method for producing an invisible element is usually required, since the values to be ordered may be expected to include positive numbers, negative numbers, and zero. If we are using a largest-number strategy to put the list in order, then a number smaller than any number in ths list will serve as a place-filler that is invisible to the selection routine. The obvious way to produce such a number for a particular list is to determine the smallest number in the list and then subtract some constant such as 10.

Using a modification of this design technology, devise a pseudocode program to produce an 'invisible element' for use in a two-array sort using a smallest-number strategy to put the list in order. Use a twenty-element array which is filled from an appropriate card deck.

10.3 Using a smallest-number selection strategy and an appropriate means of selecting an invisible filler, devise a two-array pseudocode program that will read a 20-card deck with cards containing any number (positive, negative or zero). Sort these into an order with the smallest number on top and print out the list as it appeared before ordering and after sorting.

10.4 You have a deck of 40 cards containing one number per card. This deck is read into a 40-element array called JAKE. The values in JAKE should then be transferred to a second 40-element array called GEORGE. However, the order of the values as seen in GEORGE must be the reverse of the elements in JAKE. That is, the contents of the first element of JAKE must be entered into the last element in GEORGE; the contents of the next element in JAKE must go into the second-to-last element in GEORGE; and so on.

Construct a pseudocode program including all declarations, which loads the 40 cards into JAKE, accomplishes the proper transfer to GEORGE, prints out the contents of the two arrays and signs off with the message 'Inversion Complete'.

*10.5 You have an array 20 elements long. Assume it is already loaded with the values assigned as follows. The first eight elements each have a value of 1. The remaining elements have values of 0 (zero). The name of the array is HOUSE. Each element may be thought of as a room with no more than two doors. If an element has a value of 0 (zero), the associated room might be thought of as having only one door. On the other hand, if an array element has a value of 1, the associated room could be thought of as having two doors.

A little analysis suggests that this system is a pretty good model of the simplified version of the example in Chapter 1 in which we tried to turn out all the lights in a house.

We enter this house represented in the elements of the array HOUSE, by reading the value of the first element of the array. Since the value is 1, we know there are two doors. Since we came in through one door, we know there is another one, so we can go on to the next room. If we had found a 0 (zero), we would have known that there was only one door, which was the way we came in. We could turn out the light in this room, but we could go no further.

The program you design should read an element of the array starting with the first element. If the value is 1, then turn out the lights by setting the value of the element to 5, print the message 'Lights out in room number', and then print the pointer number of the array element the value of which was just changed to 5. Since the value of the element representing the room was 1, the program should evaluate the next element or room. If the value of the room had been a zero, no further advance into another room would have been possible, since the room under investigation only had one door. However, the lights can be turned off, When dealing with an element presenting a room with only one door, after turning out the lights the program should 'leave' the house by 'going back' through the rooms that have been examined and converting the contents from 5 to −5. It should announce reaching each room and specifically announce exiting the house to the 'outside'.

The actions of the program should be controlled by the room contents, not by the pointer number of the elements, and should work for any number of two-door rooms, which can be represented by a one-dimensional array.

*10.6   Each of two decks of cards (called deck A and deck B) contains 50 cards. Each card contains a number. No end-of-data card is necessary, because we know how many cards are in each deck. The numbers on the cards are members of a small set of numbers. For example, the members of the set might be 3, 22, 8, 15 and 4. The actual values are immaterial. Any individual number may appear more than once in either or both of the decks, but there is no requirement that a particular number appear at all.

Your problem is to compare the two decks, determine those cases where the same number occupies the same location in each deck and then present this information in a clear way. Obviously, you will load each deck into a separate array. Comparison will determine if elements of the same position in each array have the same content. When this is the case, appropriate action will be taken.

One way to organize the information output is to have a third 50-element array that starts out entirely filled with zeroes. Each time comparison of the two test arrays indicates identity between their elements for a particular pointer value, the corresponding element of the third array is altered to serve as a marker. When the entire comparison is complete, the third array is printed out in order, giving a visual display of the pattern of duplication. The same effect could be achieved by printing a symbol when each comparison is complete. The symbol would indicate whether the test revealed identity or lack of identity.

Your task is to devise a pseudocode program that will load the test arrays, run the comparisons and print out a display of the comparison results.

10.7   Design a pseudocode program to check passwords according to the following specifications. The program asks for the account number of the individual. The program then searches an array that contains all the account numbers registered in the system. If the account number is not found, the client is notified that he is not registered in the system. If the account number is found, the client is asked for his pass number. The array holding the pass numbers is not totally searched. The pass number must be in the position of the pass number array that exactly corresponds to the position of the associated account number in the account number array. If the pass number is found to be correct, the client is welcomed to the system. If the pass number is not correct, an error message is printed.

10.8   You have a single array. You are to construct an interchange program written in pseudocode in which the first element becomes last and the last element becomes first. The reversal is a complete one. For example, the second element becomes the second-to-last element, and the second-to-last element becomes the second element. Assume a 51-element array that has already been loaded. Design the control loops on the basis of the total number of elements in the array instead of doing arithmetic in your head outside of the program. You should declare and load the array as a part of the program.

Warning: Check the operation of your program in a short 5-element array to see that it really works. In an odd-numbered array, there is one position that will be the same before and after reversal. Be careful that you do not interchange any elements twice, leaving them in their original positions.

*10.9   The grades of a given class are held in arrays. One array holds the identity numbers of the students. Three arrays hold the grades of each of the three exams given in the course. A fifth array will hold each student's final average in the course when it is calculated. Devise a pseudocode program that will average the three examination grades for each student and place the average in the appropriate element of the array holding final averages. When all the grades have been averaged, it should determine the class average by averaging all of the individual average grades. It should search the individual final averages and print out the identity number and final grade of all persons having an average higher than 95. These should be identified as honors students. It should then print out the class average with an appropriate identification.

You may assume that all arrays have been declared and that the raw grades data has already been loaded into the arrays holding the examination scores.

*10.10   The two-array insertion sort is good as simple sorts go, but it takes up a lot of space because it uses two arrays. It can be modified to use only one array. This modification is important, since it serves as the basis for much more sophisticated sort designs that are beyond the scope of this text, but which are quite important in computing.

In providing the program specifications a largest-element selection routine identical to the one used in this chapter will be assumed; however, the program could just as easily be written using a smallest-element selection routine. To conduct this sort, the array is searched for the largest element. When it is found it is interchanged with the first element of the array. This new arrangement contains all of the values present in the original arrangement, has no additional values, and contains no invisible markers.

This new arrangement is again searched for the largest element. However, we already have the absolutely largest element in the top position. We thus begin our new search for a largest element with the second position of the array. The first position is left alone. Again with the new arrangement, but starting with the second position, we select the largest number. When it is found it is interchanged with the first element of this new, limited array. Of course, this element is the second element of the overall array. Thus, the second largest element of the total array has been found and installed in the second position of the array.

We now have another, newer arrangement in which the top position is the largest element, the second position is the second largest element, and beginning with the third element, there is no special arrangement. Considering the array as a whole, no elements have been lost and none have been added. This process can be continued until the entire array has been sorted. Of course, the smallest element will be forced into the last position in the array.

Design a pseudocode program using this method, which loads the values on 5 cards into a 5-element array and sorts them into an arrangement beginning with the largest value in the first element and the smallest value in the last element. At the end, it should print a message stating that the sort is complete and print out the array in its sorted arrangement.

Using five real values, produce diagrams showing the arrangement of elements in the array before sorting is started and at the end of each pass of the sort. You should produce the diagram by running the values through the pseudocode program rather than just drawing the arrangements based on theoretical prediction.

CHAPTER ELEVEN

The DOFOR *Control Structure and Two-Dimensional Arrays*

WHEN WE use DOWHILE as a counting loop, it needs two particular statements. The first sets the value of the variable used in controlling the loop. The second increments that variable just before the ENDDO is reached. It is quite common for a loop to provide a fixed number of repetitions, as shown in the DOWHILE applications in the last chapter. By 'fixed number of repetitions' we mean that the number of repeats is determined by conditions that are not modified by the program steps that are being repeated. An example of this is repeating an input process a sufficient number of times to load all the elements of a linear array.

Most computer languages provide a control structure specifically designed to do this. Although this device is not part of the Bohm-Jacopini set, it is usually included in pseudocode because of its convenience. This special structure is designed so that the statement setting the initial value of the loop-control variable and the statement that increments the loop-control variable are both built into the statement syntax. Such an arrangement eliminates statements and makes certain types of loop structure much easier to write. It is of particular importance in manipulating arrays.

This is usually spoken of as a DOFOR, although in some variations of pseudocode it has other names. The first line of DOFOR sets the initial value of the loop variable, defines the limiting value, and may also define the incrementing interval if this is not unity. In the following sample DOFOR line, a loop variable named ZEBRA begins at 1 and goes to 25. Since no value for the incrementing step is included, it is assumed to be 1.

$$\text{DOFOR ZEBRA} := 1 \text{ TO } 25$$

A second example shows a DOFOR in which the looping variable SPOTS starts at 1 and advances by an increment of 3 until it reaches 25.

$$\text{DOFOR SPOTS} := 1 \text{ to } 25 \text{ STEP } 3$$

The values SPOTS takes on will be 1, 4, 7, 10, 13, 16, 19, 22, and 25. The usual STEP will be 1, although even negative values may be used, if the initial value for the loop variable is larger than the final value. Decimal fractions may also be used, but would not be appropriate in cases where an array will use the loop variable as a pointer. If a special step option is used, it is important to determine exactly what will happen. If the looping variable will not exactly equal the final limit, that final limit should be considered as a value that the looping variable cannot exceed.

In order to see the DOFOR in operation, we will replace the DOWHILE counting structures of the sorting program from Chapter 10 with DOFOR structures.

DESCRIPTION: Take a list of five numbers that are all positive and put it in order, with the largest first and the smallest last.
INPUT DATA: Five numbers larger than zero
OUTPUT DATA: The same five numbers ordered from largest to smallest
PROCEDURE:

1.	DECLARE BOX (5)	
2.	DECLARE FRAME (5)	
3.	MARK := 0	⟨**end initiation module**⟩
4.	DOFOR K := 1 TO 5	⟨**begin loading module**⟩
4.1.	Read a number, assign value to BOX (K)	
4.2.	ENDDO	⟨**end loading module**⟩
5.	DOFOR KOUNT := 1 TO 5	⟨**begin sort module**⟩
5.1.	LARGST := 1	
5.2.	DOFOR ZIP := 1 TO 5	⟨**begin select-max**⟩
5.2.1.	IF BOX (LARGST) < BOX (ZIP)	
5.2.1.1.	THEN	
5.2.1.2.	LARGST := ZIP	
5.2.1.3.	ENDIF	
5.2.2.	ENDDO	⟨**end select-max**⟩
5.3.	FRAME (KOUNT) := BOX (LARGST) ⟨**move max**⟩	

5.4.	BOX (LARGST) := MARK	⟨**zero replaces max**⟩
5.5.	ENDDO	⟨**end sort module**⟩
6.	DOFOR I := 1 TO 5	⟨**begin print module**⟩
6.1.	Print FRAME (I)	
6.2.	ENDDO	⟨**end print module**⟩
7.	END	

The utility of the DOFOR structure is obvious. This version of the sort program is more concise, more compact, and the modules stand out more clearly.

The simple one-dimensional array we have already examined gets its inspiration from the numbered elements of a list. It could, of course, be a grocery list, but it is still a list. The second type of array we will consider is derived from a table of values or information. In fact, this type of array is called a 'table' in the language COBOL.

An important use of a table is to look up information. The information might be located in an element identified as being at the intersection of a particular row and a particular column. This is analagous to saying that a certain house is at the intersection of Marvin Avenue and East 16th Street on a city map.

If we had a table in which values of some sort were entered, it would be perfectly normal to locate a particular entry by giving the row of the table and the column where it would be found. To locate the entry from this information, we would move down until we had counted off the required number of rows and then count inward until we had reached the proper column as given by the second number. Such a simple procedure would give us the proper entry. A particular entry in such a table could be designated by a variable of the form TABLE (3,5), which would refer to the entry found in the third row at the fifth column. A simple numerical table is shown in Figure 11.1, as is the search for the entry in the third row and the fifth column.

When studying arrays, the usual place to start is with programs that will load an array. One logical way to load a two-

COLUMN	1	2	3	4	5	6
ROW						
1	22	71	9	58	37	37
2	69	32	75	29	6	18
3	3	18	98	83	(15)	62
4	16	55	12	32	77	29

Fig. 11.1   Searching a two-dimensional array

dimensional array is to consider it as a table written on a piece of paper. We could imagine having a list of numbers that would be written into the table one at a time. The first number would be entered in the top left box, and each successive number would be entered in the next place in the top row until we ran out of spaces in the top row. Then we would start on the second row and continue until the table was filled.

Of course, the table might be filled by starting at the upper left-hand corner and going down one column until the end was reached and then starting at the top of the next column. There are a number of other patterns that could be developed. We will fill a two-dimensional array by rows and then proceed to do the same thing by columns. The table or two-dimensional array will be the same in both cases. This will be an array with 5 rows and 3 columns. Just as with one-dimensional arrays, the array must be declared. The set of numbers to put in is: 14, 3.8, −0.7, 138, 77.3, 13.1, −12.5, 0.05, 19.46, −44, −107, 8, −0.36, 71, and 63. For a start, we will load the array row by row. Note that the pointer variable to be used will be called ROW in the case of pointing to rows, COLUMN in the case of pointing to columns. As is always the case, these are just variables like any other variable and may have any legal variable name.

DESCRIPTION: This program creates a two-dimensional array with 5 rows and 3 columns. It then loads it with 15 numbers (presumably on cards in a card reader), and provides a message to indicate that loading is complete. Each row is loaded in turn from left to right, the way in which English is read.

INPUT DATA: A set of 15 numbers in order as follows: 14, 3.8, −0.7, 138, 77.3, 13.1, −12.5, 0.05, 19.46, −44, −107, 8, −0.36, 71, 63.

OUTPUT DATA: The product of this program is the completely filled array, but it will not be printed out. Only a message will appear, indicating that loading is complete.

PROCEDURE:

1.   DECLARE FRAME (5, 3)
2.   DOFOR ROW := 1 TO 5
2.1.   DOFOR COLUMN := 1 TO 3
2.1.1.   Read value assign to FRAME
                (ROW, COLUMN)
2.1.2.   ENDDO
2.2.   ENDDO

3.   Print 'The array is loaded'
4.   END

This is a much shorter program than seems possible for creating an array and loading it with 15 numbers. Note that although a DOWHILE loop could be used instead of the DOFOR, the absence of the initiation steps and the incrementing steps that is inherent in the DOFOR structure makes the structuring much less cluttered.

The system consists of two nested counting loops. After declaration of the two-dimensional array, control enters the outermost loop (the 2 structure). Here, the value of ROW is set to 1. Control is then passed to the inside loop (the 2.1 structure). The value of COLUMN is then set to 1, which designates an array element FRAME (1,1), which is the one in the upper left-hand corner of the array. A value of 14 is read and assigned to this array element. Control now reaches the ENDDO at 2.1.2. This is the ENDDO of the 2.1 DOFOR structure, which controls column selection. The pointer variable COLUMN is incremented by 1, taking on the value 2, and the content of this loop, beginning at 2.1, is repeated. Note that the value of ROW has not been changed because we have not gotten to the ENDDO at 2.2. Thus we read the next value (3.8) and assign it to FRAME (1,2), which is the second element of the first row of the array.

Once again, we do not escape from the inner loop, but merely increment the pointer COLUMN to a value of 3 and pass through the read step again. This time, the value −0.7 that the read step collects from its external source is assigned to FRAME (1,3). Examination of the initial line of the inside DOFOR loop indicates that the upper limit of 3 has been reached. This means that control will be transferred out of the inner loop at the ENDDO of the inner loop (2.1.2). It will then immediately reach the ENDDO (2.2) marking the end of the other loop. This will cause the pointer variable ROW to be incremented, bringing its value to 2 and again starting processing of the contents of the outer loop, which will immediately bring control to the first step of the inner loop (2.1). Here, the pointer COLUMN will be reset to 1 and the element of the array selected for read and assignment will be FRAME (2,1). Once again, the inner loop will be repeated while FRAME (2,2) and FRAME (2,3) are processed by the read and assign statement. When the upper allowable limit of ROW (which is 3) has been reached, control will again transfer out of the inner loop, the value of COLUMN will be incremented to 3 and the inner loop will take over to do read and assign for FRAME (3,1), FRAME (3,2) and FRAME (3,3).

The cycle of process and control transfer will continue until COLUMN takes on a value of 3 after ROW has taken a value of 5. This will cause FRAME (3,5) to be processed and control will exit the inner loop at its ENDDO and, finally, exit the outer loop at the ENDDO of the outer loop, which will cause accessing of the print statement (3). This in turn will print out the message announcing that the array has been filled and then close things out with the END statement (4).

Figure 11.2a shows the array FRAME (), with each element labeled by row and column. Figure 11.2b shows the array FRAME (), with each element loaded as it would be, when using the previous program to load the elements of each row completely from left to right before shifting to the next row.

(1,1)	(1,2)	(1,3)
(2,1)	(2,2)	(2,3)
(3,1)	(3,2)	(3,3)
(4,1)	(4,2)	(4,3)
(5,1)	(5,2)	(5,3)

Fig. 11.2a   Element labels for the array FRAME ( )

14	3.8	−0.7
138	77.3	13.1
−12.5	0.05	19.46
−44	−107	8
−0.36	71	63

Fig. 11.2b   The array FRAME ( ) loaded by rows

A contrast to this program, which loads each row of an array before going to the next, would be a program that would load each column of the array from the top down, starting with the left-hand column. When a column is completed it would shift to the top of the next column and start again. To see how this would work, and to gain somewhat more depth of understanding in the processing of arrays, we will do the column-by-column loading operation with the same data set on the same array.

DESCRIPTION: This program creates a two-dimensional array with 5 rows and 3 columns. It then loads it with 15 numbers (presumably on cards in a card reader), and provides a message to indicate that loading is complete. Each column is loaded in turn from top to bottom.

INPUT DATA: A set of fifteen numbers in order as follows: 14, 3.8, −0.7, 138, 77.3, 13.1, −12.5, 0.05, 19.46, −44, −107, 8, −0.36, 71, 63

OUTPUT DATA: The product of this program is the completely filled array, but it will not be printed out. Only a message will appear, indicating that loading is complete.

PROCEDURE:

1.	DECLARE FRAME (5,3)
2.	DOFOR COLUMN := 1 TO 3
2.1.	DOFOR ROW := 1 TO 5
2.1.1.	Read value assign to FRAME (ROW, COLUMN)
2.1.2.	ENDDO
2.2.	ENDDO
3.	Print 'The array is loaded'
4.	END

The loaded array is shown in Figure 11.3. To see how this system operates, a partial trace diagram is included below.

14	13.1	−107
3.8	−12.5	8
−0.7	0.05	−0.36
138	19.46	71
77.3	−44	63

Fig. 11.3   The array FRAME ( ) loaded by columns

Step	Statement	Pointer value ROW	COLUMN	Array element filled	Contents
1	1.	0	0	−	−
2	2.	0	1	−	−
3	2.1.	1	1	−	−
4	2.1.1.	1	1	FRAME (1,1)	14
5	2.1.2.	1	1	−	−
6	2.1.	2	1	−	−
7	2.1.1.	2	1	FRAME (2,1)	3.8
8	2.1.2.	2	1	−	−
9	2.1.	3	1	−	−
10	2.1.1.	3	1	FRAME (3,1)	−0.7

11	2.1.2.	3	1	–	–
12	2.1.	4	1	–	–
13	2.1.1.	4	1	FRAME (4,1)	138
14	2.1.2.	4	1	–	–
15	2.1.	5	1	–	–
16	2.1.1.	5	1	FRAME (5,1)	77.3
17	2.1.2.	5	1	–	–
18	2.2.	5	1	–	–
19	2.	5	2	–	–
20	2.1.	1	2	–	–
21	2.1.1.	1	2	FRAME (1,2)	13.1
22	2.1.2.	1	2	–	–
23	2.1.	2	2	–	–

Clearly, two-dimensional arrays can be used with nonnumerical or alphanumeric data. Such structures form the basis for many data-base systems, although the array nature of the data records or files is not always obvious. The calling and searching routines are usually arranged to give the effect of a special language, which is tailored for simplified interaction between the data base and the operator.

The data in the data base are usually held on some external storage device such as cards, magnetic tape or magnetic disk. They are loaded into an array inside the program, which is used to manipulate them when needed. Of course, with extremely large files only a portion of the file is loaded at a time, or the sorting program may work through an index system that is also contained in array form. This data base is going to be used for a simple search routine. It will be a sequential search in which all the rows are examined. Each row corresponds to qualification data on a particular individual. The order of rows, one above another, is not in any way related to the contents. With files containing more than 100 or so individual records (rows, in this case) some ordering routine should be used to make searching more efficient.

As a background for our data base, we will imagine a secretarial employment agency that specializes in replacements for persons on leave or supplies workers to augment the regular work force at times of high activity. The pertinent data for these people will be contained in a file that may be automatically loaded into an array when a search is necessary. To allow us to concentrate on the search process, all data will be held in numerical form. To safeguard the privacy of the members of the employment pool, the file listing the professional qualities will use a registration number instead of a name. The registration number is also part of a second file that lists name, address, telephone number and other information, which in combination with professional qualifications might compromise the privacy of pool members. This technique is actually used in business. A search for a combination of requirements will provide a list of registration numbers that would be used to print out the names of suitable applicants. We will not concern ourselves with the name and address file, which to safeguard security will remain imaginary.

The array of information will consist of one row for each file member. Each column within the array with contain the indicator for a separate property. Numerical entries will be used for all information. 'Yes' will be coded '1', 'no' will be coded '0', 'female' will be coded '1' and 'male' will be coded '0'. The row numbers and corresponding properties are as follows:

Column number	Property
1	Registration number
2	Year of birth
3	Sex
4	Married
5	Typing
6	Word processor experience
7	Good telephone voice
8	Particularly attractive
9	Will work evenings
10	Public relations experience
11	Bookkeeping experience
12	General office work
13	Supervisory experience

A set of data for 11 persons follows:

4783	1925	1	0	1	1	1	0	0	0	1	1	0
52963	1953	0	0	1	1	1	0	0	1	0	1	1
2834	1935	1	1	1	1	0	0	1	1	0	1	1
37823	1962	0	0	1	1	1	1	1	0	0	1	0
2974	1931	0	1	0	0	1	1	0	1	1	1	1
1049	1933	1	0	0	0	1	1	1	1	0	1	1
38742	1945	1	1	1	0	0	0	0	1	1	1	0
39286	1955	0	1	1	1	1	1	0	0	1	1	1
46287	1965	1	0	0	0	1	1	1	1	0	1	0

28435	1958	0	1	1	1	1	0	1	0	1	1	1
2759	1938	0	0	1	0	0	0	1	0	1	1	0
0000	1066	0	0	0	0	0	0	0	0	0	0	0

The twelfth line in this data base is the 'trailer' line, which indicates an end of file. Here, certain data have been included that cannot be mistaken. Since this is a numerical file, the registration number is zero and, to avoid mistakes, the birth year is given as 1066, which is the year of William the Conqueror's critical battle in England. Other numbers could have been used, like 9999, but the important thing is that it is a birth year that cannot possibly be introduced by accident in association with a real member of the employee pool. The end of the file is now marked, and records may be introduced or subtracted without altering the way in which a search is made, since the searching facility can recognize the end of the file. Of course, in a more general data file the end of file would be indicated by a line or data element that specifically states 'End of File'. The phrase 'End of File' is usually shortened to EOF.

In the following program we will assume that a search is to be made for single people who are female, over 40 years of age, and have bookkeeping and word-processing experience. The program we produce will be specifically designed for this particular search. In the not-too-distant past it was actually necessary to write a similar program to search a set of data. Of course, this was not too difficult, because models of virtually all programs were available. Eventually programs were developed that operated like a menu. These greeted the user politely, gave him or her a choice of procedures, asked what properties the operator wished to search for, conducted the search based on the answers provided and wrote out the results. All modern data-base systems have these automatic searching procedures, which provide information and statistics, and even write reports.

We have included an array in our load-and-search program that is larger than the file we will load. This is just to suggest some of the options that could be developed for more complex file structures.

DESCRIPTION: This program loads a file held on some form of card file or on a disk file, which operates roughly like a card file. It then searches the file for a particular set of descriptors and prints out a list of registration numbers representing file members who fit the description.

INPUT DATA: A set of records from secondary storage. Year of birth before 1945, sex descriptor with value 1, word-processor descriptor with value 1, bookkeeping descriptor with value 1.

OUTPUT DATA: A list of registration numbers of persons with the desired characteristics

PROCEDURE:

1. Load the external file into a matching array.
2. Search the matching array for rows that contain all of the desired characteristics.
3. When a match is found, print out the registration number found in the particular row.
4. At completion of search, finish the program.

The rough outline of the procedure section may now be expanded.

PROCEDURE:

1.	DECLARE FRAME (20, 13)	
2.	DOFOR ROW := 1 TO 20	⟨**begin loading array**⟩
2.1.	DOFOR COLUMN := 1 TO 13	
2.1.1.	Read value assign to FRAME (ROW, COLUMN)	
2.2.	ENDDO	
2.2.	IF FRAME (ROW, 2) = 1066	⟨**begin shortstop**⟩
2.2.1.	THEN	
2.2.2.	ROW = 20	
2.2.3.	ENDIF	⟨**end shortstop**⟩
2.3.	ENDDO	⟨**finish loading array**⟩
3.	DOFOR ROW := 1 TO 20	⟨**begin searching array**⟩
3.1.	IF ((FRAME (ROW, 2) < 1945) AND (FRAME (ROW, 3) = 1) AND (FRAME (ROW, 6) = 1) AND (FRAME (ROW, 11) = 1))	
3.1.1.	THEN	
3.1.2.	Print FRAME (ROW, 1)	
3.1.3.	ENDIF	
3.2.	IF FRAME (ROW, 2) = 1066	⟨**begin shortstop**⟩
3.2.1.	THEN	
3.2.2.	ROW = 20	
3.2.3.	ENDIF	⟨**end shortstop**⟩
3.3.	ENDDO	⟨**finish searching array**⟩
4.	END	

There are a number of features that are worth comment. The 2 block is used to load the contents of the external file into the array FRAME () in order. This presents no problem. However, the external file may be shorter than the array declared for it in the loading module. This will often be the case because we may be dealing with the last section of a file that is loaded in sections, or we may be using a search program that is designed to handle any of a number of different files. If the file were not completely loaded, we would miss some of the entries. Thus, we are often stuck with an array that is larger than the file we load into it. It is useful to include the trailer line that marks the end of file. For this reason a device is included that will detect this line after it has been loaded and stop further loading. This is the 'shortstop' device.

This device could simply be a GOTO statement that would cause control to leave the loading loop of 2, but if this were done, there would be two ways out of the loading module. This is a poor way to design a program.

In a simple program like this, the result is messy, but remains understandable. In a more complex program the result is chaos. To avoid this incipient spaghetti programming, we use a shortstop that merely sets the loop control variable ROW to its upper limit 20 and thus causes control to exit the DOFOR structure at the next ENDDO.

The DOFOR structures used to control loading (2) and the actual search (3) are identical. There is no logical reason why the load and search procedures could not be combined. The procedure section of the altered program follows:

PROCEDURE:

1.	DECLARE FRAME (20, 13)	
2.	DOFOR ROW := 1 TO 20	⟨**start load-search**⟩
2.1.	DOFOR COL := 1 TO 13	
2.1.1.	Read value assign to FRAME (ROW, COL)	
2.1.2.	ENDDO	
2.2.	IF (FRAME (Row, 2) < 1945) AND (FRAME (ROW, 3) = 1) AND (FRAME (ROW, 6) = 1) AND (FRAME (ROW, 11) = 1)	
2.2.1.	THEN	
2.2.2.	Print FRAME (ROW, 1)	
2.2.3.	ENDIF	
2.3.	IF FRAME (ROW, 2) = 1066	⟨**start shortstop**⟩
2.3.1.	THEN	

```
2.3.2.              ROW := 20
2.3.3.    ENDIF                          ⟨ end shortstop ⟩
2.4.   ENDDO                             ⟨ end load-search ⟩
3.     END
```

This program is six lines shorter than the version that repeats the loop twice. Although it is a bit trickier to write (and, later, to read), the complexity induced by the compactness is probably justified by the 20% reduction in size and the retention of proper structuring.

In these crude approximations of data-base processing, it should be noted that since the array pointers will be used to control the search, the file from external storage must be loaded into an array before it can be searched. Continuing to load an external file after the file has ended can cause error notices in many working languages and systems, and leaves a kind of uncertainty about the meaning of subsequent operations in pseudocode. For this reason the end-of-file trailer has been detected by a system that operates after the end-of-file marker is actually loaded into the array. In this way it could be used to stop processing in the array as required by the amount of data read in.

Before leaving our concentrated consideration of two-dimensional arrays, a type of processing should be considered that is common in the real world (and is used a great deal as an example in textbooks).

In schools, grade records must be recorded and processed. A series of exam grades must be averaged in each course for each student. Grades are returned to the main office as lists of numbers organized in groups according to the individual courses. They must be averaged, reassembled and combined to provide grade reports for all the courses that an individual student has taken. Finally, lists combined in various forms must be searched to determine who has honors-level grades and who must be warned for low grades, and to provide information about many other administrative and personal problems. These requirements are within the experience of students. It really invites creative programming.

We will consider a simple program that calculates grade averages. The same technology could be used in connection with measurement apparatus to average the results of groups of physical measurements and provide statistical information regarding their reliability.

The program in question uses two two-dimensional arrays. One array holds the first name, last name and student registration number of the student in a particular class. The second contains the student registration number and the grade for each of the three examinations in the course. The rows of the arrays are organized in exactly the same order. Thus, the name of the person in the names array will correspond to his or her grades in the grades array, and the same row pointer may be used to access names in one array and grades in the other.

The assumption that the arrays have already been filled will be included in the input specification. The registration number, both in the list of names and in the list of grades, is used in a check routine to see that the grades and the associated names have not been mixed up. In the event that a mismatch of name and grades occurs, the grades for this person are not printed and a variable within the program is set. At the end of the program this variable is checked. If it has been set to the value 1, an error message regarding matching entries is produced.

An internal variable that triggers special behavior at a later time in the program is called a 'flag'. To emphasize this, we will call the variable FLAG.

DESCRIPTION: This program reads an array, averages three numerical values in the array and returns this average to a particular column of the array. It then writes out the name of the person corresponding to the name and checks the registration number from the names file against the registration number from the grades file. If the numbers check, it prints the corresponding average beside the name. In the event of a mismatch between the registration numbers in the two files, no average is printed next to the name and an error message is printed at the end of the list of averages. If everything checks, a notification of correct match is printed out at the end of processing.

INPUT DATA: Two arrays, one containing student names and registration number (last, first, registration number), the second containing the registration number, the grades for three examinations and a column containing zeroes that will be replaced by the final average (registration number, exam grade, exam grade, exam grade, 0000). The arrays will be assumed to have been loaded by a loading routine before the grade evaluation routine. The array containing persons' names will be called NAMES. The array containing grades will be called GRADES. They will each have 35 rows and will have already been dimensioned as NAMES (35, 3) and GRADES (35, 5).

OUTPUT DATA: A course average inserted into the grades card (file), a printed list of people with their final averages, written notification if there has been a mismatch between registration numbers in the grade file and registration numbers in the name files.

PROCEDURE:

1. Initialize necessary variables and set FLAG to zero.
2. Do the average preparation, comparison and output for 35 pairs of values.
3. Print out control message and end program.

We may expand this to give the detailed pseudocode program:

PROCEDURE:

1.   FLAG := 0
2.   DOFOR ROW := 1 TO 35   ⟨**start evaluation loop**⟩
2.1.   GRADES (ROW, 5) :=((GRADES (ROW, 2) + GRADES (ROW, 3) + GRADES (ROW, 4))/3
2.2.   IF NAMES (ROW, 3) = GRADES (ROW, 1)
2.2.1.   THEN
2.2.2.   Print NAMES (ROW, 1), NAMES (ROW, 2) GRADES (ROW, 5)
2.2.3.   ELSE
2.2.4.   FLAG := 1   ⟨**set flag**⟩
2.2.5.   Print NAMES (ROW, 1), NAMES (ROW, 2)
2.2.6.   ENDIF
2.3.   ENDDO   ⟨**end evaluation loop**⟩
3.   IF FLAG = 1
3.1.   THEN
3.2.   Print 'NAME-REGISTRATION MISMATCH'
3.3.   ELSE
3.4.   Print 'CORRECT NAME CHECK'
3.5.   ENDIF
4.   END

The flag, as used in this program, is set once, indicating one error. It then stays set. Flags may be programmed to work according to other patterns. Another more complicated check procedure would be to use markers for the end of the class list of names and the list of grades. Then notification could be made to appear for cases in which the name list for the class did not have the same number of entries as the grades list for the class.

In this chapter we have worked with counting loops using a DOFOR structure. These were applied to two-dimensional arrays. Similar technology can be applied to arrays with three or more pointers. Three-dimensional space may be represented by an array with three pointers corresponding to length, width and height, or the x, y, and z coordinates. Appropriate manipulation of these arrays corresponds to the solution of problems in three-dimensional movement and perspective, but such studies are beyond the scope of a beginning text.

Even if we cannot imagine 'space' with more than three dimensions, we can describe events in such a space using arrays with one pointer or subscript corresponding to each dimension. Thus, the ability to manipulate arrays and the DOFOR statement that facilitates this are extremely important in modern computational activities.

In these programs DOWHILE might have been easier to use in cases where we did not know how many items were available. It was not used because DOWHILE needs an initial read operation to prime it. The read operations in these programs involve a loop that reads the contents of the various columns of the row. These had to be in place before the trailer (or end-of-file indicator), which is part of the DOWHILE condition, could be tested. Because this read statement with its included loop is so long, it gets rather tedious to write twice. However, this problem can be avoided if there is some single statement that can replace a complete set of statements when this set of statements is repeated. This structure will be presented in the next chapter.

PROBLEMS

Opportunities exist all around us to use two-dimensional arrays to solve real-world problems. This is because two-dimensional arrays may not only be thought of as data tables with rows and columns, but may also be thought of as maps with map coordinates. I have tried to supply a rather wide range of problems to let you see simple examples of what can be done. Even the simple examples are rather complex, however, and you may have to refer to the sample problems given in the text to get the nested loops operating exactly the way you wish. In general, these problems will take more experimentation than any others you have had. Problems 11.2, 11.7, 11.8 and 11.9 are designated as challenge problems. Programs satisfying the conditions of Problems 11.1, 11.3, 11.5, 11.7 and 11.10 will be found at the end of the book.

*   *   *

11.1 You wish to create a two-dimensional array with 5 rows and 5 columns. In this array all the elements are equal to 0 (zero), except those on the diagonal that connects the upper left-hand element (row 1, column 1) with the lower right-hand element (row 5, column 5). The elements on the diagonal should have the value 1.

Write a complete pseudocode program, including declaration of the array, that will produce this array. The values are not loaded from an external card set, but generated by the program. At the completion of the program, it is not necessary to write out the values of the elements. The message 'Array Complete' will be sufficient.

It should be noted that along the diagonal of a two-dimensional array, the row and column pointers maintain a specific relation to each other. If this is not clear to you, draw a set of squares in a square pattern with 5 elements on each side. Shade in the diagonal elements as defined above and note the relation between the row pointer and column pointer of each case.

*11.2 Design a pseudocode program that loads the values of a pack of 50 cards, each of which contains one number, into a 50-element, one-dimensional array. The program should then load the values of the elements in the one-dimensional array into the elements of a two-dimensional array with 5 rows and 10 columns. The elements should be loaded from left to right in the same way one reads a page in English. When the last element on the right end of each line is reached, the program should load the next value into the first element at the left-hand element of the next line. When the loading is complete, a message should indicate this fact.

11.3 We wish to model the plowing of a field. When a field is plowed, the plow starts at one corner of the field. It goes down one side of the field. When it reaches one boundary it turns around and starts plowing back in the direction it came from, but in a path one step farther into the unplowed region than the path that brought the plow to the boundary at which it turned. This is a back-and-forth movement. There are other plowing patterns, but this one is very old, and still, probably, the most common.

It is the 'ox plow' pattern, which goes back to the start of agriculture.

To model this, we could use a two-dimensional array. We could begin at the corner with pointers (1,1) and proceed in a plowing fashion, going back and forth until the entire field is plowed.

Given a field that we model as an array called FIELD which has 70 rows and 25 columns, design a pseudocode program that will start reading the elements of the array at the element FIELD (1,1). It should move in a field-plowing fashion until it has traversed the entire array. Each time it accesses an element it should assign it a value of 7 to show that it has been plowed. When the entire field has been plowed, the program should print out a message 'Ready for Planting', and finish.

11.4   You wish to design a program to draw a type of checker or chess board. In this board, black squares might be designated by elements having a value 7 and white squares might be designated by elements having the value 0 (zero).

You will have to use some kind of pattern to reach every square on the board. This pattern could be a row-by-row movement from left to right and top to bottom, just as you read a newspaper. It could also be a plowing pattern as in the previous problem. Whichever way you decide to do it, you will always pass through alternate black and white squares. This means that you will have to use a type of 'flasher technology' to set the values of the squares as you access them. A checker or chess board has 8 rows and 8 columns.

Design a pseudocode program that will declare an appropriately sized array. Begin at the element in the first column of the first row and, selecting the elements of the array according to a pattern of your own choice, create a chess board as described above. At the completion of the construction the program should print out the message 'Your move'.

11.5   You wish to add the elements of one square array to the elements of another square array. Both arrays have exactly the same dimensions. You wish to perform the addition element by element. That is, an element from one array will be added to the element of the second array that has the same pointers as the element of the first array. The sum of each addition will be stored in a third array. This element will have the same pointers as those of the two elements that were added.

Assume that you are working with arrays that have 5 rows and 5 columns. Design a pseudocode program that will add the elements of two arrays and store the sums in the corresponding elements of a third similar array. Your program should include array declarations and loading routines for the first two arrays, with appropriate prompts. Addition should proceed automatically after the prompt that indicates that the second of the two arrays is loaded. Upon completion of addition a prompt should state that addition is complete.

11.6 Given a square array with 5 rows and 5 columns, assume that it is already loaded with the first row all zeroes, the second row all ones, the third row all twos, the fourth row all threes and the fifth row all fours. Design a pseudocode program that will interchange the values in the rows with the values held in the columns by loading the appropriate rows into the corresponding columns of a second array. You may assume that the first array is declared and loaded and the second array is declared. At the completion of the copy of rows to columns an appropriate message should be written.

*11.7 Consider the game of 'battleship'. In this game, two persons lay out a fleet consisting of ships. The ocean is a square of graph paper or a set of squares arranged like a checkerboard, but without coloring. The usual size is 10 rows by 10 columns. The ships are designated by blackening squares on the grid. The squares that make up a particular ship must be in a line and in contact. They must all be in the same row, or all in the same column; a diagonal relationship is not allowed. The number of squares in the marker determines the kind of ship. A battleship might be three squares in line, a cruiser might be two squares in line and a destroyer might be one marked square all by itself.

Using the above conventions, design a pseudocode program that will set up the ships for one array of a game of battleship. It asks for the pointers of the elements making up a battleship (3 elements), a cruiser (2 elements) and a destroyer (1 element). If the positions selected overlap, the assignment process is indicated as defective and the whole process of arranging the fleet must begin again. If any of the pointers refers to locations that are not within the 10 row, 10 column array that constitutes the ocean, then the assignment process is indicated as defective and the whole process of arranging the fleet must begin again. When all three ships are in place, an appropriate message is written.

*11.8 Consider an array with 30 rows and 20 columns. It may be thought of as related to a giant checkerboard in which all the squares are the same color and the number of rows is not the same as the number of columns. It might also be thought of as a street plan showing the housing blocks, or it might be thought of simply as a grid. Assume that marks or markers have been placed in some of the squares of this checkerboard or grid. The rules are these: Each square that has a marker is adjacent to either one or two other squares with markers; it does not have three neighboring squares that have markers. Thus, a line of these marked squares forms a kind of river or snake or string. It does not overlap and double up. It may wander about. The neighboring squares may be either on the same row, the same column, or on a diagonal.

The start of such a snake is an array element that is at the edge of the array and connects to one element farther in. Obviously, this second element will be connected to the first, but will also be connected to another element. This next element will also be connected to another element. However, sooner or later there will be no 'next' element, and the string or snake of elements will end.

Your task is to design a pseudocode program that will start at the element that is at the edge of the array and follow the chain of elements until it ends. Each time it reaches a new element of the chain, it changes the way the marking is done. For example, if the chain is marked by always giving the elements a value of 3, this process might change the marking number from 3 to 22 each time it accesses a new member of the chain. When it has changed the marker of an element, it uses the coordinates of this newly changed element as a basis for the detection of an adjacent element that is marked with a 3. This process continues until no marked element is found. At this time, what was a string of 3's wandering through the array or grid plan has become an identically arranged string of 22's. When all the markers are changed, the program should write a message indicating this fact.

*11.9   Return to the battleship game. Assume you already have a 10 × 10 array loaded with a battleship (three connected squares), a cruiser (two connected squares) and a destroyer (a single square). Of course, the coordinates of each of the structures are recorded. Thus if another player were to enter a set of two pointers (a row and a column) in some way, the entered values could be compared with the pointers of the elements in the three structures. If a match occurs, then the player entering the pointers scores a hit on one of the ships designated by the recorded pointers. If a hit is scored, then the marker at the matched pointers is changed. If a hit is not scored, the contents of the designated element are changed to record the fact that this element has been 'called'. When 6 hits have been made, then clearly there are no more 'ships' with sections that have not been hit. This indicates the end of a battle. A player who has lost all his or her ships has lost the game.

Design a pseudocode program that asks for a pair of row and column pointers. If they match part of a ship, this fact should be announced by printing 'HIT', and an appropriate alteration should be made in the contents of the element designated by the matched pointers. If they do not match, they should be recorded and a message 'MISS' is printed. In the event that a set of pointers is called that has already been called, then a special message such as 'You did this before' should be printed out. When six hits have been recorded, the message 'NO MORE SHIPS' should be printed out.

You may design this program assuming that the ships have already been loaded into the array. Further, you need only ask for one pair of pointers. It is not necessary to do a repeat loop. This program, though it is rather large, is just a fragment that would be used as a subroutine in a larger program controlling the entire game.

11.10 Using a 5 row, 5 column square array, design a pseudocode program that converts the rows to columns and the columns to rows, as in Problem 11.6. However, in this case do not use a second array. Use a modification of the 'lobster' technology of Problem 1.3.

CHAPTER TWELVE

The Subroutine

IF ONE is working on a project such as building a doghouse out of wood, there comes a time when it is necessary to drive some nails. In fact, there will be a number of times when it is necessary to drive nails. One approach to this is to buy or build a new hammer each time one has another nail to drive. Besides being expensive and time-consuming, this method means that all those used hammers take up a lot of space.

Of course, the solution was discovered a long time ago. One has a toolkit that contains each of the tools one is likely to use. The time comes to hammer a nail. We stop worrying about any other job, select the hammer from the toolkit, transfer our self-control to the problem of using the hammer and do it. We do not do anything else at the same time because this might cause us to hit our thumb or drop the hammer on our foot. When the hammering task is finished, we can return the hammer to the toolkit and return control to the continuing job at hand.

This makes good sense for people building wooden doghouses, and it makes good programming sense as well. One divides the problem up into tasks and does them one at a time. Then one has a good overall view of the problem and can pay attention to the details of the individual task as well. Perhaps this chapter should have been given an up-market name like 'Modular Programming and the Top-Down Wooden Doghouse'.

We have the same type of toolkit in programming and all formal programming languages. A module or program part that must be run several times is set up as an individual package and used over and over again without being rewritten. When this module begins its task, it is given control. When the task is completed, control is returned to the main program. Typical examples are subroutines that read in data from external sources, output routines that deliver results to external storage or printers, testing routines that establish the existence of certain conditions, and processing routines that conduct a set of often repeated steps as a part of a larger processing procedure. There are many examples of situations where this toolkit mentality is ideal. The technology used in pseudocode is similar to that in most formal programming languages.

Essentially, the concept of subroutines involves three parts: (1) a method of calling the procedure we wish to use, (2) giving control of program operation to that procedure, and (3) returning control to the main program at the end of the procedure in question. This is accomplished in the following way.

Imagine some routine we know is going to be repeated in the course of the program. We give this program a name like HAMMER. To make it clear that what follows this catchy title is a subroutine, we give it a marker of some sort. In this case, we mark it as a subroutine. The first (or title) line of the subroutine called HAMMER will look like this:

SUBROUTINE: HAMMER

Following this title line are the necessary statements of the subroutine, organized just as they would be in an ordinary program. When the last step is reached (which would normally be END in a standard program) we put in the statement RETURN. This is to remind us to return control to wherever we were in the main program. Our subroutine now looks like this:

SUBROUTINE: HAMMER
    Statement line
    Statement line
    Statement line
RETURN

It is a good idea to indent the contents of the subroutine relative to the subroutine title line and match the position of the RETURN with the title.

Yes, but how do we get the thing into action? At the place in the program where we wish to run it, we call it by using the statement.

CALL: HAMMER

This call statement is just like any other statement. When the subroutine HAMMER has done its job and reached the RETURN, control is returned to the main program immediately following the CALL statement. It is exactly as if we had wedged the sequence of program statements open and written the set of statements contained in HAMMER into the main program. Calling the subroutine is just easier than a wedging-and-writing tactic.

There are a few more details to consider before starting to write examples of subroutines. Discussion of the way in which line numbering will be used is worthwhile. Location in the program is also important.

Usually the best place to locate one or more subroutines is at the end of the program right *after* the END statement. This keeps things out of the way and lets us concentrate on the main program. In this case the END serves to separate the main program clearly from the subroutines and simplify the assignment of line numbers.

Once one has adopted the line numbering conventions we have in use, the simplest procedure is to start renumbering at the beginning of each subroutine, but to start at 10 for the first subroutine, 20 for the second subroutine, 30 for the third and so on. Of course, if we have already reached 10 in the main program, then we will have to start higher, but this is not too serious.

Let's look at one of the earlier programs that may be simplified by using subroutines. In Chapter 5 a program was written that accepted an upper and a lower limit and then printed out all integers between the two limits, including the lower limit but not the upper one. Three versions of this program were written. The third form, shown in Figure 5.8c, was structurally optimal.

The module to input the two limits was rather long, and the third version of this program required it to be repeated twice. The program itself is repeated below for convenience. The original form of this program is then followed by a version in which the repeated block of input and screen information statements is turned into a subroutine. This is located at the end of the overall program and is called when needed.

DESCRIPTION: The program accepts two integers, which serve as lower and upper limits. It then writes out all integers, including the lower limit and up to but not including the upper limit

INPUT DATA: Two integers, one as lower limit, one as upper limit

OUTPUT DATA: Two prompts to identify lower and upper limits: the series of all integers lying between lower and upper limits and including lower limit

PROCEDURE:

1.   Print to screen, 'Enter lower limit – must be an integer'
2.   Read number from screen, place in LOWERLIMIT.
3.   Print to screen, 'Enter upper limit – must be an integer'
4.   Read number from screen, place in UPPERLIMIT.
5.   DOWHILE UPPERLIMIT <= LOWERLIMIT
5.1.   Print to screen, 'Lower limit must be less than upper limit'
5.2.   Print to screen, 'Enter lower limit – must be integer'
5.3.   Read number from screen, place in LOWERLIMIT.
5.4.   Print to screen, 'Enter upper limit – must be integer'
5.5.   Read number from screen, place in UPPERLIMIT.
5.6.   ENDDO
6.   DOWHILE LOWERLIMIT < UPPERLIMIT
6.1.   Print LOWERLIMIT
6.2.   LOWERLIMIT := LOWERLIMIT + 1
6.3.   ENDDO
7.   END

This will now be repeated using a subroutine called INFLOW to replace the series of screen messages and read statements that introduce the upper and lower limits into the program. These blocks are seen above as Steps 1, 2, 3 and 4 at the start of the program and 5.2, 5.3, 5.4 and 5.5 within the DOWHILE that starts at 5.

PROCEDURE:

1.   CALL : INFLOW   ⟨**input**⟩
2.   DOWHILE UPPERLIMIT <= LOWERLIMIT
                                                         ⟨**test output**⟩
2.1.   Print to screen, 'Lower limit
            must be less than upper limit'
2.2.   CALL : INFLOW
2.3.   ENDDO
3.   DOWHILE LOWERLIMIT < UPPERLIMIT
        < UPPERLIMIT   ⟨**produce series**⟩
3.1.   Print LOWERLIMIT
3.2.   LOWERLIMIT := LOWERLIMIT + 1
3.3.   ENDDO
4.   END
10.   SUBROUTINE: INFLOW

10.1.   Print to screen, 'Enter lower limit – must be an integer'

10.2.   Read number from screen, place in LOWERLIMIT.

10.3.   Print to screen, 'Enter upper limit – must be an integer'

10.4.   Read number from screen, place in UPPERLIMIT.

10.5. RETURN

The program version using subroutines is more compact than the one that does not. Of course, this follows almost automatically from the concept of a subroutine. Moreover, the structure and purpose of the program comes out more clearly in the subroutine version. There are two reasons for this. First, the name of the subroutine itself contains information and acts like a comment line built right into the program. Second, what is supposed to happen is indicated in the proper place in the program's structure, and then the structure is not obscured by all the logical gears, pulleys and drive belts that make it operate. Using subroutines not only avoids the need for writing each reuse of a repeated module in detail; it smooths out the logical organization of the program and provides a set of meaningful internal labels attached directly to the device they describe.

The subroutine concept may be used in two other ways that are not completely obvious. First of all, a subroutine may be called from inside another subroutine. Thus, for example, if there is some kind of safety check or shortstop device that may be useful in several structures of a program, and if each of these structures is presented as a subroutine, then it may be useful to embed the safety or shortstop device in subroutine form, within each of these two subroutines.

There is no problem with this. As the outermost subroutine is called, control is transferred to it. Within this first subroutine, when the call for the second subroutine is met, control is transferred to it. When, within the second-level subroutine, the RETURN statement is met, control is transferred back to the first-level subroutine. Within the first-level subroutine, when the RETURN is met, control is transferred back to the main program. We will see this in the next example.

Another use of the subroutine and the subroutine call is to

clarify structure. In this case, the subroutine that is called may not be a structure that repeats. The first part of the program is a set of subroutine calls that call each function that will be required in the program. Such a module at the beginning of the program is called a 'top module' or 'calling module'. It facilitates a top-down structure in that the program is broken up into tasks, and each task is then accomplished in order.

The second verison of the search program in Chapter 11 is used as an example. The procedure block as it was written is repeated for convenience, but the description, input and output blocks are not included.

Before using the subroutine treatment, the search program is modified to make it more general. The array has a row size called ROWSIZE and a column size called COLSIZE. The value of these variables is assigned in the initiation section of the program.

Since the variable names for these limits are used throughout the program, changing the constant values at initiation ensures that they are changed throughout the program. The column containing the end-of-file marker is also handled in a general way from the initiation module by setting the value of STOPCOL to indicate the location and STOPMARK to indicate the marker value. The values are used in the same way as in the simplified program. Here is the program as previously written, but with the generalized variables in place:

PROCEDURE:

1.	ROWSIZE := 20	⟨**max number of rows**⟩
2.	COLSIZE := 13	⟨**max number of cols**⟩
3.	STOPCOL := 2	⟨**file end col**⟩
4.	STOPMARK := 1066	⟨**file end marker**⟩
5.	DECLARE FRAME (ROWSIZE, COLSIZE)	
6.	DOFOR ROW := 1 TO ROWSIZE	
		⟨**begin array load**⟩
6.1.	DOFOR COLUMN := 1 TO COLSIZE	
6.1.1.	Read value assign to FRAME (ROW, COLUMN)	
6.1.2.	ENDDO	
		⟨**begin shortstop**⟩
6.2.	IF FRAME (ROW, STOPCOL) = STOPMARK	
6.2.1.	THEN	
6.2.2.	ROW := ROWSIZE	
6.2.3.	ENDIF	⟨**end shortstop**⟩

6.3.	ENDDO	⟨finish loading array⟩
		⟨begin array search⟩
7.	DOFOR ROW := 1 TO ROWSIZE	
7.1.	IF ((FRAME (ROW, 2) < 1945) AND (FRAME (ROW, 3) = 1) AND (FRAME (ROW, 6) = 1) AND (FRAME (ROW, 11) = 1))	
7.1.1.	THEN	
7.1.2.	Print FRAME (ROW, 1)	
7.1.3.	ENDIF	
		⟨begin shortstop⟩
7.2.	IF FRAME (ROW, STOPCOL) = STOPMARK	
7.2.1.	THEN	
7.2.2.	ROW := ROWSIZE	
7.2.3.	ENDIF	⟨end shortstop⟩
7.3.	ENDDO	⟨end array search⟩
8.	END	

This program will now be written using a calling or top module. When it is necessary to modify the program for a particular matrix or search, the programmer can enter the initiation module to change the variables that are assigned there, or the search module itself can be entered to change the items that constitute the pattern of responses sought.

PROCEDURE:

1.	CALL : INITIAL	⟨set limiting variables⟩
2.	CALL : RAYLOAD	⟨load array from file⟩
3.	CALL : RAYSEARCH	⟨search array⟩
4.	END	

10.	SUBROUTINE : INITIAL	⟨set limiting variables⟩
10.1.	ROWSIZE := 20	⟨max row pointer⟩
10.2.	COLSIZE := 13	⟨max col pointer⟩
10.3.	STOPCOL := 2	⟨end marker column⟩
10.4.	STOPMARK := 1066	⟨end marker value⟩
10.5.	DECLARE FRAME (ROWSIZE, COLSIZE)	
10.6.	RETURN	

20.	SUBROUTINE : RAYLOAD	⟨load the array⟩
21.	DOFOR ROW := 1 TO ROWSIZE	
21.1.	DOFOR COLUMN := 1 TO COLSIZE	
21.1.1.	Read value assign to FRAME (ROW, COLUMN)	

```
21.1.2.              ENDDO
                             ⟨finish load at file end⟩
21.2.                CALL : SHORTSTOP
21.3.                ENDDO
22.        RETURN

30.        SUBROUTINE : RAYSEARCH   ⟨search the array⟩
31.                DOFOR ROW := 1 TO ROWSIZE
31.1.                  IF (FRAME (ROW, 2) < (1945)
                       AND (FRAME (ROW, 3) = 1) AND
                       (FRAME (ROW, 6) = 1) AND
                       (FRAME (ROW, 11) = 1)
31.1.1.                   THEN
31.1.2.                       Print FRAME (ROW, 1)
31.1.3.                   ENDIF
31.2.                  CALL : SHORTSTOP
                             ⟨finish search at file end⟩
31.3.                  ENDDO
32.        RETURN

40.        SUBROUTINE : SHORTSTOP
                             ⟨stop action at file end⟩
41.                IF FRAME (ROW, STOPCOL) = STOPMARK
41.1.                  THEN
41.2.                      ROW := ROWSIZE
41.3.                  ENDIF
42.        RETURN
```

This organization means that the individual subroutines are much less complex structures than the overall program as designed without top modules. In the case of larger and more complex programs, it means that the modules themselves may be written more easily than a single nonmodular version of the program. This has many advantages. The choice of when to use a top-module-type structure, however, will depend on the individual programmer, the nature of his or her colleagues and supervision, the complexity of the program and the environment in which it will be used. Just the same, when a program looks tough, top-module technology is a good approach.

Before looking at one last program focusing on subroutines, some possible extensions of the subroutine concept may be considered.

Could a subroutine call itself? The answer is yes. This is

possible in a limited number of languages. It is rather special and will not be discussed here.

The second question is more general. This is whether the variables in a particular subroutine represent a particular population of variables that cannot be 'seen' by the main program or the rest of the subroutines. We can imagine cases where we wish to have individual data structures that are seen or altered only by a single subroutine.

Then values used in a particular subroutine would be passed from the main program to the subroutine when that subroutine was called. Within this subroutine, these values would be assigned to variables unrelated to any variables named in the main program. The results of this work would be passed back to the main program and assigned to variables there that were different from any in the subroutine. Thus operations in the subroutines would not produce 'side effects' on variables in the main program. This option is available in a number of languages and is often used. It is not needed for the level of programming used in this text and will be excluded to avoid needless complexity. All variables used in our programs have been and will be 'global'. That is, they may be used, accessed, assigned or changed by the main program or any subroutine.

The last program discussed in this chapter makes good use of subroutines to conduct a task that otherwise would clutter up the main program. Although the operation done in the subroutine is relatively obvious, the use of subroutine structuring (handling tasks one at a time) will simplify our thinking.

Let us suppose that we have a series of numbers in a linear array. They are not in any particular order. We wish to have them in order of decreasing size as the array pointer increases. If we imagine these numbers in a single row that we read from left to right, a simple procedure may be used to put them in order.

Passing along the row from left to right, we compare the first value with the second. If the second value is less than the first, that is as it should be, since we wish things to decrease from left to right, in the same direction in which we would read the line. If things are in order, we just go on to check the relation between the second and third elements.

On the other hand, if the first and second elements are in the wrong order we interchange them, bringing them into the correct relationship. The pointer numbers of the positions are the same; it is only the contents of the positions which have changed. The contents of successive array variables have been interchanged, but the variables and their subscripts remain the same.

When the interchange of the contents of the first and second variables has been completed, we consider the second and third elements of the row. If the contents are in order, comparison is made of the next pair; if not, an exchange is made and after the exchange the comparison proceeds to the next pair.

In the following table we examine the sorting process outlined above. Each line shows the contents of the linear array. For simplicity, the variable names and pointers have been excluded. All we see are the contents of the variables as if they were arranged in cans and we were looking through some kind of fluoroscope. The position of the cans and their labels will not change, only the contents.

The first line shows the contents of the array as the sort started. These contents are, reading from left to right, the integers: 6, 8, 5, 7, 9. In this first line the first two numbers are underlined, indicating that they are being compared. In the second line we write the entire contents of the array, including the results of the comparison. If an interchange was required, it has happened. If the order of the inspected pair was correct, nothing is changed. Then, in the third line, the next pair under comparison is indicated, and the fourth line shows the results. Things continue in this way until the entire array has been inspected.

$$\begin{array}{l}
\underline{6\ 8}\ 5\ 7\ 9\\
\underline{8\ 6}\ 5\ 7\ 9\\
8\ \underline{6\ 5}\ 7\ 9\\
8\ \underline{6\ 5}\ 7\ 9\\
8\ 6\ \underline{5\ 7}\ 9\\
8\ 6\ \underline{7\ 5}\ 9\\
8\ 6\ 7\ \underline{5\ 9}\\
8\ 6\ 7\ \underline{9\ 5}
\end{array}$$

Notice that the smallest number (5) in the array has migrated to the position farthest to the right (that is, to the position it will occupy in the final order). It will not have to move again. The other elements have in some cases been rearranged, but the overall order remains jumbled.

We have made one pass through the array with our test-and-interchange routine. We will now make another pass. Note, however, that it is not necessary to include the last element of the array in the comparison because we already know it is the smallest.

$$8\underline{}6\,7\,9\,5$$
$$8\,6\,7\,9\,5$$
$$8\,6\,7\,9\,5$$
$$8\,7\,6\,9\,5$$
$$8\,7\,6\,9\,5$$
$$8\,7\,9\,6\,5$$

As we indicated, one less test and interchange sequence was needed to complete this second pass. Now, on to the third pass! Remember, the last two elements are now in place, so the next pass will again use one less test-interchange combination than the one just completed.

$$8\,7\,9\,6\,5$$
$$8\,7\,9\,6\,5$$
$$8\,7\,9\,6\,5$$
$$8\,9\,7\,6\,5$$

This pass is now complete and we can do the last pass, which will be quite short.

$$8\,9\,7\,6\,5$$
$$9\,8\,7\,6\,5$$

That's it! The array is now in the desired order. Remember, in this case we have not looked at the pointers. We are just examining the contents of each of the array variables. The pointers will remain the same. The first element, whatever its value, will have a pointer 1, and so forth. The pointers will be used to manipulate the element contents just as pointers have been used in the preceding examples.

Now let us see how many repetitions of the various steps are forced on us by the nature of the process. If we have 20 elements in the array, then the worst case we will have is to move one element into place with each pass. Of course, the last element will have no place else to go, so only 19 passes will be required. This is the general rule. We must make one less pass than the total number of elements in the array.

The passes themselves will also become progressively shorter. A set of 20 elements consists of 19 side-by-side pairs, if you produce the pairs by going along the row of elements making up all the pairs of adjacent elements that can be made. However, at the end of each pass you will have put one element into place, so the pass following that will involve one less comparison. Of course, you could make the same number of compare-interchange actions all the way through, but in this case a number of the elements you were comparing would already be officially in place. That is, you would know they were in the right place because you had put them there, and there would be no reason to compare them.

Any initial distribution is possible. It would be a waste of time if we were to go on sorting a list after it was in order. This involves a question: How do we know that a list is in order? The answer is that if on a given pass there are no interchange steps, the array must be in order. This sounds pretty obvious. It is. Until such a pass is made, we must just go on making passes, but when such a pass has been completed, there is no need to make any more passes, even if we had made only one pass and there were several hundred elements in the array. But how do we know that there was no exchange made in a given pass? Naturally, whenever an exchange is made we set a flag. Each time a pass is completed the flag is tested. If it has not been set, then no further passes are executed. Of course, at the beginning of each pass, just after the flag has been tested, it must be returned to its initialized or 'unset' form so the effect of setting it will show. Once it has been set, if it is set again during a pass, nothing happens; it is just brought to the value it already has.

In writing the first version of this program, we will assume a 5-element list. We will also assume that this list is being loaded from the screen. We will not worry, at this time, about end-of-file technology. There is some type of mechanism by which we know the list length and can set the array length and other variables accordingly.

The shortstop technology used in this version involves a flag that is set when an interchange is made. Control of the passing loop will be accomplished by a DOWHILE structure with a compound condition. One part of the condition will be examination of the looping variable. The other part of the condition will determine whether the flag has been set.

Many of you probably realize that this is that classical tool of computer programming instruction, the 'bubble sort'. (In case you don't, that is what it is called.) The name derives from the way the larger or smaller elements move through the mass of values, much as heavier or lighter particles are separated in certain types of flotation device.

A tricky aspect of bubble sort itself is the interchange of

elements. If you have two elements and use an assignment statement to convert the first to the second and then repeat the technology backwards, you will have two variables containing the same value. You have to transfer the value of the first variable to a holding variable. Then the value of the second variable can be put into the first variable. The original value of the first variable is not lost because it is in the holding variable. This value of the holding variable is then placed in the second variable. The result is that everything swaps around in a circle.

A more detailed discussion of the bubble sort technique will be put off until after the top-module treatment of the program.

In the following version a maximum amount of nesting is used, and subroutines are not used at all, even though they might be helpful. Even so, the modular structure of the program is evident, and the only complicated section is the bubble sort itself.

DESCRIPTION: This program loads five variables from the screen, puts them in order from largest to smallest and prints out the ordered list.

INPUT DATA: Five numbers

OUTPUT DATA: The output is the same five numbers, beginning with the largest and going to the smallest.

PROCEDURE:

1. Initialize the program.
2. Load the constants from the screen.
3. Sort the constants in order from largest to smallest.
4. Print out the ordered list of numbers.
5. End of program.

The procedure is now expanded:

PROCEDURE:

1.   RAYSIZE := 5   ⟨**number of elements**⟩
2.   DECLARE CRATE (RAYSIZE)   ⟨**working array**⟩
3.   DOFOR I := 1 TO RAYSIZE   ⟨**start array load**⟩
3.1.   Print to screen: 'Enter list element #', I
3.2.   Read value from screen, assign to CRATE (I)
3.3.   ENDDO   ⟨**end array load**⟩
4.   K := 1   ⟨**initialize counter**⟩
5.   BANNER := 1   ⟨**set flag**⟩
6.   DOWHILE (K < = (RAYSIZE −1)) AND
       (BANNER = 1)   ⟨**start pass loop**⟩

6.1.   BANNER := 0   ⟨**reset flag**⟩
6.2.   DOFOR N := 1 TO (RAYSIZE −K)
                                          ⟨**start pair select**⟩
6.2.1.   IF CRATE (N) < CRATE (N + 1) ⟨**start test**⟩
6.2.1.1.   THEN
6.2.1.2.   BANNER := 1 ⟨**set flag if exchange**⟩
                                          ⟨**start interchange**⟩
6.2.1.3.   HOLDER := CRATE (N)
6.2.1.4.   CRATE (N) := CRATE (N + 1)
6.2.1.5.   CRATE (N + 1) := HOLDER
                                          ⟨**end interchange**⟩
6.2.1.6.   ENDIF   ⟨**end test**⟩
6.2.2.   ENDDO   ⟨**end pair select**⟩
6.3.   K := K + 1   ⟨**increment pass counter**⟩
6.4.   ENDDO   ⟨**end pass loop**⟩
7.   DOFOR L := 1 TO RAYSIZE   ⟨**start printout**⟩
7.1.   Print CRATE(L)
7.2.   ENDDO   ⟨**end printout**⟩
8.   END

Notice that by using DOWHILE instead of DOFOR, a compound condition may be used. Before entering the DOWHILE loop at 6, it is necessary to initialize the loop counting variable K (line 4), as is always the case when DOWHILE is used to control a counting loop. However, in this case the flag BANNER must be changed to its set position to permit entrance to the loop. It is changed to its unset value at 6.1 to permit it to respond to the interchange sequence (or its absence), which goes from 6.2.1.2 to 6.2.1.5.

In writing the program with a complete top-down treatment, the top module itself takes the place of the initial rough program written in rather crude English. The description, input data and output data are as for the preceeding example.

PROCEDURE:

   1.   CALL : INITIAL   ⟨**set internal constants**⟩
   2.   CALL : LISTLOAD   ⟨**load working array**⟩
   3.   CALL : BUBSORT   ⟨**sort by bubble technique**⟩
   4.   CALL : PRINTLIST   ⟨**print sorted array**⟩
   5.   END

   10.   SUBROUTINE : INITIAL
   11.   RAYSIZE := 5   ⟨**array size**⟩

```
12.              DECLARE CRATE (RAYSIZE)
13.              RETURN

20.         SUBROUTINE : LISTLOAD
21.              DOFOR I := 1 TO RAYSIZE
21.1                 Print to screen: 'Enter list element #', I
21.2                 Read value from screen, assign to CRATE (I)
21.3             ENDDO
22.         RETURN

30.         SUBROUTINE : BUBSORT
31.              DOFOR K := 1 TO RAYSIZE −1
                                              ⟨start passes⟩
31.1             BANNER := 0              ⟨initialize flag⟩
31.2                 DOFOR N := 1 TO RAYSIZE −K
                                              ⟨select pair⟩
31.2.1.                 IF CRATE (N) < CRATE (N + 1)
                                              ⟨test⟩
31.2.1.1.                  THEN
31.2.1.2.                     CALL : SWITCH
                                              ⟨exchange pair⟩
31.2.1.3.                  ENDIF
31.2.2.                ENDDO
31.3.                CALL : SHORTSTOP
                              ⟨stop action if list in order⟩
31.4.             ENDDO              ⟨end passes⟩
32.         RETURN

40.         SUBROUTINE : PRINTLIST
41.              DOFOR L := 1 TO RAYSIZE
41.1.                Print CRATE(L)
41.2.            ENDDO
42.         RETURN

50.         SUBROUTINE : SWITCH
51.              BANNER := 1                      ⟨set flag⟩
52.              HOLDER := CRATE(N)
53.              CRATE (N) := CRATE (N + 1)
54.              CRATE (N + 1) := HOLDER
55.         RETURN

60.         SUBROUTINE : SHORTSTOP
61.              IF BANNER = 0
61.1.                THEN
61.2.                   K := RAYSIZE −1
```

61.3.   ENDIF
62.   RETURN

Most of the subroutines require little or no explanation; however, BUBSORT is a bit complicated. The key lies in line 31.2. We are going through the elements of the list, designating the pairs of adjacent elements in order. We must designate a pair by either the first or the second element of the pair. We have chosen to designate the elements by the first element of the pair. This means that our first pair will be designated by N := 1 and our last pair by N := RAYSIZE −1, which stands for the next-to-last element in the array. This is only for the first pass, when the pass-counting variable K from line 31 has the value 1. Thus on the first pass we will examine all the pairs, and the value of the marker element of the pair will run from 1 to RAYSIZE −1. On the second pass (when K is 2) we do not wish to compare the final pair on the list. Our final marker will designate the next-to-last pair, and so this marker will be the pointer to the last element but 2. That is, it will be RAYSIZE −2. Since this is the second pass, this could as well be RAYSIZE −K. Would this have worked back at the first pass? Yes, because there the pointer was RAYSIZE −1, and K had a value of 1. Notice that from our original verbal analysis we knew that the number of pairs had to change as a function of the number of the current pass.

We thus started out with a general statement of the rule defining the pair to be compared and looked for an involvement with the counter that determined the pass number. To see more exactly how this works, we will change a few conditions and derive a new control function that makes things happen in exactly the same fashion.

Suppose we had decided to mark the pairs selected in line 31.2 by focusing on the second element of each pair to be compared. Then line 31.2 would read

DOFOR N := 2 to RAYSSIZE + 1 −K

In this case, we would also have to change the designations of the elements in line 31.2.1 to

IF CRATE (N − 1) < CRATE (N)

It will be necessary to work through both versions several times to get the feel of how the designators work. The whole idea is that each time a new pass is made, one less element is examined. This is effectively examining one pair less, based on the way pairs are defined. Thus, the number of the pass being run must be related to the number of the element being used as a pair designator in any comparison. Don't become too depressed. Developing a feel for handling the subscripts in a bubble sort is not difficult. It just requires a bit of pencil work. Once you have it in hand, you will find that most aspects of pointer manipulation will seem much more natural. The way to handle this is to write trace tables for several different examples of each designation technique.

In examining the subroutine SHORTSTOP, it is worth reviewing the technique we use to go to the end of the program when it is shown that the array is in order before the theoretical number of passes are completed. A GOTO could be used. This would mean that the DOFOR loop controlling the number of passes would have two exits. One exit is the natural exit at the corresponding ENDDO. The second is the GOTO activated by a flag test routine. As we get into more complex programs, it is clear that having two exits to a single module often leads to 'tangled wires'. The simplest solution is to avoid the GOTO by having an assignment statement that sets the looping variable to its final value. In this case, the loop control structure will 'think' that the proper number of repetitions has been completed and cause control to leave the loop at the natural location, which is the ENDDO.

Once the logic is understood, the details present no problem. The flag (BANNER) that actuates SHORTSTOP is set within the SWITCH subroutine. Thus, if SWITCH is not called in a particular pass, BANNER is never set to 1. If a complete pass beginning at 31.2 is run without calling SWITCH, then BANNER, which was set to 0 at 31.1, is never set to 1. Then when that particular pass is exited at the ENDDO of line 31.2.2, SHORTSTOP, which is called at 31.3, sees a value of 0 for the flag BANNER and boosts the looping variable K to its limiting value RAYSIZE −1, which causes the sort to be exited immediately at 31.4.

This top-module version of the program is quite straightforward. The bubble sort module itself, BUBSORT, contains subroutines SHORTSTOP and SWITCH, but the essential nested loop organization has not been changed. It is hard to be certain whether breaking down BUBSORT further with subroutines would be a simplification or whether highly nested compact structures are better treated as single units.

It is clear that there are a great many more algorithms that would be fun to develop and write in pseudocode, but in a book we must stop somewhere.

Remember, the purpose is to help in designing and understanding the design of algorithms and to present them in compact, well-structured code. Pseudocode is not an end in itself.

To aid in bridging the gap between pseudocode and conventional machine languages, the Appendix considers the translation of pseudocode logical structures into equivalent structures in the languages BASIC, FORTRAN, COBOL and Pascal.

I hope you will continue to practice writing programs and developing algorithms in pseudocode. It helps. You can improve your analytical powers and refine your structural presentation, even when the hardware is down.

PROBLEMS

All of the problems of Chapter 12 look rather formidable. However, now that we have subroutines, it is possible to write fully modular, top-down programs with top modules at the beginning to make analysis of algorithms and allocation of tasks relatively straightforward. I have designated Problems 12.2, 12.6, 12.7 and 12.8 as challenge problems. You will note that a number of the problems are actually reassignments of older problems under conditions where more advanced solving and processing technology is used. In general this provides greatly increased clarity and efficiency. Answers to Problems 12.1, 12.3, 12.5, and 12.9 will be found at the end of the book.

* * *

12.1   Consider the two-array sort used as a model in Chapter 10. In the text example, a zero was used as the invisible value that escapes the selection routine. In Problem 10.6 a routine for producing a generalized invisible value was discussed.

Basing your design on a 25-element array, design a pseudocode program that describes a complete two-array sort, including the initial reading of the values from cards, the selection of an invisible element, the sort procedure itself and a printout routine that prints the sorted array in order. Subroutines should be used as much as possible. In particular, a 'top module' or 'calling module' should be used at the start of the program to 'call' the various routines.

*12.2   Conducting the transactions of a bank account is a common programming problem. Ideally, the first thing such a program would do is to print a set of choices on the screen. These might be 'Make a Deposit', 'Make a Withdrawal', 'Print Out the Balance', and 'List Most Recent Transactions'. These titles would each be accompanied by a number. A prompt following the list of choices should ask for the number of the activity you wish to perform. When this number is entered, the program would do the things you have chosen. This is a 'menu'. Such programs are described as 'menu-driven programs'.

The technology of making a deposit is fairly clear. One merely enters the date and the amount. The date can be entered numerically as Month: Date: Year, in the US fashion. Each time period can be requested separately and assigned to a variable. Thus no confusion results. The amount in dollars and cents presented as a decimal without a dollar sign is also clear.

The technology for a withdrawal is the same except that if the account does not hold sufficient funds, this should be noted and no action taken. Again, a date would be entered using the same routine as before. Asking for the balance is no problem, and since no change is made in the account status, no date need be presented.

The 'most recent transactions' option seems a bit difficult, but is not. We can assume that the date information (month, date, year) is held numerically in an array, as well as an indicator showing whether a withdrawal or a deposit occurred, the amount and the balance. The withdrawal or deposit indicator could merely be a 1 or a −1. The historical data could be held in a 10-row matrix with an appropriate number of columns for the necessary information.

At the time of a transaction, the information-holding array or arrays would be altered in the following fashion. The contents of those elements with pointer 1 would be transfered to elements with pointer 2. The elements with pointer 2 would be transferred to elements with pointer 3. This would proceed in the same way down to the elements with pointer 10, which would be discarded. The elements with pointer 1 would be left empty to accept the new transaction, data, transaction symbol and balance. On a call for transactions, the contents of these holding arrays would be printed out in an appropriate format.

All of these various menus and operations are obvious applications of modular programming with subroutines. Design a pseudocode program that describes this menu-driven banking system and that uses subroutines, nested subroutines and a calling module at the start of the program.

12.3   In Problem 10.8 you constructed a kind of pseudocode program designed for use in a type of hand-held computer. This computer and its program were intended to handle the house-number problem discussed in Chapter 1.

Rewrite the house-number program. You may assume it is provided with information by an operator who is actually experiencing the problem. The hand-held computer is telling the operator what to do. This time, use subroutines to improve the design of the program. You may also wish to introduce Boolean operators to simplify the nesting structures.

12.4 In Problem 3.10 an exercise was presented in which a cube was repeatedly divided. The surface area was calculated after each division. This was a relatively hard task. It was quite easy to become confused. Write a pseudocode program to describe the calculation of the surface area as the cube is divided. You may assume seven division cycles, but need not actually calculate the surface area this time. Use subroutine technique to present the changes in the various dimensions and the associated calculations.

12.5 A common device in computer design is a 'stack'. It works like this: A value is presented to the stack for storage. The stack has a pointer that is pointing at a storage location. You may think of this storage location as an element of a one-dimensional array. The value is stored at the location defined by the pointer and the pointer is incremented. It is then pointed to a new empty position. A second value might be stored. The procedure would be the same. The value would be stored at the location indicated by the pointer and the pointer would be incremented.

Items must be removed from the stack in the reverse order in which they were put into the stack. That is, the last item we put into the stack is the first one we take out. In the example above, if we remove an item from the stack, we first decrement the pointer variable so it points to the location where the second value was stored and we can then remove the second value. Now that the second value has gone, we can remove the first value. We decrement the pointer variable again and we point to the first value stored in the stack so we can now remove it.

This can be thought of as a spring-loaded tube for storing ping-pong balls. One ball is pushed in and stored in the tube. A second ball is pushed into the tube and stored on top of the first. A third ball is pushed into place and goes in on top of the second. The second ball cannot be removed until the third ball has been removed, and the first ball cannot be removed until the second ball has been removed. The first ball stored is the last one that can be recovered. The first one in is the last one out, and the last one in is the first out.

This last-in–first-out (LIFO) technology is characteristic of stack structures and is achieved by pointer manipulation. The pointer variable of a one-dimensional array may be used exactly like the pointer on a stack, and the array can be made to serve as a model of a stack.

Design a pseudocode program that uses a one-dimensional array to simulate a stack. Use menu technology to call a routine that asks for a value and pushes it onto the stack or pops the 'top' item of the stack and prints it out. Assume you have a 10-element array. When the pointer variable can no longer be incremented, the stack is full and an appropriate prompt should be printed out. The program should also make it impossible to increment the stack pointer beyond a value of 10 or decrement the pointer below a value of 1.

*12.6   In Problems 5.7 and 4.9 we discussed a change-making machine that accepted a value in coins called 'Drips' and converted it to 'Drips', 'Globs' and 'Hunks'. We must now design a more advanced machine for the same market. This machine asks for the value of a piece of merchandise. The value of the bill in Drips, Globs and Hunks is typed in. The machine then asks for the value of the money presented to pay the bill. This amount is also entered in Drips, Globs and Hunks. The machine then prints out the value of the bill, the value given in payment and the amount of change to be returned to the purchaser. This is also in Drips, Globs and Hunks.

Note that the easiest way to handle this is to convert the bill and the payment to Drips, calculate the change and then convert the result back to Drips, Globs and Hunks. Note also that there should be a test to ensure that the customer has paid enough. If he/she has not paid enough, he/she should be informed.

Write a pseudocode program that describes the operation of this machine. The program should ask for the amount of the bill and the payment and print the value of the change. A 'calling module' design can be used for this, and subroutines may be employed both to save space and increase clarity.

*12.7   Problem 11.7 dealt with a program that enabled a player to set up three ships for a game called 'Battleship'. Problem 11.9 dealt with the task of recording hits and misses from one of the players. We now have a setup routine and a playing routine for a one-player situation.

In a normal game, each player would set up his or her fleet. When both fleets were properly set up, the players would alternately call pairs of pointers indicating locations in their opponent's 'ocean'. This would continue until one or the other of the two fleets was sunk.

Design a pseudocode program that will enable each player to set up his or her fleet in separate arrays, will control the alternation between players calling pointers, and which will determine hits, misses and the destruction of one fleet or the other. The alternation between players should go on until one or the other wins. This program will be simplified by extensive use of subroutines.

*12.8   In Chapter 1 an extension of the house-rooms problem was discussed in which rooms might have as many as three doors, one of which had to be a closet. It was further suggested that a method of marking doors each time they were passed through might be a useful way to handle the problem.

It is intended to design a hand-held computer for leading people through such house problems. The computer will ask things like how many doors are seen, how many doors have one marker, and how many doors have two markers. It will give instructions concerning going through doors, going back through doors that have already been used, when to drop a marker and when to turn out lights.

Design a pseudocode program for use in this hand-held computer to be used in the special case of the house-room problem as it is described in Chapter 1 and above. It should start at the outside and return to the outside through the same door. You will probably wish to design this program in terms of relatively simply activities, which may then be refined into subroutines.

12.9   Design a device like a stack. This is a device in which a number of values may be stored, but instead of LIFO (last-in–first-out) it is FIFO (first-in–first-out). It is, of course, also last-in–last-out. It may be imagined as a kind of stack in which the items are pushed on at one end of the stack, but popped off at the other end.

Try to imagine a physical design that works like this. Assume it has a capacity of 10 numbers. It is based on array technology, but will 'push' and 'pop' at different ends of the stack of values. It will also need some type of routine to inform itself which element contains a value, which can be removed next and which will be filled with a new variable.

When you have a reasonable physical image of the device, build a pseudocode program that shows how it works. This will be driven by a simple menu that gives the choice of pushing or popping. Use a 10-element, one-dimensional array.

12.10   Design a version of the one-array insertion sort that makes use of subroutines to clarify the actions of the nested loop structure. Use a 10-element, one-dimensional array.

Answers to Selected Problems

CHAPTER TWO

2.1 *a.* OK
    b. '–' not legal
    c. OK
    d. 'Lower Case' not legal
    e. OK
    f. 'Start with number' not legal
    g. '+' not legal
    h. 'Lower Case' not legal
    i. OK

2.2 *a.* 8
    b. 8
    c. 19
    d. 2
    e. 8
    f. 9

2.3 *a.* 45
    b. 20
    c. 20
    d. 21

2.4 *a.* 4
    b. 25
    c. 14.82
    d. 111

2.5 *a.* $6 * (8 - 3)$
    b. $((17 + 6)/6)/8$
    c. $(8 * 14) - (15/4)$
    d. $8 - 2/(2 + 3)$

2.6 *a.*

$(3 + 12) * 8 + 3 - 5/(8 + 6)$	122.64
$(3 + 12 * 8) + 3 - (5/8 + 6)$	12.83
$3 + (12 * 8 + 3)15/8 + 6$	−0.83
$(3 + 12) * 8 + (3 - 5/8 + 6)$	128.38

    b.

$6 * (3/4 - 3) + 5 * (3 - 1 + 4)/3$	−3.5
$(6 * 3/4 - 3) + 5 * (3 - 1) + 4/3$	12.83
$6 * (3/4 - 3) + 5 * 3 - (1 + 4/3)$	−0.83
$(6 * 3/4) - (3 + 5) * 3 - (1 + 4/3)$	−21.83

There are many more combinations; these are only a few.

2.7 *a.*

Miles driven by car on its own	150
Miles to go after engine failure	$375 - 150$
Miles driven by truck carrying car	$375 - 150$

216

Gallons gas used by car 150/22
Gallons gas used by truck (375 − 150)/7
Total gas used 150/22 + (365 − 150)/7
Cost (150/22 + (365 − 150)/7) * 1.10
Calculated cost is: $42.86

    b. (CARMILES/CARMPG + (CITYDIS − CARMILES)/TRUCK-MPG) * GASCOST

2.8 *a.* 3.67
    b. 107
    c. 70
    d. 132

2.9 *a.* ((3 + 12) * 8 + 3 − 5)/8 + 6   20.75
       (3 + (12 * 8 + 3) − 5)/(8 + 6)   6.93
       (3 + 12) * (8 + (3 − 5/8)) + 6   161.62
       ((3 + 12 * 8) + 3 − 5)/(8 + 6)   6.93

    b. (6 * (3/4 − 3) + 5) * (3 − 1 + 4)/3   −17
       (6 * (3/(4 − 3)) + (5 * 3) − 1 + 4)/3   12
       (6 * (3/4 − (3 + 5 * 3) − 1) + 4)/3   −104.17
       (((6 * 3)/4 − 2) + 5 * 3 − 1) + 4/3   17.83

2.10 *a.* NUMTRAINS * KARTSINTRAIN * CARTONSINKART * EGGPERCARTON
    b. 3 * 4 * 62 * 12
       or 8,928 eggs

CHAPTER THREE

3.1 *a.* Not proper; plus sign on left side.
    b. Not proper; equal sign, not assignment operator.
    c. OK
    d. OK
    e. OK
    f. Not proper; constant on left side.
    g. OK
    h. Not proper; constant on left side.

3.2 *a.* DROPSY := 5
    b. PIP :=K
    c. NAN := NAN + 1
    d. ZIP := X54 + BETA5
    e. STING := STING − FROST

3.3 1. FONT := 7
   2. Print FONT
   3. FONT := FONT + 2
   4. GOTO Step 2
   5. END

3.4 1. DIG := 23
   2. Print 'No Joy'
   3. Print DIG
   4. DIG := DIG + 5
   5. GOTO Step 2

3.5 42

3.6 1. FLOURCOST := 35
   2. EGSCOST := 89
   3. MILKOST := 45
   4. GROCBIL := FLOURCOST + EGSCOST + MILKOST
   5. Print GROCBIL
   6. END

3.7 1. BUGSNUM := 3
   2. TIME := 20
   3. Print BUGSNUM, TIME
   4. BUGSNUM := BUGSNUM * 2
   5. TIME := TIME + 20
   6. GOTO Step 3
   7. END

3.8 12

3.9 1. TREEWT := 1.5
   2. YEARS := 0
   3. Print TREES, TREEWT
   4. YEARS := YEARS + 1
   5. TREEWT := TREEWT * 2
   6. TREEWT := TREEWT − TREEWT/3
   7. GOTO Step 3
   8. END

COMMENT   I have assumed you planted the tree the moment the termites went on vacation and then weighed it at that time, yielding the seedling at zero years. After that the weighings occurred on the same date. The tree had grown another season and the termites had worked on the tree after weight doubling, but before weighing.

3.10 1. CYCLENUMB := 0
    2. KUBNUMBERS := 1

3.   KUBEDGE := 2
4.   FACEAREA := KUBEDGE * KUBEDGE
5.   KUBAREA := 6 * FACEAREA
6.   TOTAREA := KUBAREA * KUBNUMERS
7.   Print CYCLENUMB. KUBEDGE, TOTAREA
8.   CYCLENUMB := CYCLENUMB + 1
9.   KUBNUMBERS := KUBNUMBERS * 8
10. KUBEDGE :=KUBEDGE/2
11. GOTO Step 4
12. END

CYCLENUMBERS	KUBEDGE (feet)	TOTAREA (sqfeet)
0	2	24
1	1	48
2	.5	96
3	.25	192
4	.125	384
5	.0625	768

CHAPTER FOUR

4.1

4.2

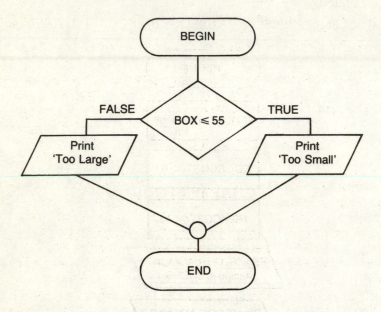

4.3 *1.* FLOURCOST := 35
  2. EGGSCOST := 89
  3. MILKCOST := 45
  4. Assign value to FLOURPNDS
  5. Assign value to EGGBOXES
  6. Assign value to MILKBOTTLES
  7. GROCBIL := FLOURCOST * FLOURPOUNDS + EGGSCOST * EGGBOXES + MILKCOST * MILKBOTTLES
  8. Print GROCBILL
  9. END

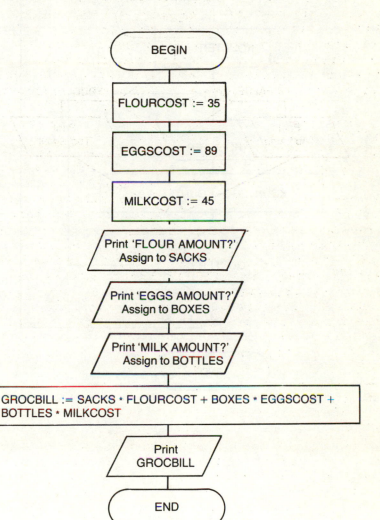

4.4

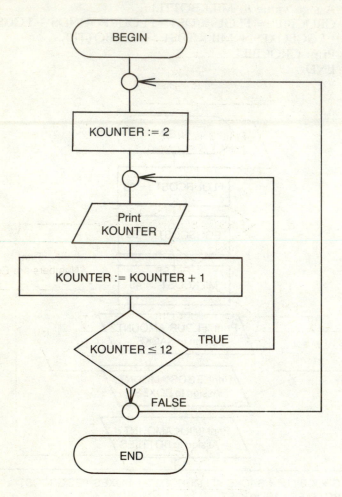

4.5

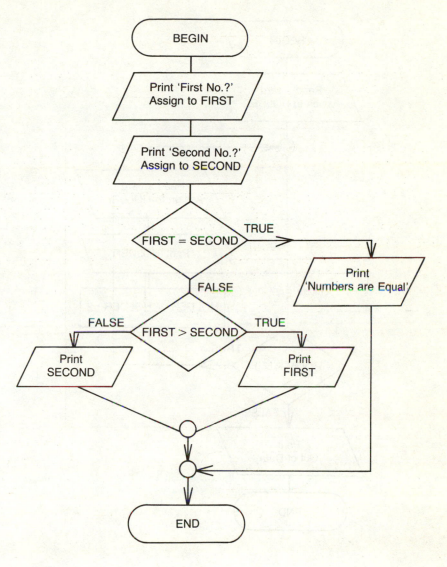

4.6

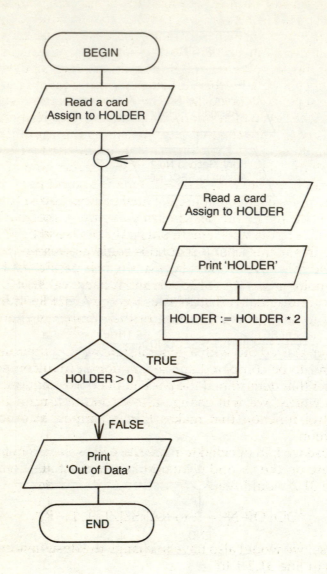

4.7

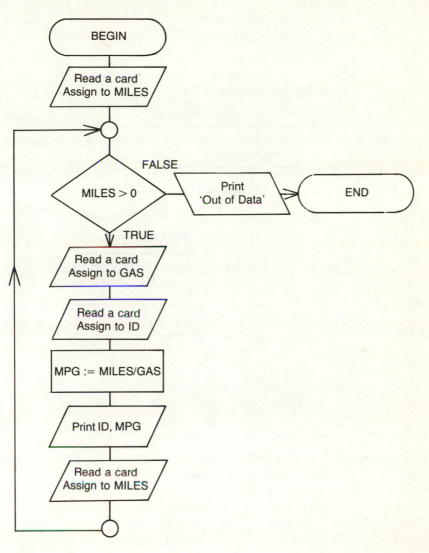

4.8

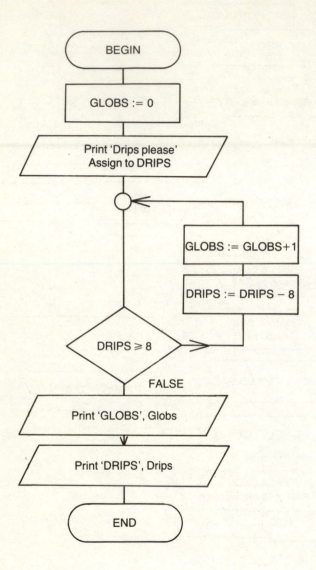

4.9

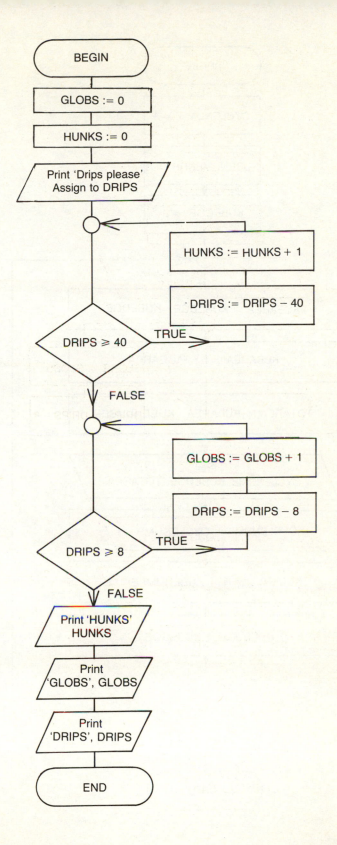

4.10

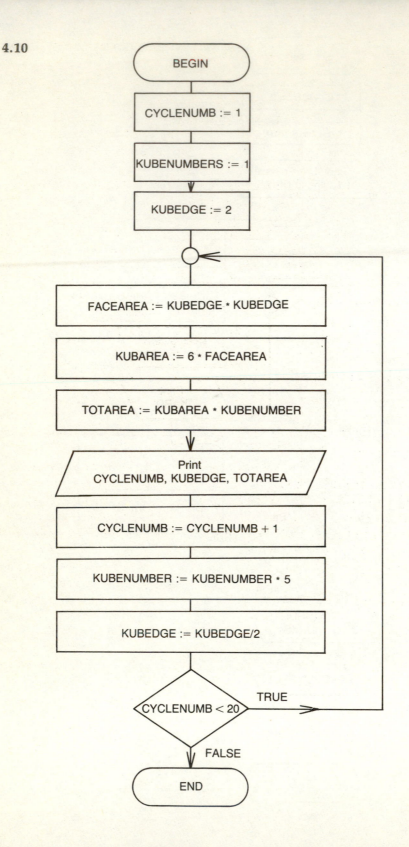

BEGIN

CYCLENUMB := 1

KUBENUMBERS := 1

KUBEDGE := 2

FACEAREA := KUBEDGE * KUBEDGE

KUBAREA := 6 * FACEAREA

TOTAREA := KUBAREA * KUBENUMBER

Print
CYCLENUMB, KUBEDGE, TOTAREA

CYCLENUMB := CYCLENUMB + 1

KUBENUMBER := KUBENUMBER * 5

KUBEDGE := KUBEDGE/2

CYCLENUMB < 20   TRUE

FALSE

END

CHAPTER FIVE

5.3

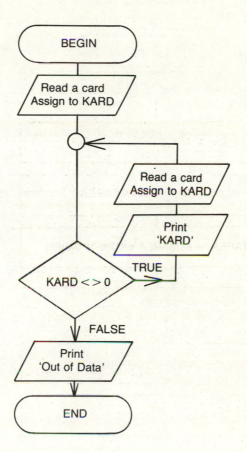

5.5

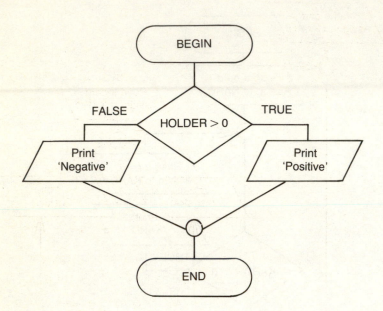

5.6

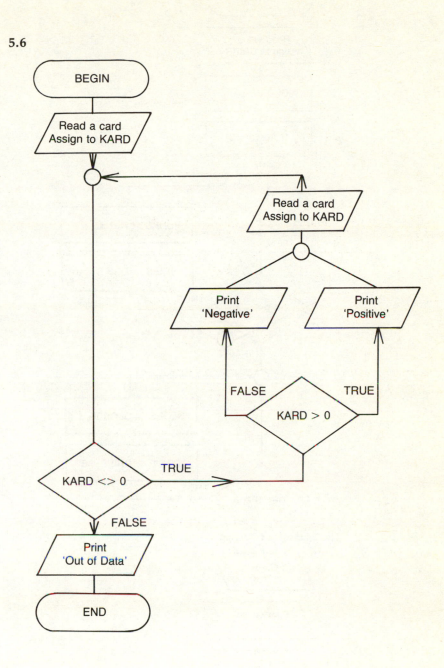

5.7

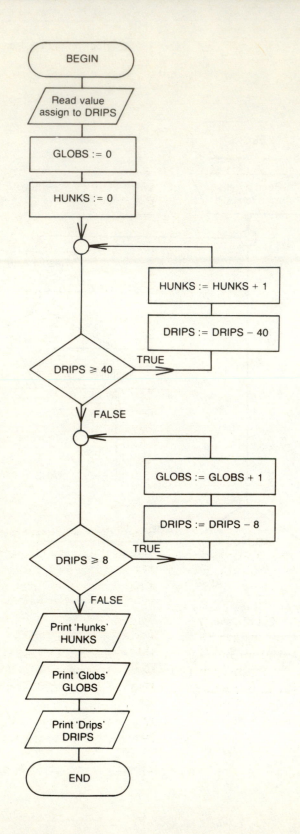

5.10

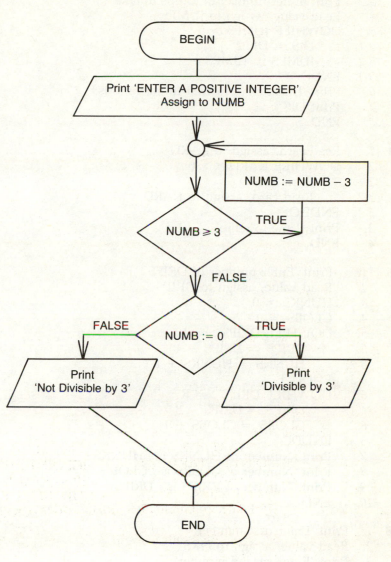

CHAPTER SIX

6.2 *1.* Print 'Enter distance to wall'
2. Read value, Assign to DIS
3. Print 'Enter number of jumps to take'
4. Read value, assign to JUMPS
5. DOWHILE JUMPS > 0
5.1. DIS := DIS/2
5.2. JUMPS := JUMPS − 1
5.3. ENDDO
6. Print 'Distance from wall to machine is:'
7. Print DIS
8. END

6.4 *1.* Read card, assign to KARD
2. DOWHILE KARD < > 0
2.1. Print KARD
2.2. Read card, assign to KARD
2.3. ENDDO
3. Print 'Time to retire'
4. END

6.6 *1.* Print 'Enter number of DRIPS'
2. Read value, assign to DRIPS
3. HUNKS := 0
4. GLOBS := 0
5. DOWHILE DRIPS >= 40
5.1. DRIPS := DRIPS − 40
5.2. HUNKS := HUNKS + 1
5.3. ENDDO
6. DOWHILE DRIPS >= 8
6.1. DRIPS := DRIPS − 8
6.2. GLOBS := GLOBS + 1
6.3. ENDDO
7. Print 'Number of HUNKS is', HUNKS
8. Print 'Number of GLOBS is', GLOBS
9. Print 'Number of DRIPS is', DRIPS
10. END

6.8 *1.* Print 'Enter first number'
2. Read value, assign to FIRST
3. Print 'Enter second number'
4. Read value, assign to SECOND
5. TEMP := FIRST
6. FIRST := SECOND
7. SECOND := TEMP
8. Print 'Switch completed'
9. ENDS

Statement	First	Second	Temp
1.	–	–	–
2.	20	–	–
3.	20	–	–
4.	20	45	–
5.	20	45	20
6.	45	45	20
7.	45	20	20
8.	Print 'Switch completed'		
9.	END		

6.10 *1.*   IF FLASHER = 8
    1.1.   THEN
    1.2.   Print 'RED'
    1.3.   FLASHER := 10
    1.4.   ENDIF
    2.   IF FLASHER = 10
    2.1.   THEN
    2.2.   Print 'GREEN'
    2.3.   FLASHER := 8
    2.4.   ENDIF

    1.   KOUNTER := 1
    2.   FLASHER := 10
    3.   DOWHILE KOUNTER <= 10
    3.1.   IF FLASHER = 8
    3.1.1.   THEN
    3.1.2.   Print 'RED'
    3.1.3.   FLASHER := 10
    3.1.4.   ENDIF
    3.2.   IF FLASHER = 10
    3.2.1.   THEN
    3.2.2.   Print 'GREEN'
    3.2.3.   FLASHER := 8
    3.2.4.   ENDIF
    3.3.   KOUNTER := KOUNTER + 1
    3.4.   ENDDO
    4.   END

CHAPTER SEVEN

7.2 *1.*   Print 'Enter initial deposit'
    2.   Read value, assign to PRINCIPLE
    3.   Print 'Enter interest rate (as decimal, 10% is 0.10)'
    4.   Read value, assign to RATE

     5.   Print 'Enter number of years the account runs'
     6.   Read value, assign to TIME
     7.   TOTINT := 0
     8.   YEAR := 1
     9.   DOWHILE YEAR <= TIME
     9.1.   INTEREST := PRINCIPLE * RATE
     9.2.   TOTINT := TOTINT + INTEREST
     9.3.   PRINCIPLE := PRINCIPLE + INTEREST
     9.4.   Print 'Account value is', PRINCIPLE
     9.5.   Print 'This years interest', INTEREST
     9.6.   Print 'Interest paid to date', TOTINT
     9.7.   Print 'Number of years the account has run', YEAR
     9.8.   YEAR := YEAR + 1
     9.9. ENDDO
     10.   END

Year	Account value	Interest	Total interest
1	2,120	120	120
2	2,247.20	127.20	247.20
3	2,382.03	134.83	382.03
4	2,524.95	142.92	524.95
5	2,676.45	151.50	676.45

7.4 COMMENT We solve this without nesting or Boolean technology; thus some of the thinking appears clumsy. This is particularly true in considering conditions where a negative (and hence impossible) tax increment is obtained. This is why the technique of converting negative tax increments is used. With more advanced logical structures, writing this program becomes much more straightforward.

     1.   Print 'Enter gross income'
     2.   Read value, assign to GROSS
     3.   IF GROSS <= 1500
     3.1.   THEN
     3.2.   TAX1 := GROSS * 0.10
     3.3.   ELSE
     3.4.   TAX1 := 1500 * 0.10
     3.5. ENDIF
     4.   IF GROSS <= 5000
     4.1.   THEN
     4.2.   TAX2 := (GROSS − 1500) * 0.15
     4.3.   ELSE
     4.4.   TAX2 := 3500 * 0.15
     4.5. ENDIF
     5.   IF GROSS <=10000
     5.1.   THEN

```
5.2.            TAX3 := (GROSS − 5000) * 0.22
5.3.       ELSE
5.4.            TAX3 := 5000 * 0.22
5.5.    ENDIF
6.      TAX4 := (GROSS − 10000) * 0.27
7.      IF TAX2 < 0
7.1.        THEN
7.2.            TAX2 := 0
7.3.    ENDIF
8.      IF TAX3 < 0
8.1.        THEN
8.2.            TAX3 := 0
8.3.    ENDIF
9.      IF TAX4 < 0
9.1.        THEN
9.2.            TAX4 := 0
9.3.    ENDIF
10.     TOTALTAX := TAX1 + TAX2 + TAX3 + TAX4
11.     NET := GROSS − TOTALTAX
12.     Print 'For gross income equal to', GROSS
13.     Print 'Income tax is', TOTALTAX
14.     Print 'Net income is', NET
15.     END
```

Calculation based on GROSS = 2200
    TAX1 = 150, TAX2 = 105, TAX3 = 0, TAX4 = 0
    TOTALTAX = 255, NET = 1945.
Calculation based on GROSS = 1100
    TAX1 = 110, TAX2 = 0, TAX3 = 0, TAX4 = 0
    TOTALTAX = 110, NET = 990.

7.6
```
1.      Read value, assign to BIGGEST
2.      Read value, assign to NORMAL
3.      IF NORMAL > BIGGEST
3.1.        THEN
3.2.            HOLDER := BIGGEST
3.3.            BIGGEST := NORMAL
3.4.            NORMAL := HOLDER
3.5.    ENDIF
4.      Print 'The larger value is', BIGGEST
5.      Print 'The smaller value is', NORMAL
6.      END
```

7.8 Version 1

```
1.      Print 'Enter lock code number'
2.      Read value, assign to KEY
```

    3.   IF KEY := TUMBLER
    3.1.   THEN
    3.2.   Print 'The lock is open'
    3.3.   ENDIF
    4.   END

Version 2

    1.   Print 'Enter lock code number'
    2.   Read value, assign to KEY
    3.   IF KEY := TUMBLER
    3.1.   THEN
    3.2.   LATCH := 1
    3.3.   ELSE
    3.4.   LATCH := 0
    3.5.   ENDIF
    4.   IF LATCH := 1
    4.1.   THEN
    4.2.   Print 'The lock is open'
    4.3.   ENDIF
    5.   END

7.10   1.   Print 'Enter supervisor's code number'
        2.   Read value, assign to SUP
        3.   IF SUP < > TUMBLER1
        3.1.   THEN
        3.2.   Print 'This key is not correct'
        3.3.   ELSE
        3.4.   Print 'OK, enter operator code number'
        3.5.   Read value, assign to OPKEY
        3.6.   IF OPKEY = TUMBLER2
        3.6.1.   THEN
        3.6.2.   Print 'Door unlocked'
        3.6.3.   ENDIF
        3.7.   ENDIF
        4.   Print 'Lock test procedure is complete'
        5.   END

CHAPTER EIGHT

8.1   1.   Read a card, assign to FUZE
        2.   DOWHILE FUZE < > 0
        2.1.   KOUNTER := 0
        2.2.   DOWHILE KOUNTER <= 10
        2.2.1.   NUMBER := FUZE + KOUNTER

2.2.2.   Print NUMBER
2.2.3.   KOUNTER := KOUNTER + 1
2.2.4.   ENDDO
2.3.   Read a card, assign to FUZE
2.4.   ENDDO
3.   Print 'No more data'
4.   END

8.3 1.   Read value, assign to FIRST
2.   Read value, assign to SECOND
3.   IF FIRST < SECOND
3.1.   THEN
3.2.   Print FIRST, SECOND
3.3.   ELSE
3.4.   Print SECOND, FIRST
3.5.   ENDIF
4.   END

8.5 1.   POS := 0
2.   NEG := 0
3.   Read a card, assign to KARD
4.   DOWHILE KARD < > 0
4.1.   IF KARD > 0
4.1.1.   THEN
4.1.2.   POS := POS + 1
4.1.3.   ELSE
4.1.4.   NEG := NEG + 1
4.1.5.   ENDIF
4.2.   Read a card, assign to KARD
4.3.   ENDDO
5.   IF POS = NEG
5.1.   THEN
5.2.   Print 'Number of pos. and neg. values is equal'
5.3.   ELSE
5.4.   IF POS > NEG
5.4.1.   THEN
5.4.2.   Print 'More pos. than neg. cards'
5.4.3.   ELSE
5.4.4.   Print 'More neg. than pos. cards'
5.4.5.   ENDIF
5.5.   ENDIF
6.   END

8.7 1.   PERIOD := 1
2.   DOWHILE PERIOD <= 5
2.1.   HOURS := 0

2.2.   DOWHILE HOURS <= 11
2.2.1.   MIN := 0
2.2.2.   DOWHILE MIN <= 59
2.2.2.1.   SEC := 0
2.2.2.2.   DOWHILE SEC <= 59
2.2.2.2.1.   Print HOURS, ':', MIN, ':', SEC
2.2.2.2.2.   SEC := SEC + 1
2.2.2.2.3.   ENDDO
2.2.2.3.   MIN := MIN + 1
2.2.2.4.   ENDDO
2.2.3.   HOURS := HOURS + 1
2.2.4.   ENDDO
2.3.   PERIODS := PERIODS + 1
2.4.   ENDDO
3.   Print 'Wind me, please'
4.   END

8.9 1.   BIGGEST := 0
2.   MIDDLE := 0
3.   SMALLEST := 0
4.   Read value, assign to FIRST
5.   Read value, assign to SECOND
6.   Read value, assign to THIRD
7.   IF FIRST > SECOND
7.1.   THEN
7.2.   IF FIRST > THIRD
7.2.1.   THEN
7.2.2.   BIGGEST := FIRST
7.2.3.   ELSE
7.2.4.   BIGGEST := THIRD
7.2.5.   ENDIF
7.3.   ELSE
7.4.   IF SECOND > THIRD
7.4.1.   THEN
7.4.2.   BIGGEST := SECOND
7.4.3.   ELSE
7.4.4.   BIGGEST := THIRD
7.4.5.   ENDIF
7.5.   ENDIF
8.   IF BIGGEST = FIRST
8.1.   THEN
8.2.   IF SECOND > THIRD
8.2.1.   THEN
8.2.2.   MIDDLE := SECOND
8.2.3.   SMALLEST := THIRD
8.2.4.   ELSE

8.2.5.	MIDDLE := THIRD
8.2.6.	SMALLEST := SECOND
8.2.7.	ENDIF
8.3.	ENDIF
9.	IF BIGGEST = SECOND
9.1.	THEN
9.2.	IF FIRST > THIRD
9.2.1.	THEN
9.2.2.	MIDDLE := FIRST
9.2.3.	SMALLEST := THIRD
9.2.4.	ELSE
9.2.5.	MIDDLE := THIRD
9.2.6.	SMALLEST := FIRST
9.2.7.	ENDIF
9.3.	ENDIF
10.	IF BIGGEST = THIRD
10.1.	THEN
10.2.	IF FIRST > SECOND
10.2.1.	THEN
10.2.2.	MIDDLE := FIRST
10.2.3.	SMALLEST := SECOND
10.2.4.	ELSE
10.2.5.	SMALLEST := SECOND
10.2.6.	MIDDLE := FIRST
10.2.7.	ENDIF
10.3.	ENDIF
11.	Print 'The order of numbers entered is:'
12.	Print FIRST, SECOND, THIRD
13.	Print 'Arranged from greatest to smallest is:'
14.	Print BIGGEST, MIDDLE, SMALLEST
15.	END

CHAPTER NINE

9.1 Written without NOT:

$$(BIRK >= 7) \ AND \ (BIRK <= 15)$$

$$BIRK := 5$$

$$(5 >= 7) \ AND \ (5 <= 15)$$
$$FALSE \ AND \ TRUE$$
$$FALSE$$

$$BIRK := 22$$

$$(22 >= 7) \ AND \ (22 <= 15)$$

TRUE AND FALSE
FALSE

Written with NOT:

NOT ((BIRK < 7) OR (BIRK > 15))

BIRK := 4

NOT ((4 < 7) OR (4 > 15))
NOT ((TRUE) OR (FALSE))
NOT (TRUE)
FALSE

BIRK := −3

NOT ((−3 < 7) OR (−3 > 15))
NOT ((TRUE) OR (FALSE))
NOT (TRUE)
FALSE

9.2 Written without NOT (when these conditions are met, the system operates):

(KRONCH <= 8) OR (KRONCH >= 45)

KRONCH := 78

(78 <= 8) OR (78 >= 45)
FALSE OR TRUE
TRUE

KRONCH := 16

(16 <= 8) OR (16 >= 45)
FALSE OR FALSE
FALSE

Written with NOT:

NOT ((KRONCH > 8) AND (KRONCH < 45))

KRONCH := −3

NOT ((−3 > 8) AND (−3 < 45))
NOT (FALSE AND TRUE)
NOT FALSE
TRUE

KRONCH := 30

NOT ((30 > 8) AND (30 < 45))
NOT (TRUE AND TRUE)
NOT TRUE
FALSE

9.3 1.   SOUGHT := 33.2
 2.   Read a card, assign to TEST
 3.   DOWHILE ((TEST < > SOUGHT) AND (TEST < > 0))
 3.1.   Read a card, assign to TEST
 3.2. ENDDO
 4.   IF TEST = 0
 4.1.   THEN
 4.2.   Print 'The desired number is absent.'
 4.3.   ELSE
 4.4.   Print 'The desired number is present.'
 4.5. ENDIF
 5.   END

9.4

A	B	NOT (A)	NOT (B)	(NOT (A) AND NOT (B))
T	T	F	F	F
T	F	F	T	F
F	T	T	F	F
F	F	T	T	T

9.5 1.   EXTEMPLIM := 105
 2.   INTEMPLIM := 325
 3.   INPRESLIM := 400
 4.   Read internal temperature, assign to INTEMP
 5.   Read internal pressure, assign to INPRES
 6.   Read external temperature, assign to EXTEMP
 7.   IF ((EXTEMP > EXTEMPLIM) AND ((INTEMP >
         INTEMPLIM) OR (INPRESS > INPRESLIM)))
 7.1.   THEN
 7.2.   Print 'DANGER'
 7.3.   ELSE
 7.4.   Print 'System ok'
 7.5. ENDIF
 8.   END

To alter the conditions as indicated in the second part of the problem, change line 7 and only line 7 to read IF ((EXTEMP > EXTEMPLIM) AND ((INTEMP > INTEMPLIM) AND (INPRES > INPRESLIM))).

COMMENT   The Boolean statement used in the two versions of line 7 is clear, but a bit complicated. It would be a great deal better as code if one level of nesting was used. That is, the external temperature test would constitute either a DOWHILE or an IF–THEN structure, and the test of internal temperature and internal pressure would constitute an IF–THEN–ELSE nested in the outer statement. The control conditions of the internal selection for the two examples would be, respectively:

(INTEMP > TEMPLIM OR INPRES > PRESLIM)

for the first case, and

(INTEMP > TEMPLIM AND INPRES > PRESLIM)

for the second.

9.6

A	B	NOT (A)	NOT (B)	NOT (A) OR NOT (B)	NOT (NOT (A) OR NOT (B))
T	T	F	F	F	T
T	F	F	T	T	F
F	T	T	F	T	F
F	F	T	T	T	F

9.7
1. Read value, assign to FIRST
2. Read value, assign to SECOND
3. Read value, assign to THIRD
4. BIGGEST := 0
5. MIDDLE := 0
6 SMALLEST := 0
7. IF ((FIRST > SECOND) AND (FIRST > THIRD)
7.1. THEN
7.2. BIGGEST := FIRST
7.3. ENDIF
8. IF ((SECOND > FIRST) AND (SECOND > THIRD))
8.1. THEN
8.2. BIGGEST := SECOND
8.3. ENDIF
9. IF ((THIRD > FIRST) AND (THIRD > SECOND))
9.1. THEN
9.2. BIGGEST := THIRD
9.3. ENDIF
10. IF BIGGEST = FIRST
10.1. THEN
10.2. IF SECOND > THIRD
10.2.1. THEN
10.2.2. MIDDLE := SECOND
10.2.3. SMALLEST := THIRD
10.2.4. ELSE
10.2.5. MIDDLE := THIRD
10.2.6. SMALLEST :=SECOND
10.2.7. ENDIF
10.3. ENDIF
11. IF BIGGEST = SECOND
11.1. THEN
11.2. IF FIRST > THIRD

11.2.1.   THEN
11.2.2.   MIDDLE := FIRST
11.2.3.   SMALLEST := THIRD
11.2.4.   ELSE
11.2.5.   MIDDLE := THIRD
11.2.6.   SMALLEST := FIRST
11.2.7.   ENDIF
11.3.   ENDIF
12.   IF BIGGEST = THIRD
12.1.   THEN
12.2.   IF FIRST > SECOND
12.2.1.   THEN
12.2.2.   MIDDLE := FIRST
12.2.3.   SMALLEST := SECOND
12.2.4.   ELSE
12.2.5.   MIDDLE := SECOND
12.2.6.   SMALLEST :=FIRST
12.2.7.   ENDIF
12.3.   ENDIF
13.   Print 'The variables listed as entered are'
14.   Print FIRST, SECOND, THIRD
15.   Print 'The variables as put in order are'
16.   Print 'BIGGEST, MIDDLE, SMALLEST'
17.   END

COMMENT   Notice that the use of Boolean structures produced clearer organization. It is not necessary to replace all nesting by Boolean statements. The main purpose is clarity and ease of analysis.

9.8 While Boolean techniques can be used with counting structures, they complicate things. Hence, a program is not included.

9.9   *1.*   Read a card with three values on it
     2.   Assign first value to ADOOR
     3.   Assign second value to BDOOR
     4.   Assign third value to CDOOR
     5.   ADOOR := ADOOR + 1
     6.   Print 'Entering room'
     7.   IF ((BDOOR = 5) AND (CDOOR = 5))
     7.1.   THEN
     7.2.   Print 'This is a closet. I leave as I came'
     7.3.   ADOOR := ADOOR + 1
     7.4.   ENDIF
     8.   IF ((BDOOR = 0) AND (CDOOR = 5))
     8.1.   THEN
     8.2.   Print 'I am leaving by the only other door'
     8.3.   BDOOR := BDOOR + 1

8.4.   ENDIF
9.   IF ((BDOOR = 5) AND (CDOOR = 0))
9.1.   THEN
9.2.   Print 'I am leaving by the only other door'
9.3.   CDOOR := CDOOR + 1
9.4.   ENDIF
10.   IF ((BDOOR = 0) AND (CDOOR = 0))
10.1.   THEN
10.2.   Print 'Leaving by one of the other two doors'
10.3.   BDOOR := BDOOR + 1
10.4.   ENDIF
11.   Print 'What Next?'
12.   END

9.10   *1.*   Read card from A-deck and assign to A
2.   Read card from B-deck and assign to B
3.   DOWHILE (A < 0 AND B < 0)
3.1.   DOWHILE A = B
3.1.1.   Read from A-deck and assign to A
3.1.2.   ENDDO
3.2.   IF A > B
3.2.1.   THEN
3.2.2.   Print A
3.2.3.   Read card from A-deck, assign to A
3.2.4.   ELSE
3.2.5.   Print B
3.2.6.   Read card from B-deck, assign to B
3.2.7.   ENDIF
3.3   ENDDO
4.   DOWHILE A <> 0
4.1.   Print A
4.2.   Read card from A-deck, assign to A
4.3.   ENDDO
5.   DOWHILE B <> 0
5.1.   Print B
5.2.   Read card from B-deck, assign to B
5.3.   ENDDO
6.   Print 'Data Merge Complete'
7.   END

CHAPTER TEN

10.2   *1.*   DECLARE SHELF (20)
2.   KOUNTER := 1
3.   DOWHILE KOUNTER <= 20

3.1.   Read card, assign to SHELF (KOUNTER)

3.2.   KOUNTER := KOUNTER + 1

3.3.   ENDDO

4.   BIGGEST := SHELF (1)

5.   ZIP := 1

6.   DOWHILE ZIP <= 20

6.1.   IF BIGGEST < SHELF (ZIP)

6.1.1.   THEN

6.1.2.   BIGGEST := SHELF (ZIP)

6.1.3.   ENDIF

6.2.   ZIP := ZIP + 1

6.3.   ENDDO

7.   INVIS := BIGGEST + 10

8.   END

10.4 1.   DECLARE GEORGE (40), JAKE (40)

2.   I := 1

3.   DOWHILE I <= 40

3.1.   Read card, assign to JAKE (I)

3.2.   ENDDO

4.   ZILCH := 1

5.   DOWHILE ZILCH <= 40

5.1.   GEORGE (ZILCH) := JAKE (41 − ZILCH)

5.2.   ZILCH := ZILCH + 1

5.3.   ENDDO

6.   K := 1

7.   DOWHILE K <= 40

7.1.   Print JAKE (K), GEORGE (K)

7.2.   K := K + 1

7.3.   ENDDO

8.   Print 'Inversion Complete'

9.   END

10.6 1.   DECLARE ABLE (50), BAKER (50), CHUCK (50)

2.   K := 1

3.   DOWHILE K <= 50

3.1.   Read card from deck-A, assign to ABLE (K)

3.2.   Read card from deck-B, assign to BAKER (K)

3.3.   K := K + 1

3.4.   ENDDO

4.   I = 1

5.   DOWHILE I <= 50

5.1.   IF ABLE (I) = BAKER (I)

5.1.1.   THEN

5.1.2.   CHUCK (I) := 1

5.1.3.   ELSE

5.1.4.		CHUCK (I) := 0
5.1.5.	ENDIF	
5.2.		I := I + 1
5.3.	ENDDO	
6.	ZIP := 1	
6.1.	DOWHILE ZIP <= 50	
6.2.		Print CHUCK (ZIP)
6.3.		ZIP := ZIP + 1
6.4.	ENDDO	
7.	END	

10.8

1.	DECLAR RADAR (51)
2.	IKON := 1
3.	DOWHILE IKON <= 51
3.1.	Read value, assign to RADAR (IKON)
3.2.	IKON := IKON + 1
3.3.	ENDDO
4.	N := 1
5.	DOWHILE N <= 25
5.1.	FLOP := RADAR (N)
5.2.	RADAR (N) := RADAR (52 − N)
5.3.	RADAR (52 − N) := FLOP
5.4.	N := N + 1
5.5.	ENDDO
6.	END

10.10

1.	DECLARE RACK (5)
2.	MARK := 1
3.	DOWHILE MARK <= 5
3.1.	Read value, assign to RACK (MARK)
3.2.	MARK := MARK + 1
3.3.	ENDDO
4.	START := 1
5.	DOWHILE START < 5
5.1.	BIGPOINT :=START
5.2.	ZIP := START
5.3.	DOWHILE ZIP <= 5
5.3.1.	IF RACK (BIGPOINT) < RACK (ZIP)
5.3.1.1.	THEN
5.3.1.2.	BIGPOINT := ZIP
5.3.1.3.	ENDIF
5.3.2.	ZIP := ZIP + 1
5.3.3.	ENDDO
5.4.	TEMP := RACK (START)
5.5.	RACK (START) := RACK (BIGPOINT)
5.6.	RACK (BIGPOINT) := TEMP

5.7.   START := START + 1
5.8.   ENDDO
6.   Print 'Sort Complete'
8.   ZIP := 1
9.   DOWHILE ZIP <= 5
9.1.   Print RACK (ZIP)
9.2.   ZIP := ZIP + 1
9.3.   ENDDO
10.   END

CHAPTER ELEVEN

11.1 *1.*   DECLARE BOX (5,5)
2.   DOFOR ROW := 1 TO 5
2.1.   DOFOR COL := 1 TO 5
2.1.1.   IF ROW = COL
2.1.1.1.   THEN
2.1.1.2.   BOX (ROW, COL) := 1
2.1.1.3.   ELSE
2.1.1.4.   BOX (ROW, COL) := 0
2.1.1.5.   ENDIF
2.1.2.   ENDDO
2.2.   ENDDO
3.   Print 'Array Complete'
4.   END

11.3 *1.*   DECLARE FIELD (70,25)
2.   FLAG := 1
3.   DOFOR ROW := 1 TO 70
3.1.   IF FLAG := 1
3.1.1.   THEN
3.1.2.   DOFOR COL := 1 TO 25
3.1.2.1.   FIELD (ROW, COL) := 7
3.1.2.2.   ENDDO
3.1.3.   FLAG := 10
3.1.4.   ELSE
3.1.5.   DOFOR COL := 25 TO 1 STEP −1
3.1.5.1.   FIELD (ROW, COL) := 7
3.1.5.2.   ENDDO
3.1.6.   FLAG := 1
3.1.7.   ENDIF
3.2.   ENDDO
4.   Print 'Ready to Plant'
5.   END

11.5 *1.* DECLARE BOX1(5,5), BOX2(5,5), HOLDER(5,5)
2. Print 'Loading Arrays'
3. DOFOR ROW := 1 TO 5
3.1. DOFOR COL := 1 TO 5
3.1.1. Print 'Loading element into Array 1'
3.1.2. Read value, Assign to BOX1(ROW, COL)
3.1.3. Print 'Loading element into Array 2'
3.1.4. Read value, Assign to BOX2(ROW, COL)
3.1.5. ENDDO
3.2. ENDDO
4. Print 'Loading Complete'
5. DOFOR ROW := 1 TO 5
5.1. DOFOR COL := 1 TO 5
5.1.1. HOLDER (ROW, COL) := BOX1(ROW, COL) +
BOX2(ROW, COL)
5.1.2. ENDDO
5.2. ENDDO
6. Print 'Addition Complete'
7. END

11.7 The important part of this program is the technology used to achieve control without resorting to GOTO or having the use of subroutine structures. In this answer we will suggest a type of program that will achieve the desired result, but the actual construction of the program will be left to the student.

Each ship will be represented by a two-dimensional array consisting of two columns and a sufficient number of rows to account for the number of points the particular ship requires. Three points for a battleship, two points for a cruiser and one point for a destroyer means that these ships will be represented by two-dimensional arrays with three rows, two rows and one row, respectively. The coordinates of the points representing the ship in question will be stored in the appropriate array for that ship. Thus, to designate a battleship's position, we must load the coordinates for three points into the elements of an array having three rows. Each row contains one pair of coordinates.

There will be one additional array. This will have a row for each of the coordinates used to represent a ship. Thus, if you have one battleship, one cruiser and one destroyer, there will be six rows. This array will also have two columns, providing space for each of the two coordinates of the points in question. Where the ship arrays are used to establish the locations of the ships, the array containing all the points representing locations occupied by ships is used to avoid overlap of ships.

Assume the playing field to be filled will contain three ships: one battleship, one cruiser and one destroyer. This means that there will be three ship assignment routines. The first will announce itself and go through a three-step loop to load three coordinates, one pair at a time. This will load the battleship's position markers into the corresponding array. At the same time it will load the same three pairs of coordinates into the first three pairs of elements in the array that controls overlaps. The cruiser will be located next by loading two pairs of coordinates, which will be entered into the array representing the cruiser and into the fourth and fifth pairs of elements in the array used in overlap checking. The destroyer would be handled in the same way.

Let us now examine the actual entering of coordinates. Each time a pair of coordinates is requested by a loading sequence and entered, it will first reside in a pair of variables represented as a simple array with one row and two columns. Of course, this is really a one-dimensional array with two elements. The coordinates will first be tested to see if one of them is larger than 10. If they pass the test, they will be tested against the pairs of values held in the array used to check for ship overlap. If at the same time (Boolean AND) both the new coordinates correspond to a pair of coordinates already residing in the overlap-testing array, the entered points are unacceptable. Thus, there are two ways entered coordinate pairs may be unacceptable. One of the coordinates may be larger than 10, or the pair of coordinates entered may exactly match a pair of coordinates already entered.

For the moment, assume the entered coordinates are acceptable. In this case, they will be transferred from the holding array to the next available pair of positions in the array representing the ship being filled and to the next available pair of positions in the overlap array. Appropriate messages will announce that the ship is now filled, and refer control to the next ship, or will request another pair of coordinates for the ship in question.

In the event that a pair of coordinates entered is not acceptable, two things will happen. First, the variable controlling the loop used to load the ship array will be set to its limit, thus transferring control out of the loading loop. Second, a variable called CLEARANCE (or some similar name) will be set to 1. This variable is a flag that was set to 0 at the beginning of the entire loading program.

We now have a situation in which an unacceptable coordinate pair has caused control to go out of the loading loop in service. Further, a flag has been set. Each loading loop after the first one is protected by a DOWHILE that requires the flag to unset (value should be 0). If this is not the case, control passes to the next loading loop. Of course this next loading loop is also protected, so control passes through all loading phases to the end of the program. The end of the program is also protected by a test block in the form of an IF–THEN–ELSE. This tests the flag. If the flag has not been set (value is 0), the program assumes all ships have been set up, announces this and ends. If the flag has been set (value is 1), it is clear that a coordinate pair was not acceptable. Hence, this alternative prints a notice that an unacceptable variable has been used and advises the user to start the loading program again and ends.

You should be at a level of development where the pseudocode writing will cause few difficulties. It is hoped that this detailed discussion of a useful set of routines to provide good structure while avoiding GOTO will permit you to write the program. This problem will be developed further in Chapter 12. However, at that time you will have subroutines to work with and will have a bit more experience. Using what you know from this example, you should start from scratch rather than patching up the program you have created here.

11.10 *1.* DECLARE RACK (5,5)
 2.   DOFOR ROW := 1 TO 5
 2.1.   DOFOR COL := 1 TO 5
 2.1.1.   Read value, assign to RACK (ROW, COL)
 2.1.2.   ENDDO
 2.2. ENDDO
 3.   Print 'Array Loaded'
 4.   DOFOR ROW := 1 TO 5
 4.1.   DOFOR COL := 1 TO 5
 4.1.1.   IF ROW < COL
 4.1.1.1.   THEN
 4.1.1.2.   HOLDER := RACK (ROW, COL)
 4.1.1.3.   RACK (ROW, COL) := RACK (COL, ROW)
 4.1.1.4.   RACK (COL, ROW) := HOLDER
 4.1.1.5.   ENDIF
 4.1.2.   ENDDO
 4.2. ENDDO
 5.   Print 'Inversion Complete'
 6.   END

CHAPTER TWELVE

12.1 I feel that by this time, a general indication of the type of program should be sufficient to permit problem solution. For this reason, the problem solutions presented here will consist of the calling module and a few comments about additional subroutines to include within those subroutines activated directly by the calling module. This method of providing an answer will be followed for the rest of the problem solutions.

   1. DECLARE CRATE (25), FRAME (25)
   2. CALL: CRATELOAD
   3. CALL: INVISIBLE
   4. CALL: TWORAYSORT
   5. CALL:OUTPRINT

REMARK   In the subroutine TWORAYSORT there is a time when you have completed the selection of the present largest element when you transfer this element to the second array, and replace it in the original array with the invisible element. You may or may not wish to make this an additional subroutine. The routine used to select the largest element within each sorting pass is used again and again. It is a candidate for separate subroutine structure, but it is very short. This is up to you.

   My own opinion is that, considering the size of this program and the size of the optional subroutines suggested, the use of these optional subroutines does not add to the clarity of the program as it would for a larger program.

12.3 *1.* CALL: BUSSTOP
   2. CALL: FIRSTTEST
   3. CALL: DIRECTION
   4. CALL: ROUTINETEST
   5. CALL: ADVENTURESEND

REMARK   I would group the receipt of the house number and its entry to the machine via a question with the test of the first house encountered as the bus is left. This would be BUSSTOP. FIRSTTEST is a subroutine used for the test of the second house number. Provided neither the test included in BUSSTOP nor the test included in FIRST-TEST is positive, the data from these two subroutines will be used in conjunction with a subroutine called DIRECTION that determines whether the person conducting the investigation is moving in the correct direction and reverses his or her direction if necessary. From here until the testing routine either meets the right house or reaches the end of the street, the testing will be routine, so we have a sub-routine called ROUTINETEST.

   In a single test like BUSSTOP or FIRSTTEST, only one test is run. At the end of this test, whether it is successful, or shows the end of the street or does neither, control must return to the main program. In the event of no result, it does this with a normal RETURN. In the event of a result, it will call a routine called SUCCESS or STREET-SEND. These subroutines will provide a suitable message and set a variable (which might be called NECESSARY) to a value of 1. This is because if the end of the street has been found, or the correct house number has been found, it is not necessary to do any of the remaining subroutines except ADVENTURESEND. Thus, after BUSSTOP, the actual operational part of each subroutine will be protected by a DOWHILE whose condition is that NECESSARY have a value of zero. NECESSARY is set at 0 at the start of BUSSTOP and will be set to 1 only when the SUCCESS subroutine or the ENDOFSTREET subroutine is called by a test sequence.

This subroutine design allows control to proceed smoothly along the top module, avoids ending the program inside one of the subroutines and always ensures that the termination subroutine (in this case ADVENTURESEND) is run exactly in the sequence shown in the top module. Within those modules involving a test, you may wish to refer to a common TEST subroutine, or you may not. In any event, remember that the complete test may be positive involving success, negative involving the end of the street, or neutral involving neither. In the event of no decision, you will leave the subroutine in the case of BUSSTOP and FIRSTTEST, and you will be told to go to the next house and enter its number in the case of ROUTINETEST.

12.5 1. CALL: STACKBILT
2. CALL: MENU
3. CALL: SIGNOFF

The subroutine STACKBUILT declares the array and sets the pointer to its initial position. Setting this pointer merely involves assigning the value 1 to a variable that will serve to designate a particular position in the array serving as a stack.

Since this is a demonstration model, empty spaces in the stack should be indicated by the value 0. Thus, only nonzero numbers should actually be stored in the stack. This technique of using zero is convenient. In the case of a real stack, a special symbol is used, or each stack location has a real physical location in the computer hardware and may thus actually be empty.

The subroutine MENU offers the user a choice of activities. These are PUSH, POP, DISPLAY and QUIT. In the case of all choices except QUIT, completion of the requested activity returns control to the MENU subroutine. At the beginning of the stack program, the stack pointer points at an empty space. This is a another way of saying that the variable that holds the stack pointer contains the number 1, the pointer of the first element of the array. If the choice POP is called, subroutine presents a prompt indicating that the stack is empty. If values have been entered into the stack, the pointer will point to the empty element immediately above the space occupied by the last number entered. If a POP is then requested, the pointer value will be reduced in value by 1 and the value corresponding to that position printed out, after which a value of 0 is placed in that position. Thus, at the end of a POP, the pointer will point to an empty space. If the pointer value is 1, then the stack is empty and a notice to that effect is displayed.

If the activity PUSH is requested, the program asks for a value to be pushed and places it in the location indicated by the pointer value in the stack pointer variable. The value of the stack pointer will be increased by one, so that it points to an unoccupied space in the array respresenting the stack. If incrementing the stack pointer variable causes it to reach a value one greater than the highest allowable pointer for the array serving as stack, then the stack has been filled and no empty space remains. Notice should be given of this position and attempts to call PUSH should only get this message.

DISPLAY should cause the stack to be printed out as a column of numbers. The stack pointer position should be indicated.

QUIT is obvious. It should cause control to return to the main program leading to the SIGNOFF call, which ends the program.

12.9   The calling module of this FIFO device is identical to that of a stack. The choices within the menu are also the same. The trick is to know where the earlier entries are and to arrange space so that after a number of PUSH and POP operations new space is not lost. A good way to accomplish this is the following.

The array is always organized with the value that has been stored the longest at the location with pointer value 1 and the remaining stored values arranged in order of decreasing residence time above this location. When a number is pushed onto the array it will be entered in the first empty location following the filled position having the highest value pointer.

When a number is popped from the array, it will always be the value stored at the position pointed to by the array pointer value of 1, since this position contains the oldest resident. When a number is popped from the array, the location where it was stored will become empty, since when the value is printed out its location will be cleared. At this time a subroutine should be called automatically that will cause each value resident in the array to be shifted into the adjacent location that is one position nearer the first position of the array. The array is thus reordered so that the oldest resident is again in the first position. At the same time, the pointer locating the next available position for loading must be changed. All these adjustments can be produced by the shifting subroutine, which you may wish to call SHIFT. Of course, you will have to have notification routines that will be called in the event the array is completely full or completely empty. The automatic decision to call these subroutines will depend on the location of the pointer, which shows the next position available for filling. If this location is that with array pointer 1, then the array is empty and a POP request should cause this response. If the pointer indicating the next position to be filled contains a value one greater than the number of elements in the array, then no position is available for filling and a notice should be printed. The same notice should be printed on any attempt to introduce a new value.

The DISPLAY option should cause the array contents to be listed in order. The pointer locating the next position to be filled should be indicated.

APPENDIX

Translating Pseudocode into Computer Languages

IF YOU have written a well-organized meaningful essay in English, you may wish to translate it into French or German without losing the subtleties of structure and content. A comprehensive phrasebook and a detailed two-language dictionary will be of little help if you do not already have a good knowledge of the foreign language. However, if you do have some skill with the foreign language, then the phrasebook and dictionary can be an immense help, because they ensure that the precise meaning and evocative structure you produced in the English masterpiece will be carried over to the new language to delight your readers.

The same approach applies to the translation between pseudocode and computer languages. You used pseudocode to help in the analysis of some problem. The structural features helped you provide a clear, well-organized masterpiece of a program. Now you are ready to transform it into a computer language so that it may be run on the hardware. Since the structure and logic are already properly designed in the pseudocode program, you can devote maximum attention to the grammar and punctuation of the computer language to avoid error notices during the preparation phase or when the program is finally run. Before you can hope to start on such a translation, you need to know the desired computer language fairly well.

What this appendix provides is a set of translations of the common control devices of pseudocode into well-structured modules written in selected computer languages: BASIC, FORTRAN, COBOL and Pascal. The structures considered will be selection (IF–THEN–ELSE, IF–THEN), DOFOR and DOWHILE. The structure DOUNTIL will be examined only during consideration of Pascal. This language makes specific use of this construction, but it is not part of the direct or implied system of control in the other three languages we consider in this text.

The optional structure CASE, though quite useful, is not particularly common in general programming and will be excluded. If a language has major variants differing in their use of statements related to the

257

pseudocode control structures, then the significant variations will be considered. In those cases where a GOTO structure is required, its use will be localized within a specific module.

It will sometimes be necessary to use some form of subroutine to produce the desired control effects. Where this is necessary, the process of subroutine definition will be discussed. Further, such aspects of variable passing as are necessary will be discussed, but the subject will not be treated in its own right, because the technology of passing variables between main program and subroutines is specific to each higher language.

Three considerations should be kept in mind. First, the use of standardized computer language structures corresponding to the pseudocode control structures facilitates rapid coding by reducing much of the translation to a process of simple substitution. Second, the translator should have a good knowledge of the computer language to be used. Third, the translation structures presented below work quite well and have been tested in the classroom; however, you may know of or invent one that you like better. Use the translation that you find is comfortable, but stick to a standard form, whatever the source. Standardization simplifies substitution technology and lets you concentrate on the computer language grammar and the special problems inherent in using the particular computer language under consideration.

Section 1: Pseudocode into BASIC

Most versions of BASIC available today have a full selection (IF–THEN–ELSE) statement, a statement corresponding exactly to DOWHILE and a statement corresponding to DOFOR. Earlier versions, a few of which are still running, have a limited selection form corresponding to IF–THEN, the structure mentioned above which is very close to DOFOR, and nothing even vaguely like DOWHILE.

In BASIC, all variables may be used by both the main program and any subroutines that are created. For this reason, there is no special procedure for passing variables between the main program and any subroutines, and at the same time, there is no problem in passing values from the subroutines back to the main program.

For our first replacement examples we will use the more primitive form of BASIC. Since this is a subset of the more advanced BASIC language sets, these techniques will always work. However, whenever you have a BASIC interpreter or compiler of the more modern variety, by all means make use of the more modern control structures. The degree to which they improve programming speed and clarity is almost beyond belief.

SELECTION (IF–THEN)

Pseudocode	BASIC
IF A LARGER THAN K THEN Z := 5 ENDIF	100 IF A > K THEN Z = 5

Suppose the activity to undertake when the control condition is satisfied is a multi-line process. In the simple form of BASIC, this can often best be done in the form of a subroutine. In writing the IF–THEN statement in BASIC, note that it may be written 'IF ⟨condition⟩ THEN 700' or 'IF ⟨condition⟩ GOTO 700', where ⟨condition⟩ represents the test to be is carried out and 700, which may be any valid line label, is the line label to which control should be transferred. In the case of other statements to be executed, including GOSUB, a THEN is required.

Pseudocode	BASIC

IF A LARGER THAN K
    THEN
        Z := 5
        PRINT Z
ENDIF
	100 IF A > K THEN GOSUB 2000
	    .
	    .
	900 END
	2000 REM SUBROUTINE FOR A > K
	2010 Z = 5
	2020 PRINT Z
	2030 RETURN

A less desirable way to write this module is to use a GOTO. This has a drawback in that it involves inverting the logical condition in the control statement, which makes the BASIC program harder to understand.

Pseudocode	BASIC

IF A LARGER THAN K
    THEN
        Z := 5
        PRINT Z
ENDIF
	100 REM IF–THEN (A > K)
	110 IF A <= K GOTO 150
	120 REM THEN
	130 Z = 5
	140 PRINT Z
	150 REM ENDIF

As a general rule, a subroutine call in the IF statement seems preferable.

SELECTION (IF–THEN–ELSE)

The simplest way to handle an IF–THEN–ELSE in primitive BASIC is with two consecutive IF statements:

Pseudocode	BASIC
IF A LARGER THAN K	100 REM IF–THEN–ELSE (A > K)
THEN	110 IF A > K THEN GOSUB 2000
Z := 5	120 REM ELSE
PRINT Z	130 IF A <= K THEN GOSUB 3000
ELSE	140 REM ENDIF
K := 25	:
PRINT 'No Sale'	900 END
ENDIF	2000 REM SUBROUTINE FOR A > K
	2010 Z = 5
	2020 PRINT Z
	2030 RETURN
	3000 SUBROUTINE FOR Z <= K
	3010 K = 25
	3020 PRINT 'No Sale'
	3030 RETURN

To avoid the use of two successive IF–THEN structures, a single control block may be used. Once again, this involves the GOTO. Here, there are two GOTOs in addition to an inverted control condition. This arrangement works and it is sometimes seen in textbooks, but the combination of two GOTOs as well as an inverted control condition seems an invitation to confusion. Here is an example:

BASIC
```
100 REM IF–THEN–ELSE (A > K)
110 IF A <= K GOTO 160
120 REM THEN
130          Z = 5
140          PRINT Z
150 GOTO 190
160 REM ELSE
170          K = 25
180          PRINT 'No Sale'
190 REM ENDIF
```

DOWHILE

In the more limited versions of BASIC, where the statements WHILE and WEND do not exist, the DOWHILE control structure may be emulated in two different ways. One involves the use of a subroutine and one GOTO. The action of the GOTO is restricted to two lines. The logic of the control condition remains as written in the pseudocode design program.

Pseudocode	BASIC
DOWHILE Z < 35	100 REM DOWHILE (Z < 35)
Print Z	110 IF Z < 35 THEN GOSUB 2000
Z := Z + 1	120 IF Z < 35 GOTO 110
ENDDO	130 REM ENDDO
	⋮
	⋮
	⋮
	900 END
	2000 REM SUBROUTINE FOR Z < 35
	2010 PRINT Z
	2020 Z = Z + 1
	2030 RETURN

In the BASIC emulation of DOWHILE above, note the unusual way the IF statement repeats itself in lines 110 and 120. Running a trace on the module will show that this rather odd structure, in conjunction with a subroutine, provides a satisfactory result. I prefer it to the more usual form shown below, in which the control statement is inverted relative to that used in the pseudocode design program or flowchart documentation. This is because the preferred structure not only keeps all the GOTOs in one place, but also avoids any temptation to invert the logical condition that controls the module. Here is the more usual form:

Pseudocode	BASIC
DOWHILE Z < 35	150 REM DOWHILE (Z < 35)
Print Z	110 IF Z >= 35 GOTO 150
Z := Z + 1	120 PRINT Z
ENDDO	130 Z = Z + 1
	140 GOTO 110
	150 REM ENDDO

DOFOR

The DOFOR structure causes a loop to be repeated a fixed number of times, depending on the values assigned to a set of counting variables. There is a structure, even in the primitive versions of BASIC, that takes care of this directly. It is called the FOR–TO–NEXT statement and operates as shown below.

Pseudocode	BASIC
DOFOR K := 1 TO 5	110 FOR K = 1 TO 5
$\quad$ Z := Z + 1	110 $\quad$ Z = Z + 1
$\quad$ Print Z	120 $\quad\quad$ PRINT Z
ENDDO	130 NEXT K

This completes the emulation of the fundamental control structures in the less sophisticated forms of BASIC. The more advanced form will now be examined. This is typical of most BASIC programming systems found on computers today. There are a number of differences between older versions of BASIC and the modern forms of the language. One difference is that the variables may consist of more than one or two letters and thus approximate meaningful words. From our point of view, the most important reforms are the addition of a selection structure that is much like the IF–THEN–ELSE and a structure that is essentially identical to DOWHILE.

The IF–THEN–ELSE will be considered first. The same conditions will be used that were used in the consideration of more primitive BASIC technology, but in this case the improved variable designation rules will be used, as well as the more advanced control structures.

Before demonstrating the use of the IF–THEN–ELSE structure, the specific definition usually found in advanced versions of BASIC should be discussed. The entire IF–THEN–ELSE structure is only one statement. Although it may occupy several programming lines, it will have only one line label number for the entire multi-line structure. If a statement to be executed by the THEN clause or the ELSE clause is more than one statement line, or is actually another multi-line control structure, the size of the selection statement may exceed the limits placed on it by the compiler or interpreter rules. In general, these rules state that the entire selection statement may occupy no more than 255 spaces. Since the usual computer screen has 80 spaces per line, this means roughly three physical lines of code. In some versions of BASIC this is improved by having spacing lines automatically inserted. These lines do not allow more code to be entered, but they do improve the layout of the selection spacing without using up any of the precious 255 spaces. In general, if the statements to be executed as choices are more than one line in length, subroutine technology should be used. This also applies in the case of nested control structures. Of course, when subroutines are used, program clarity is facilitated by using appropriate REM comments to identify the subroutine calls and the subroutines themselves.

Two selection examples will be presented. The first uses single-line statements that correspond to the tasks of the THEN and ELSE clauses. In the second, multi-line statements will be required for the choices, hence subroutine technology will be used.

SELECTION (IF–THEN–ELSE)

Pseudocode	Advanced BASIC
IF ALDO LARGER THAN KING	100 IF ALDO > KING
THEN	THEN ZEBRA = 5
ZEBRA := 5	ELSE KING = 25
ELSE	110 REM ENDIF
KING := 25	
ENDIF	

The organization of selection with multi-line options uses subroutines, as follows:

Pseudocode	Advanced BASIC
IF ALDO LARGER THAN KING	100 IF ALDO > KING
THEN	THEN GOSUB 2000
ZEBRA := 5	ELSE GOSUB 3000
Print ZEBRA	110 REM ENDIF
ELSE	:
KING := 25	:
Print 'No Sale'	:
ENDIF	900 END
	2000 REM SUBROUTINE,
	ALDO > KING
	2010 ZEBRA = 5
	2020 PRINT ZEBRA
	2030 RETURN
	3000 REM SUBROUTINE
	ALDO <= KING
	3010 KING = 25
	3020 PRINT 'No Sale'
	3030 RETURN

DOWHILE

The logical structure we have call DOWHILE in pseudocode is perfectly emulated in advanced versions of BASIC. The statement that begins the block is separate from the one that ends the block. Even though they are required to work in concert and may not be used independently, they each have separate line numbers. This makes it possible to use multi-line statements or nested control structures without recourse to subroutine technology. A single example of this structure is presented below:

Pseudocode	Advanced BASIC
DOWHILE ZEBRA LESS THAN 35	100 WHILE ZEBRA < 35
Print ZEBRA	110 PRINT ZEBRA
ZEBRA := ZEBRA + 1	120 ZEBRA = ZEBRA + 1
ENDDO	130 WEND

This completes the treatment of conversion of pseudocode control structures to BASIC.

Section 2: Pseudocode into FORTRAN

The translation of the major logical control structures from pseudocode into FORTRAN presents problems analogous to those we met in BASIC. There have been many versions of the language. FORTRAN 66 is the basic set of FORTRAN commands and is a subset of all FORTRAN variants. The first part of the section on FORTRAN will show the translation of selected control structures from pseudocode into FORTRAN 66.

The notation 66 refers to the year in which the American National Standards Institute (ANSI) released this standard. It is still sometimes referred to as Standard FORTRAN. It was recognized that a number of specific changes could be introduced to improve various aspects of the language. For this reason ANSI released an updated standard in 1977 known as FORTRAN 77. In addition to this, a number of variants of FORTRAN have been released with special features. These include such languages as WATFIV (University of Waterloo, Ontario, Canada) and M77 (University of Minnesota). Since any structure presented in FORTRAN 66 syntax will run in any of the variants, we have used this for our fundamental FORTRAN. Since FORTRAN 77 is also considered a general standard and is widely available, it is used as our 'advanced' version.

In some cases we will make use of subroutine technology. FORTRAN poses a slight problem in presenting such structures. All variables must be formally passed by one method or another between the main programs and any subprograms or subroutines. We will use the so-called COMMON method. In this case, a particular location in the main storage of the machine is designated to hold a variable that may be designated by one name in the main program and by the same or another name in a subprogram. No matter what the variable name used, the reference is to the same location in machine memory. To simplify reference we will use the same name in both the main program and the subroutine. Both the main program block and the subroutine must have a COMMON notification to identify the technology, but otherwise the variables will act as if they were global. This approach is used to permit the user to focus on translation of a logical structure from Pseudocode to FORTRAN. An understanding of this translation process is the intent of this section of the appendix.

As in the case of BASIC, we will consider the structures selection (IF–THEN–ELSE, IF–THEN), DOWHILE and DOFOR. FORTRAN 66 in particular will require the use of the GOTO statement, but the same stratagems presented in the discussion of BASIC will be used to prevent GOTO from getting out of control. FORTRAN 66 will be discussed first; FORTRAN 77 will be treated separately.

SELECTION (IF–THEN)

Pseudocode	FORTRAN 66
IF IKE GREATER THAN KID THEN NIK := 5 ENDIF	IF (IKE .GT. KID) NIK = 5

As in BASIC, a multi-line activity may be treated with a subroutine. Here it will be necessary to include the COMMON statement in both the main program and the subroutine to pass the variables. The statement is shown to indicate the need for its presence rather than to show exactly where it would be found in the FORTRAN 66 program, since the examples shown are program fragments rather than complete programs.

Pseudocode	FORTRAN 66

IF IKE LARGER THAN KID
   THEN
       NICK := 5
       MAN := MAN + 1
ENDIF
	COMMON // NICK, MAN
	IF (IKE .GT. KID) CALL BIKE
	   .
	   .
	   .
	STOP
	END
	SUBROUTINE BIKE
	COMMON // NICK, MAN
	   NICK = 5
	   MAN = MAN + 1
	RETURN
	END

This structure may also be written using GOTO and avoiding subroutines. As seen in the similar situation with BASIC, using this technology not only introduces a GOTO that can lead to problems of clarity; it is usually written with the control condition inverted relative to the design logic to keep the controlled clause near the conditional statement.

Pseudocode	FORTRAN 66

IF IKE LARGER THAN KID
   THEN
       NICK := 5
       MAN := MAN + 1
ENDIF
	IF (IKE .LE. KID) GO TO 50
	    NICK = 5
	    MAN = MAN + 1
	00050 CONTINUE

Note that the FORTRAN reserved word CONTINUE is a statement used as an address to mark boundaries between modules or to identify modules, but that it is actually nonfunctional.

SELECTION (IF–THEN–ELSE)

The easiest way to handle IF–THEN–ELSE in FORTRAN 66 is with two consecutive IF statements and subroutines, just as in the analogous case in BASIC:

Pseudocode	FORTRAN 66

IF IKE LARGER THAN KID
  THEN
    NICK := 5
    MAN := MAN + 1
  ELSE
    NICK := 21
    MAN := MAN − 2
ENDIF
	COMMON // NICK, MAN
	C IF–THEN–ELSE CONDITION (IKE > KID)
	    IF (IKE .GT. KID) CALL BIKE
	C ELSE
	    IF (IKE .LE. KID) CALL SIKE
	C ENDIF
	  STOP
	  END
	  SUBROUTINE BIKE
	  COMMON // NICK, MAN
	    NICK = 5
	    MAN = MAN + 1
	  RETURN
	  END
	  SUBROUTINE SIKE
	  COMMON // NICK, MAN
	    NICK = 21
	    MAN = MAN − 2
	  RETURN
	  END

In FORTRAN 66, emulation of the selection (IF–THEN–ELSE) control structure without using two successive IF–THEN blocks involves inversion of the control condition and two GOTO statements. Here is the way it works. If the control condition is not inverted, the physical order of the control blocks must be interchanged:

```
C     IF-THEN-ELSE FOR THE CONDITION (IKE > KID)
          IF (IKE. LE. KID) GO TO 60
C             THEN
                  NICK = 5
                  MAN = MAN + 1
                  GO TO 90
C             ELSE
00060             NICK = 21
                  MAN = MAN - 2
C         ENDIF
00090 CONTINUE
```

DOWHILE

FORTRAN 66 has the same DOWHILE problems as the more limited forms of BASIC. The same emulation structures will be used, although the coding differs because the syntax of FORTRAN 66 is different from that of BASIC.

Pseudocode	FORTRAN 66

```
DOWHILE IKE GREATER
THAN KING                    COMMON/IKE/NICK
    NICK := 5 - IKE     C     DOWHILE IKE LARGER THAN KING
    IKE := IKE - 1      00100     IF (IKE .GT. KING) CALL LIKE
ENDDO                             IF (IKE .GT. KING) GO TO 100
                        C     ENDDO
                              STOP
                              END
                              SUBROUTINE LIKE
                                  COMMON // IKE, NICK
                                  NICK = 5 - IKE
                                  IKE = IKE - 1
                              RETURN
                              END
```

This FORTRAN 66 emulation of DOWHILE by the use of a subroutine for the body of the loop uses the same type of repeated conditional as was used in the DOWHILE emulation written in the earlier form of BASIC. The structure using multiple GOTO statements or a close relative is the one more commonly shown in texts. A version of it is shown below:

```
C     DOWHILE IKE LARGER THAN KING
00100     IF (IKE .LE. KING) GO TO 200
          NICK = 5 - IKE
          IKE = IKE - 1
          GO TO 100
```

```
00200 CONTINUE
C     ENDDO
      STOP
      END
```

DOFOR

FORTRAN 66 contains a construction that is the exact equivalent of the DOFOR loop. It permits the body of the loop to be bounded by independent statements and to contain as many statements as desired. In FORTRAN as in BASIC, the effect of the structure known as DOFOR in pseudocode can be achieved with a simple structure already present in FORTRAN 66.

Pseudocode	FORTRAN 66

DOFOR KID := 1 TO 5
    ITEM := ITEM + 3
    NICK := NICK * ITEM
ENDDO
	DO 150 KID = 1, 5
	    ITEM = ITEM + 3
	    NICK = NICK * ITEM
	00150 CONTINUE

The representation of the structures selection (IF–THEN, IF–THEN–ELSE), DOWHILE and DOFOR in FORTRAN 77 will now be examined. FORTRAN 77 contains a selection structure for both IF–THEN and IF–THEN–ELSE that enables the programmer to write these control statements in a manner virtually identical to that of pseudocode. The problem with the IF statement in FORTRAN 66 is that it can exert direct control over only a single statement. Thus, if it is desired to control a multi-statement process, recourse must be made to a GOTO statement or a subroutine call. In the FORTRAN 77 IF block, these restrictions vanish. The nature of the construction sets no limits on the number of statements that may be directly controlled. Simple examples of both the IF–THEN and IF–THEN–ELSE forms follow.

SELECTION (IF–THEN)

Pseudocode	FORTRAN 77

IF IKE LARGER THAN KING
    THEN
        NICK := 5
        MAN := MAN + 1
ENDIF
	IF (IKE .GT. KING) THEN
	    NICK = 5
	    MAN = MAN + 1
	ENDIF

SELECTION (IF–THEN–ELSE)

Pseudocode	FORTRAN 77

IF IKE LARGER THAN KING
   THEN
       NICK := 5
       MAN := MAN + 1
   ELSE
       NICK := 21
       MAN := MAN − 2
ENDIF
	IF (IKE .GT. KING)
	   THEN
	       NICK = NICK + 5
	       MAN = MAN + 1
	   ELSE
	       NICK = 21
	       MAN = MAN − 2
	ENDIF

Although the complete selection block is always available in FOR-TRAN 77, a problem arises with DOWHILE or WHILE. At the time the FORTRAN 77 standard was defined, there was sufficient disagreement among FORTRAN experts over the usefulness of this structure to have it excluded from the standard. However, at present, quite a number of FORTRAN 77 compilers include it as an addition to the ANSI standard. Although it is included here and marked as FORTRAN 77, one should be aware that it is not always present in compilers of that designation. Once again, the block structure, with its separate initial and closing statements, permits control of multi-statement blocks without destroying the structural integrity of the program, or requiring recourse to GOTO or subroutine calls.

Pseudocode	FORTRAN 77

DOWHILE IKE GREATER THAN KING
     NICK := 5 − IKE
     IKE := IKE − 1
ENDDO
	WHILE (IKE .GT. KING) DO
	     NICK = 5 − IKE
	     IKE = IKE − 1
	ENDWHILE

The DOFOR structure (the FOR loop) is the same in FORTRAN 77 as in FORTRAN 66, hence it will not be repeated here. This completes the discussion of the use of the Bohm-Jacopini control structures in FOR-TRAN 66 and FORTRAN 77 and their emulation in those cases where a specific coding statement is not available.

Section 3: Pseudocode into COBOL

The syntax of COBOL has remained very nearly the same since its initial standardization. For this reason, there will not be an elementary COBOL emulation and an advanced COBOL emulation of the pseudocode control structures. There is a special problem inherent in working with COBOL. The language has been designed to be both self-documenting and flexible in its statement construction. This means that the actual form of a particular statement may be quite similar to a description in plain English of the action undertaken. Further, the actual form in which the statement is written may vary over a rather broad spectrum.

Of course, there are a number of features in the syntax of COBOL that simplify the task of the person writing structured code. First, its beautifully defined IF–THEN and IF–THEN–ELSE constructions include a method of defining a 'domain of control' by periods(.). for the various alternatives. In this way, a multi-statement procedure may be included directly within the body of the selection block. On the other hand, a technology is included by which control may be transferred to a named 'paragraph'. This is essentially a subroutine device, but the flexible statement of COBOL, if properly used, can make the action understandable in a way that is hard to match in other languages. The PERFORM statement provides a way to run the pseudocode DOFOR and DOWHILE structures in a clear fashion.

The examples will only show control of multi-statement options, but these will be handled by including option blocks in the control statements and by referring to named paragraphs. Notice that the PERFORM statement plus a paragraph name can be used either as a subroutine type of structure or, with appropriate additions, as a loop type of structure.

SELECTION (IF–THEN)

Pseudocode		COBOL
IF MARGO LARGER THAN MUFF	20	IF MARGO > MUFF
THEN	30	MOVE 1 TO ZEBRA
ZEBRA := 1	40	MOVE MIDDLE TO CAT
CAT := MIDDLE	50	ADD MILK SUGAR
		GIVING HUG.
HUG := MILK + SUGAR		
ENDIF		

This may also be written using a PERFORM statement and a paragraph reference. We will assume that ZOO is the name of the paragraph and that it contains the three statement lines concerning ZEBRA, CAT and HUG.

```
20 IF MARGO > MUFF
30     PERFORM ZOO.
```

SELECTION (IF–THEN–ELSE)

Pseudocode	COBOL
IF IKE LARGER THAN KING	20 IF IKE > KING
THEN	30 MOVE 5 TO NICK
NICK := 5	40 ADD 1 TO MAN
MAN := MAN + 1	50 ELSE
ELSE	60 MOVE 21 TO NICK
NICK := 21	70 SUBTRACT 2 FROM MAN.
MAN := MAN − 2	
ENDIF	

Again, the PERFORM structure can be used, assuming that GROMAN is a paragraph name for the statements MOVE 5 TO NICK and ADD 1 TO MAN, and SHRINKMAN is a paragraph containing MOVE 21 TO NICK and SUBTRACT 2 FROM MAN. In this case, the COBOL fragment becomes:

```
20 IF IKE > KING
30      PERFORM GROMAN
40 ELSE
50      PERFORM SHRINKMAN.
```

DOWHILE

The DOUNTIL structure is carried out using a COBOL structure called PERFORM UNTIL. The structure works like a DOWHILE in that if the condition is already met, no action occurs. However, an inversion of the logic is required to fit things together.

Pseudocode	COBOL
DOWHILE IKE LARGER THAN KID	20 PERFORM SHRINK UNTIL IKE NOT > KID.
NICK := 5 − IKE	
IKE := IKE − 1	
ENDIF	

In this case we again assume that the paragraph reference SHRINK represents a paragraph consisting of the sentence SUBTRACT IKE FROM 5 GIVING NICK and the sentence SUBTRACT 1 FROM IKE. Although the logic of the DOWHILE must be reversed, this is done with NOT, which simplifies the conversion. Since COBOL is already rather wordy, the introduction of some form of comment line probably does not present a clarification.

DOFOR

Again, this structure is accomplished in COBOL using PERFORM with appropriate options. The only alteration is the inclusion of sentences that indicate the initial value and incrementing of the control variable. However, if the control variable is used only to control counting and will not be printed out or used in further operations, it may be excluded as in the following example:

Pseudocode	COBOL

DOFOR KID := 1 TO 5
    ITEM := ITEM + 3
    NICK := NICK * ITEM
ENDDO
	20 PERFORM GROWTH 5 TIMES.

The paragraph GROWTH is assumed to contain the sentences ADD 3 TO ITEM and ADD ITEM TO NICK.

Section 4: Pseudocode into Pascal

The conversion of a program written in pseudocode into one in Pascal is almost a trivial exercise. This is because the logical structures are virtually identical and the nomenclature is very similar. In Pascal the reserved words BEGIN and END are used to cause a block of several statements to perform as one statement. Since multi-statement activities will be used in all of our control models, BEGIN and END will always be found. If the controlled activities were only a single statement, BEGIN and END would be excluded. Semi-colons (;) are used as statement terminators.

Pascal allows free choice between capital and small letters. I have written the reserved words in all capitals and the variables completely in small letters. The use of this option varies somewhat among programmers. The THEN reserved word could be on the same line as the IF. Many programmers write this way and start the controlled statement or the BEGIN on the next line. Pascal allows great flexibility in spacing. I have used conventions that match the presentation of pseudocode in this text.

Pseudocode	Pascal

IF MARGO LARGER THAN MUFF
    THEN
          ZEBRA := 1
          CAT := MIDDLE
          HUG := MILK + SUGAR
ENDIF
	IF margo > muff
	    THEN
	    BEGIN
	    zebra := 1;
	    cat := middle;
	    hug := milk + sugar
	    END;

SELECTION (IF–THEN–ELSE)

The similarities between pseudocode and Pascal are such that there is really no need for comment.

Pseudocode	Pascal

IF IKE LARGER THAN KING
    THEN
          NICK := 5
          MAN := MAN + 1
    ELSE
          NICK := 21
          MAN := MAN − 2
ENDIF
	IF ike > king
	    THEN
	    BEGIN
	    nick := 5;
	    man := man + 1
	    END
	ELSE
	    BEGIN
	    nick := 21;
	    man := man − 2
	    END;

DOWHILE

Pascal's DOWHILE-related structure is identical to that we have used in pseudocode, except for the relative positions of DO and WHILE and the lack of the ENDDO.

Pseudocode	Pascal

DOWHILE IKE LARGER THAN KID
    NICK := 5 − IKE
    IKE := IKE − 1
ENDIF
	WHILE ike > kid DO
	    BEGIN
	    nick := 5 − ike;
	    ike := ike − 1
	    END;

DOFOR

There are two ways to write a DOFOR loop in Pascal. I have chosen the one that most closely matches the pseudocode DOFOR. There are several small differences. Pascal does not have a STEP option. The STEP is never written and is automatically 1. Further, Pascal has a slightly different order of DO and FOR.

Pseudocode	Pascal

DOFOR KID := 1 TO 5
    ITEM := ITEM + 3
    NICK := NICK * ITEM
ENDDO
	FOR kid := 1 TO 5 DO
	BEGIN
	item := item + 3;
	nick := nick * item
	END;

There a number of other structures in Pascal. It has a proper CASE structure, for instance, and a nice library of special operations. However, the major control structures are listed above.

Index

algorithm, 7, 45
  design, 103
algorithms in programs, 103
AND, 134
  truth table, 148
  Venn Diagram, 135
arithmetic
  hierarchy, 24
  operators, 23, 83
arguments, 137
arrays, 155–66, 173–88
  as tables, 175
  declaration, 156
  loading, 175, 188
  one-dimensional, 155–66
  searching, 161
  sorting, 161–7, 174
  two-dimensional, 173–89
assignment, 31–40, 82
  operator, 31
  statement, 32–40

BASIC, 68
  from pseudocode, 258–64
BEGIN, 45
binary, 4–5
  code, 4–5
  numbers, 4–5
Bohm and Jacopini, 62–3, 173
Boole, George, 132
Boolean
  algebra, 132–49
  expressions, 139–42
  operators, 134
bubble sort, 203–10

call, 195
calling module, 199
CASE, 69–70
  flowchart, 70

pseudocode, 88–9
central processing unit, 9
COBOL, 63
  from pseudocode, 269–71
column, 176
computer, 2–4, 8–9
condition, 84
connector, 47
constants, 23
control structures, 63, 84

data processing, 22–6, 185–7
database, 180–2
decision symbol, 46
DECLARE, 157
Djikstra, Edsger, 51
DOFOR, 173–5
DOUNTIL, 68
  flowchart, 68
  pseudocode, 88
DOWHILE, 67–8
  flowchart, 67
  pseudocode, 88

END, 45, 92
END-OF-FILE (EOF), 182
ENDDO, 85
ENDIF, 85
ENIAC, 3
equal sign, 28
evaluate expressions, 25–6

flag, 122, 186, 205
flowchart, 44–77
  module inversion, 98
  standard forms, 62–77
  symbols, 45–7
FORTRAN, 63, 68
  from pseudocode, 264–9

goof-proof, 54
GOTO, 35–6, 50, 95–9
grammar, 8

hardware, 9
hierarchy of operations, 24
high-level languages, 5

IF-THEN, 66
    flowchart, 67
    pseudocode, 84–6
IF-THEN-ELSE, 65–6
    flowchart, 66
    pseudocode, 84–6
initialize, 10
input, 21, 81
    duplication, 58, 75
    symbol, 46
    verification, 54
INPUT DATA, 90
    interchange, 202
IPO diagram, 90
iteration, 63

language
    elements, 36
    high-level, 5
    machine, 4
layout, 89–91
line numbers, 91, 93, 120–1, 127, 196
logical algebra, *see* Boolean algebra
lookup table, 175
loop, 11, 66–70

machine language, 5
main storage, 9
mnemonic code, 5
modular programming, 55, 116–20,
    157–9, 200–1
module, 10, 63, 77
multi-dimensional arrays, 188

nesting, 96, 111, 117–28
Newton, Sir Isaac, 104
NOT, 137
    truth table, 149
    Venn diagram, 138
numerical
    constant, 23
    variable, 25–6

OR, 135–6
    truth table, 148

Venn diagram, 135
output, 22, 81–3
    symbol, 46
OUTPUT DATA, 90

parentheses, 24
Pascal, 68
    from pseudocode, 272–3
passing variables, 202
pointer, 157–8, 163, 204
Print statement, 35, 82–3
problem
    analysis, 12–13
    description, 89
process, 21–2, 45–6
program, 8, 10
programming style, 71–2, 90–1
prompt, 52
pseudocode, 5
    advantages, 7

Racker, Ephriam, 103
ranges, 139–42
Read statement, 81–2
recipe, 10
relational operators, 85
repetition, 49
row, 176

selection, 65–7, 84
sequence, 65, 84
shortstop, 198–202, 205–8
sort, 161–7
    bubble, 203–10
spaghetti programming, 51, 99, 116
stop, 45
subroutine, 10, 77, 93, 195–210
    call, 195–7
subscript, 167–210
substitution, 25
swap, 205–6
switch, 4
syntax, 7

table production, 21
terminator, 45
top down
    design, 71–93, 103–4
    programming, 64, 207–8
top module, 199
trace, 159–61
trailer line, 182
translation, 7, 257–3

BASIC, 258–64
COBOL, 269–71
FORTRAN, 264–9
Pascal, 272–3
truth tables, 148–9

variable

assignment, 31–4
definition, 26
names, 26
verification, 54
Venn diagrams, 133–8

Wirth, Niklaus, 64